Touring the West
with Leaping Lena, 1925

D1736247

Touring the West with Leping Lena, 1925

By W. C. Clark

Edited by David Dary

UNIVERSITY OF OKLAHOMA PRESS : NORMAN

Library of Congress Cataloging-in-Publication Data
Names: Clark, Willie Chester, author. | Dary, David, editor.
Title: Touring the West with Leaping Lena, 1925 / by W. C. Clark ; edited
by
David Dary.
Description: Norman : University of Oklahoma Press, 2016. | Includes
index. Identifiers: LCCN 2015037373 | ISBN 978-0-8061-5228-8 (paperback : alk.
paper) Subjects: LCSH: West (U.S.)—Description and travel. | West
(U.S.)—History, Local. | Automobile travel—West (U.S.) | Clark, Willie
Chester—Travel—West (U.S.) | BISAC: BIOGRAPHY & AUTOBIOGRAPHY /
Personal Memoirs. | HISTORY / United States / 20th Century. | TRAVEL /
Special Interest / Family.
Classification: LCC F595 .C625 2016 | DDC 917.8/04—dc23
LC record available at http://lccn.loc.gov/2015037373

The paper in this book meets the guidelines for permanence and durability of the Committee on Production Guidelines for Book Longevity of the Council on Library Resources, Inc. ∞

1 2 3 4 5 6 7 8 9 10

Contents

Illustrations

Figures

Map

Introduction

AMERICANS TODAY THINK NOTHING OF DRIVING COAST TO COAST on the nation's interstate highways. Early in the twentieth century, however, only the brave and adventuresome would attempt such a journey on the crude, mostly unmarked, mostly dirt and gravel roads that then existed.

Americans in motorcars usually followed routes blazed earlier by pioneers on horses or in wagons pulled by oxen. In the East, some travelers followed the National or Cumberland Road, the first major improved highway built by the federal government starting in 1811. By 1837 the National Road extended from Cumberland, Maryland, west to Vandalia, Illinois, where construction stopped for lack of funding. In time, after the automobile was invented and perfected, many motorists west of the Mississippi River followed segments of the Santa Fe and Oregon Trails. Travel, however, was slow along the unmarked and poorly maintained routes. The arrival of the railroads enabled travelers to avoid such roads. Steam locomotives conquered the vast distances between cities and towns, ever growing in size and number, and carried humans faster than they could travel on horseback or in wagons or stagecoaches.

After Henry Ford introduced his low-priced Model T in 1908, the automobile caught the fancy of many Americans and they began taking to the roads. Their growing obsession with owning motorcars prompted the federal government to become more directly involved in road development, which up to then had been the purview of local and state governments.

In 1912 Carl G. Fisher, an Indiana entrepreneur, conceived the idea of creating the first improved transcontinental highway for travel between New York City and San Francisco. Fisher called it the Lincoln Highway as a national memorial to President Abraham Lincoln. The Lincoln Highway Association was formed and the idea of a coast-to-coast highway gained much support, especially in the thirteen states along its proposed route—New York, New Jersey, Pennsylvania, Ohio, Indiana, Illinois, Iowa, Nebraska, Colorado, Wyoming, Utah, Nevada, and California.

The idea for a highway across America was catching on. Also in 1912, another group of motoring enthusiasts organized the National Old Trails Road Association in Kansas City, Missouri. They sought to promote a transcontinental road from Baltimore to Los Angeles that would cross Pennsylvania, Ohio, Indiana, Illinois, Missouri, Kansas, Colorado, New Mexico, Arizona, and California. The association endeavored to capture the romance of the nation's historic trails, including the National Road and the Santa Fe Trail. Its progress, however, was slower than that of the group supporting the Lincoln Highway. Soon other groups organized, intent upon promoting highways in other areas of the nation. Better roads became an almost universal call.

The Lincoln Highway was first to become a reality. Its association's *Official Road Guide* (1916) outlined the route, noting that it was "something of a sporting proposition" that might take twenty to thirty days to travel. The *Guide* urged motorists to drive for six daylight hours and average eighteen miles an hour if they planned to make the journey in thirty days.

The Lincoln Highway Association estimated that it would cost no more than five dollars a day per person, including food, gas, oil, and even "five or six meals in hotels"; the cost of auto repairs was extra. Because service stations were rare in many areas, motorists were encouraged to top off their gas tanks whenever possible and to first wade through water crossings to make sure their autos could make it through. The *Guide* also provided a list of recommended equipment to carry.

By 1916 the public's interest in motorcar travel saw other automobile manufacturers joining Ford to satisfy Americans' demand to own autos. The growing popularity of auto travel pushed Congress to pass the Federal-Aid Road Act and create the Federal-Aid Highway Program, providing funds to state highway agencies for road improvements. The program, however, was put on the back burner when the United States entered World War I. In 1921, after the war had ended, Congress authorized what became the Bureau of Public Roads to construct national paved highways.

By 1925 there were about 250 named highways in the nation, including the Lincoln, the National Old Trails, and others laid out and marked by private-road automobile clubs. The routes were marked intermittently by signs or colored bands on utility poles, but the labeling was inconsistent and haphazard, causing much confusion.

The Federal Aid Highway Act of 1925 proposed using a nationwide grid with odd-numbered routes running north to south and even-numbered routes east and west. The legislation proposed a state-administered system to mark the highways with uniform numbers on a widely recognizable standardized shield.

Some people opposed numbers, believing their use would make highways cold and impersonal. The numbered routes were still being planned in June 1925 when W. C. Clark, sixty-three, his wife, Nevada, fifty-five, and their daughter, Florence, thirty, set out from their home in Ravenswood, West Virginia, to tour the American West.

Leaving Ravenswood in a new 1925 Chevrolet, the Clarks drove west to Kansas, then to Nebraska, Iowa, South Dakota, Wyoming, and Washington State. From there they drove south through Oregon and California before turning east through Arizona, New Mexico, Arkansas, and Missouri as they made their way back to their West Virginia home.

The Clarks traveled in a Series K Superior touring car, one of five models then manufactured by Chevrolet. The Clarks' Chevrolet had

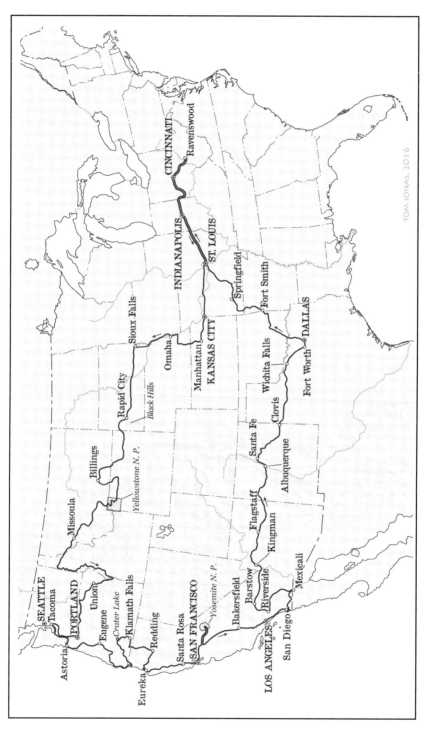

Leaping Lena's tour of the West. Cartography by Tom Jonas. Copyright © 2016 by the University of Oklahoma Press. All rights reserved.

A Chevrolet assembly line producing the 1925 Chevrolet Superior roadster or touring auto, like the one W. C. Clark drove on his western journey. *Courtesy General Motors Heritage Archives.*

an electric starter, wood-spoke wheels, and roll-down curtains on the sides. It was much improved over the 1924 model and included a three-speed manual transmission with a 171-inch four-cylinder engine that developed 26 horsepower. The wheel base was 103 inches. The Series K also had a new single dry plate clutch to replace Chevy's obsolete cone clutch. The auto had semielliptical springs, and a new, semifloating rear axle with one-piece "banjo" casings. There were new 11-inch-diameter brakes, but only on the rear wheels. Bumpers were optional. The basic 1925 Chevrolet Series K model was listed for $515, about twice as much as the comparable Ford model.

As Clark reveals in his narrative, he made some modifications to the vehicle for the journey. He added a heavy front bumper, a spotlight, and a "more melodious horn" than was standard. He also attached a grub box on one running board and bolted a large iron luggage carrier to the rear of the auto.

This 1925 advertisement offers the Chevrolet Series K Superior roadster for $525 f.o.b. in Flint, Michigan. *Courtesy General Motors Heritage Archives.*

In his narrative, Clark provides more information about his vehicle than about himself, but research has determined that his full name was Willie Chester Clark, born in Iowa about 1861. He married Nevada Cobb in Spokane, Washington, three days before Christmas in 1892. In 1895, they had a son, Carl C. Clark, and in 1896, a daughter, Florence, both born in Washington. By 1910 the family was living in Nashville, Tennessee, where the federal census that year lists

The profile of the 1925 Chevrolet Series K Superior roadster was appealing to those wanting to travel by touring auto. *Courtesy General Motors Heritage Archives.*

for Economical Transportation

CHEVROLET

The World's Finest Low Priced Touring Car

Only $525 f.o.b. Flint Mich.

Special Easy Payment Plan

Features that make Chevrolet the most popular low priced quality car.

- Modern streamline body
- Polished radiator
- Lustrous, durable Duco finish
- Cowl lamps
- Complete, fully equipped instrument board
- Powerful economical motor
- Dry plate disc clutch
- Modern sliding gear transmission
- Long, semi-elliptic springs of chrome-vanadium steel
- Big brakes, oversize for safety
- Sturdy rear axle with one-piece pressed steel housing and heavy driving gears
- Positive semi-reversible steering gear

These are but a few of 83 distinctive quality features.

Power — endurance — fine appearance — comfort and great economy! More quality features of construction than your automobile dollar can buy anywhere. This is what you get in a Chevrolet.

Nowhere else can you find so many fine car characteristics for so little money. Chevrolet sets a new standard of values, both in its low first cost and its economy of upkeep. Here is a car which will give you maximum mileage per dollar of cost.

It has a powerful economical motor—dry disc clutch that requires no lubrication—semi-elliptic springs that equal 88% of its wheel base and is finished in Duco whose color and luster last for years and can be very easily cleaned. It comes to you fully equipped and ready for thousands of miles of highly satisfactory service.

And Chevrolet is not only inexpensive to buy and inexpensive to operate but very easy to own. An exceptionally easy-payment plan makes it possible for you to start your purchase with as little as $5. See your nearest Chevrolet dealer. Ask him how easily you can get a Chevrolet.

The Roadster - - - '525	The Sedan - - - '825
The Coupe - - - 715	Commercial Chassis - 425
The Coach - - - 735	Express Truck Chassis 550

ALL PRICES F. O. B. FLINT. MICH.

Chambers Motor Sales
Gd. River and Brooklyn   Glendale 4720
Highland Chevrolet Sales Co.
12893 Woodward   Hemlock 10370
Ginn & Homer, Inc.
9258 Grand River   Garfield 5963
Central Chevrolet
Chene and Jefferson   Edgewood 4223
Superior Chevrolet Sales
8690 Twelfth   Empire 0353
A. Blessing Motor Sales
7699 Gratiot   Melrose 4695
Chevrolet Motor Co.
Detroit Retail Store
General Motors Bldg.   Northway 0500
Michigan Chevrolet Sales
6640 Michigan   Lafayette 5682
Bielman–Taube Motor Sales
8100 Gratiot   Lincoln 4701
Belle Isle Auto Sales
11300 E. Jefferson   Hickory 5684

Kessler Sales & Service
Dix at West Grand Blvd.   West 2140
Hamtramck Chevrolet Sales
11426 Jos. Campeau   Hemlock 9010
Leyes Bros., Inc.
3034 W. Lafayette   West 3009
Weisman Motor Sales
3639 Woodward   Glendale 9389
Leech Auto Sales   Redford, Mich.
507 S. Main   Royal Oak Sales   Royal Oak, Mich.
Wallace Hartman, Inc.
Woodward and 7 Mile Road, Ferndale
Wellar Chevrolet Sales
10370 W. Jefferson, River Rouge, Mich.
Down River Motor Sales
37 S. Biddle   Wyandotte, Mich.
Allison–Bachelder Motor Sales
331 Main   Plymouth, Mich.
Dearborn Motor Sales
116 E. Michigan Ave.   Dearborn, Mich.

Quality at Low Cost

Another advertisement lists the features that made the Chevrolet Series I Superior roadster a fine auto for travel. *Courtesy General Motors Heritage Archives.*

The New Instrument Board

THE instrument board on all new models has been greatly refined, both in appearance and construction. It is equipped with a paneled type ammeter and oil gauge, speedometer, switch and choke control panel, and a neat hand regulator for the automatic windshield wiper on all closed models. The instrument board has been designed to provide maximum leg room in the driving compartment.

The New Instrument Board, showing New Design and arrangement of Panel Type Instruments.

The refined instrument board on the 1925 Chevrolet Superior roadster. *Courtesy General Motors Heritage Archives.*

W. C. as a deputy in the U.S. Revenue Service, later renamed the IRS. Clark apparently retired from government service by 1914 and purchased the *Ravenswood News*, a weekly newspaper in West Virginia. The U.S. census of 1920 lists him as editor and publisher and his wife, Nevada, as a printer.

In 1928, however, the Clarks sold their weekly newspaper and moved to nearby Ripley, West Virginia. They were living there when the 1930 census was taken. Clark, then sixty-eight, listed his occupation as a writer of literature, and Nevada continued to list her occupation as a printer, though she probably no longer worked as one.

Clark's storytelling skills are evident throughout his 1925 journal as he details the trip that covered more than 12,000 miles in 123 days. His narrative takes the reader back in time before the interstate highway system, when roads were often difficult to negotiate, when motorcar travel was slow by today's standards, and when travelers stopped for the night to camp because modern motels and tourist camps were only beginning to develop.

Clark's account of his family's journey across America begins on June 3 and ends on October 5, 1925. He titled his journal "Touring with Leaping Lena," borrowing a popular slang phrase of the day

A street view of the building that housed Clark's weekly West Virginia newspaper, the *Ravenswood News,* in the mid-1920s. *Courtesy Rob Benson Collection.*

describing the bumpy motion experienced when riding in automobiles. He refers to the auto he is driving as "Lena." Instead of providing chapters, his original text was divided into eighty-three "Leaps" from one place to another along the journey. For ease of reading, I have eliminated the leaps from his narrative and divided the text into manageable chapters, each covering specific geographical areas. Otherwise, except for occasional edits for clarity, the text is exactly as Clark wrote it.

Clark had kept a journal of two other auto trips, one a belated honeymoon in 1922, and the other a tour through New England and part of Canada in 1923. He gained much experience in journal writing during both trips, and this 1925 journal hints that he was a seasoned traveler.

Each time he and his wife left for a trip, they simply closed the *Ravenswood News* office. They made arrangements for someone to come in each Saturday to receive any local news stories and to transact any business. When the Clarks returned, they would publish all of the paper's numbered issues not printed during their absence. The Clarks apparently followed this practice during each of their three known auto tours, and from all indications this arrangement was agreeable to subscribers. The Clarks really had no choice but to cease publication if they wanted a vacation. They were the ones who gathered the news,

W. C. Clark and family frequented the restaurant at the Victoria Inn in Ravenswood, West Virginia. They visited with George Long and his wife, Sarah, who owned and operated the inn. George Long suggested the Clarks visit with their son, Archie W. Long, on their western trip. The Clarks did (see chapter 1). *Collection of David Dary.*

sold advertising, hand-set the type for their weekly paper, proofed the copy, printed the paper on their press, and ultimately saw to the paper's delivery.

In this western journey, Clark captures the life and times he witnessed in the areas his family traveled through. He was a good newspaperman and a keen observer. The Clarks made their journey during what was called the Roaring Twenties, when the United States became the wealthiest country in the world and all Americans were thought to be prospering. In several passages, however, Clark points out that such prosperity was not evident everywhere, and that there were many problems. He describes one area he visited as the "land of no hope" and another where the lack of water brought many hardships to farmers and others. In the Pacific Northwest, Clark complains that farmers suffered from government interference and that "big politics" was hurting millworkers. When the Clarks reached Southern California, he observed that while fruit producers were making money, many other residents were living off the money of easterners, by either selling real estate, building houses on the lots easterners bought, or selling

The house on the left was the home of Archie W. Long on Houston Street in Manhattan, Kansas, when the Clarks made their visit in 1925 and stayed with the Long family. This photo was made during the winter following the Clarks' visit. The vehicle is a 1926 Ford. *Collection of David Dary.*

gasoline to newcomers and tourists. Clark's grasp of reality comes through in his narrative.

Every day or so Clark would mail his written accounts home. Once the family returned to Ravenswood, his narrative was typeset at the *Pittsburgh Post* less than two hundred miles to the northeast. Using a proof press, a few copies of the journal were printed for family and friends. Clark's "Apology" and "Appreciation" at the beginning of his crudely printed narrative credit daughter Florence with having set the type, and read and corrected the copy in the office of the *Pittsburgh Post,* where she worked as a proofreader. In his notes, Clark indicates she had help from friends at the newspaper in printing a small number of copies one page at a time. Perhaps no more than a dozen copies of the journal were produced, but the exact number is not known.

One of the original printed copies used to produce this work was sent by Clark to my grandfather Archie W. Long in Manhattan, Kansas. He had been born and raised in Ravenswood, where his parents had owned and operated the Victoria Inn.

In 1925, when the Clarks made their journey, Long owned and operated the Long Oil Company along with many service stations between Kansas City and central Kansas. In his narrative, Clark recounted their visit with my grandparents and their daughter, Ruth Long (my mother), in their Manhattan home before taking to the road again and heading for Iowa, where Clark had been born.

Attempts to locate other copies of Clark's journal have been unsuccessful. It is believed that my grandfather's copy may be the only surviving copy. Although Clark indicates in his narrative that the family took many photographs on the trip, they have not been located. Period photographs, however, have been included here to provide a visual sense of things seen by the Clarks on their journey. Notes have been added where it was thought additional information would help the reader.

Clark's journal captures the color, flavor, and hardships of early auto travel—the sights seen, the people met, the difficulties encountered, and the countless flat tires. His narrative draws the reader back to an earlier era when Americans were beginning to set out in their motorcars for the pleasure of seeing their country. A bit of Americana now preserved between this book's two covers for future generations to experience, Clark's "Touring with Leaping Lena" conveys the excitement of discovery and of the unexpected.

TOURING WITH LEAPING LENA

An Account of the Journeyings of Mr. and Mrs. W. C.
Clark and Their Daughter Florence,
June 3, October 5, 1925.

BY W. C. CLARK

Apology

"Touring With Leaping Lena," [original title] in its present form, was set, read and corrected in the office of the *Pittsburgh Post*, Pittsburgh, Pa., after working hours. The fatigue at the close of the day accounts for more than the usual amount of brain fag; as a proof-reader she [Florence Clark] is notoriously poor—all of which will explain, and we trust excuse, the poor style, bad divisions and typographical errors.

Appreciation

We thank the management of the *Pittsburgh Post* for their courtesy in lending their space and equipment for this work.

We are deeply grateful to the many of Florence's fellow-workers for their kindness and help with the making-up and presswork of this production.

CHAPTER ONE

West Virginia to Kansas

WITH THE FINAL ATTACHMENTS TO BE PUT ON IN MIDDLETOWN, BUT still with a rather tourist appearance, Lena stepped onto the ferry at 10:10 and five minutes later rolled up the Ohio bank with Florence at the wheel. There was no effort at speed, the purpose being merely to run to Columbus that day, and the road was a familiar one. Wheat in Great Bend was full grown but not yet beginning to "ripen unto the harvest." The road to the junction of the Pomeroy-Portland road was dry but rough, still lacking the gravel surface we hope to see on the return trip.

The heat was intense, but the road was fine until after passing Lancaster, where began a detour which came back to the regular road at Canal Winchester; a good road it was, except that it was very dusty and the heavy traffic kept feeding us more Ohio soil than we desired.

Reached the cheerful home of the Hamptons in North Columbus at 5:30 to have it announced that the man of the house would not be home until the following day. He and the scribe had been fellow laborers in Uncle Sam's revenue service, besides which he is a most companionable fellow, so the announcement was a disappointment—one not long continued, however, as a half-hour later he drove in, having run 76 miles in two and one-half hours in order to keep the dinner appointment made last Thanksgiving. In the evening, all hands went over into East Columbus to spend an hour or two with Mother Lodge and her three sons, a fourth one of whom had followed the example of the scribe years ago and married one of the Cobb girls in Washington, one of the objects of this trip being to visit them in their Tacoma home, and a failure to have seen home folks would have been a great disappointment.

The speedometer leaving Ravenswood had read 1,755 and when it went into the garage that night it was 1,894, Lena complaining of a sore foot—in other words with one front tire softer than it should have been, and the rear tire which had gone bad in Pittsburgh threatening to blow out before morning.

⁕

Lena's fever increased during the night. In other words that soft tire had become a flat one. A little air introduced before breakfast was still there after that meal, so it was inferred that the trouble had been in the valve, and a regular dose of Ohio air proved more palatable than the West Virginia kind. The threatened blowout was too apparent to be risked further, so that tire was taken off and carried as a spare, to be discarded and a new one purchased at Middletown. It is things like this that are not included in the prospectus of a trip, that add variety and surprises to the trip, even though they do not materially increase the pleasure.

The evening before, Florence had been dropped off to visit Betty Mae Sheward and her babies, and at 9 A.M. she arrived at the Hampton home and we were soon on our way with the same blistering sun as yesterday.

Lunch at Springfield and a short distance out the remains of a freshly burned car beside the road reminded us of the perils by which we were beset. A few miles farther there was another, it not being entirely gone, still furnishing food for flames.

Next came a crossing of the traction line with a sharp turn beyond and a fine tree in front of a house; its body a foot through had been stripped of its bark where a car had struck it. Some speedster had been unable to negotiate the turn and we had a vision of the appearance of his car after it had barked the tree. But his peril was not that to which we were subject, for Mrs. Clark promptly called down the driver whenever the speedometer passed the 35-mile mark, watching that instrument being one of the things she seemed fondest of!

Near Middletown was another thing which told a story far from complete—on one side of the road was a Chevrolet car on its back while in a similar position on the other side lay one of those things which made Detroit famous. Men standing by said no one was hurt, which may or may not have been true, but there was nothing to tell whether both drivers or only one had been at fault.

The day before while stopped at a filling station at Canal Winchester, the car ahead had backed up with sufficient force to bend Lena's bumper, and while Mrs. Clark was examining the extent of the injury he suddenly backed up again and almost caught her. The danger is not all to the driver and the innocent bystander frequently gets the worst of it.

The dry spell broke finally with two nice little showers between Dayton and Middletown, and a third was breaking as we pulled up in front of the youngsters' home—the latter continuing for several hours, and giving a dry country a pretty fair wetting.

Speedometer reading 2,007.

The additions to the equipment of Lena involved some fine problems, especially that of where to carry the spare tire, and as a consequence the greasing had to go over until Monday morning; and that with taking pictures of the outfit from every angle, and other things, it was 9 when the work was done, the tank filled with gas and the grand start was made.

For the information of those contemplating a similar trip I will endeavor to describe the "tout ensemble." The car was the same new Chevrolet which was driven to Pittsburgh a few weeks before, and it was equipped with many of the devices commonly attached to cars by owners who think they can improve on the work of the manufacturer. Besides the state license tags and one announcing the name of the port from which she sailed, there were other tags proclaiming the owner to be a member of two popular automobile associations. Then in the way of equipment there was a front bumper of more than ordinary weight—which same has already proven its worth. A spotlight provided light at night available anywhere about the camp ground, as well as being a "trouble lamp" when such a thing might be needed. A horn more melodious than that designed by the manufacturer was ready to warn the fellow to "lay over." An ordinary bundle carried on one running board was offset on the other by a "grub box" four feet long and 10 inches square. The latter was divided into compartments.

But the "piece de resistance" in the way of equipment was the rear luggage carrier. It was evolved from the brain of a Pittsburgh friend, Fred Schultz, and we started with the feeling that nothing more substantial in that line would be encountered on the trip. Built of heavy iron, heavily bolted throughout, the force which would demolish it or wrench it from the car would wreck any vehicle made by man. With a length of 42 inches, a depth of 18 and a width of 24, it furnished a storage room like a tobacco barn, and was admired by all who saw it and its fortunate owner envied accordingly.

By means of these various contrivances the load was pretty evenly distributed over the car, although naturally there was considerable "cutting and trying" in getting everything loaded just as it would be most satisfactory.

The kitchen department contained a camp stove made of interwoven iron rods, with sheet iron ends, sides and top, the latter being to prevent the cooking utensils getting blackened so much. Two or three small pans furnished the ware for doing the cooking, and the table "china" was a set of plates and cups made of white granite wear, the whole enclosed in a gallon bucket of the same material. A folding steel table and three folding stools were the "furniture."

The entire equipment and personal belongings weighed probably 500 pounds in addition to the three passengers—who had a gross weight of 480 when they started.

The 20 miles to Eaton took considerable time, the road being quite indifferent in quality, but from there on it was the finest road for that length that we had ever traveled. I had heard of the wonderful gravel roads of Indiana, but did not find them. We crossed the state from Ohio to Illinois, but every foot of the way was a hard surfaced road, mostly concrete but occasionally a few miles of brick. And it was good road, too. Mrs. Clark recovered from her uneasiness of the starting days and offered no objections when Lena took the bit in his teeth and paced off mile after mile at a rate of 45 miles an hour, and occasionally an even half hundred.

At Indianapolis we stopped for a few minutes to greet Ruby Wolfe, who was just finishing her sixth year as teacher in the schools of the Hoosier capital.

The good road continued on into Illinois, and in spite of the start two hours later than had been planned, we arrived at the farthermost point we had dreamed of reaching, Effingham, Ill., in the pleasant tourist camp in which I am writing by the dying rays of the sun. For mile after mile the road was as straight as the eye could see, and apparently as level as the level of a lake, but after crossing the Wabash river at Terre Haute there were several miles of rolling country, some of which even a West Virginian had to admit was "broken country." There we had an illustration of what man can do when he tries, even without much opportunity. Going down a gentle slope along a ravine we came to where a thoughtful state had erected a guard fence to keep reckless motorists from going over the bank, but one expert driver had circumvented the state road commission and plunged his Ford coupe over that bank, landing right side up in the bottom of the ravine, apparently uninjured except for a broken rear window and a bent fender.

When the festive motorist starts out to smash something, no road is good enough to defeat his purpose.

Speedometer reported the run for the day as 265 miles.

⁂

No sooner did we strike the regular Dayton branch of the Old National Road at Eaton yesterday than there began to be a good many tourists, although not nearly so many as there will be later in the season. By the time we reached camp at Effingham we had seen cars from about half the states in the Union, and of the half dozen cars which later appeared at the camp for the night no two were from the same state, those most widely separated being one from Texas and one carrying two men who said they were from NEWburyport (pronounced all as one word and accented as indicated by the syllable in capitals), Massachusetts. They were on their way to California, had been a week on the road and were so homesick that they were thinking of going back, but decided to persevere as far as St. Louis, where one of them had an aunt. When I told him I had been in his town (I did not attempt to pronounce it as he did) he took to me like a sick kitten to a warm brick, and I think it helped his homesickness a little.

For two or three days there had been a mysterious leakage in one of our tires. Sometimes it would hold all day, and again it would lose half its air over night. Removal this morning betrayed a tiny tack in the casing, and thereby part of our troubles were removed.

Our earlier miles in Illinois last night had been through a rather poor region, but soon after starting this morning there was a decided improvement in the appearance of the country, much tilled land appearing, and the season was considerably more advanced. All the way down through Ohio, Indiana and eastern Illinois the wheat had seemed just the same as at home—fully grown but not yet turning yellow—but this morning the very first crop was considerably more advanced, and many fields will fall before the reaper next week. A still more remarkable change was in the corn when we came down onto the Mississippi river bottom just out east of St. Louis. Instead of the tiny shoots just peeping forth from the ground, the stalks were more than two feet high, almost ready to tassel out. It was easily a month farther advanced.

Vandalia, Ill., broke the continuous stretch of perfect road. It announced a speed limit of 10 miles an hour, and enforced the order by the most effective speed restriction known to the tourist. I had never been in Vandalia before, and was disappointed in its poor streets, and also in its size. Giving its name to a considerable transportation system, the Vandalia Line, it had always been thought of as a town of some consequence, forgetting a fact that sometimes very small places can do that. Remember Glendale as part of the R. S. & G.!

East St. Louis also had its streets very much torn up, and detouring there may have been responsible for us crossing the bridge farthest down the river. It saved us the price of the toll, but landed us on an unknown street. Knowing that we had to go far back from the river we kept on about 40 blocks without seeing an officer or a street name. Turning north at random we met an officer who told us how to get there, we being but a short distance out of the way, and we came straight on through to the crossing of the Missouri at St. Charles 20 miles away. There a pleasant surprise came to us in learning that 33 miles more of concrete road had been put into commission last fall, reducing our dirt road by that amount. Still pleasanter was the later discovery that six or eight more miles had just been thrown open, and so courteous was the Highway Commission of the state that two more sections each of two or three miles were opened when they saw Lena coming. (Notice we spell the name of that road-making body with capital letters, contrary to all the rules of the office.)

Because of all this we are camped in a lovely tourist camp at Fulton, Mo., the former home of Howard Sutherland and are a full half day ahead of our schedule.

Speedometer says the day's run was 236 miles.

The clover on the camp ground at Fulton was about six inches high and made a splendid foundation for a bed, tempting us to sleep a little late, but somewhere on ahead was presumably mail waiting for us, and the tourist looks eagerly forward to the points where mail is due, so there was little tarrying over the morning meal and packing. The caretaker had a visitor that morning, and we had the curiosity to ask if they had any recollection of the days when Howard Sutherland was the editor of a newspaper in their town. One of them was aware of the fact, and quite accurately estimated the time at 40 years ago. Howard was just out of college then and little dreaming what the future had in store for him, nor in what locality lay the scene of his life's activities.

We had not been particularly pleased with the appearance of the "Show Me" state as we had seen it from St. Louis to Fulton. The land had been of indifferent quality, judging by the use made of it, only a small part of it being under cultivation, and at times from high points where we could see over wide areas it appeared to be mainly occupied by timber and brush. But out of Fulton there was a decided improvement, farms becoming more common, cultivation more intense and crops better.

Our general course was parallel with the Missouri river, and with roads on both sides of the river and crossings at several rival towns, there was soon an abundance of advice as to where was the most advantageous point for the traveler to cross "Old Muddy." Notified in time of our contemplated visit, the management of Yellowstone Park had been preparing for us by melting the snow from the roads and camping places, sending the resulting water down the rivers, and as a consequence the Missouri was up. It was seldom in sight from the road, but when we did see it the current was swift and the water muddier than when J. A. Fling washes the streets at home.

Rocheport had a ferry, Booneville a free bridge, Arrow Rock a ferry, and each had plenty of advertising showing why it was the best place to cross. We chose the free bridge, and the result showed that it was as expensive as free things usually are. First thing after crossing on the free bridge—and it was a beautiful and expensive structure—when buying a morning paper in a drugstore we were presented with some more free service in the way of information regarding the roads ahead, which ended in buying a package of a new medicine that store was putting on the market, and using that means to secure distribution. It was only 40 cents, and when properly applied with a hot flannel was practically certain to cure frostbite!

Next we had a big crop of detours, over quite indifferent roads, making a distance to travel of some 12 miles farther than had we gone by the Arrow Rock ferry. That would seem a big price to pay for the saving made, but in addition to that, along one detour was a piece of broken stone which made a bruise on Lena's heel which necessitated changing tires. The spare was a new tire bought since leaving home, but in less than a half mile it went bad, and we were helpless three miles from any source of possible "first aid." A dozen passing cars were stopped before a blowout patch could be obtained, two gentlemen of color finally producing one which had seen considerable service, but appeared to have a little more left in it. Thereby we arrived at Arrow Rock some three hours later than though we had gone direct to its ferry. Or possibly had we gone direct we never should have arrived. One never knows just what to write after he says if.

Anyhow we got a new tire there and prepared to ship the busted new one back home in hopes of getting our money back for it. Also we got a splendid dinner cheap, and went on our way rejoicing that it had been no worse, and at half after six rolled up in front of the home of a cousin of Mrs. Clark's 24 miles short of Kansas City, about 18 hours ahead of our schedule, but expected any minute, and in spite of the troubles noted and a few others, with a record for the day of 181 miles.

This was our first mail point since leaving home, and there was a lot of it waiting for us. Laying over here for a day while more mail arrives and Lena gets the carbon scraped out of his internal workings gives an opportunity for recording a few observations which may be of value to others who plan to come this way.

Among tourists Missouri has a bad reputation as to the roads following a rain. Undoubtedly this reputation is deserved. We were so fortunate as to be two or three weeks behind any rain, but wherever the roads are not hard surfaced—and that is much of the way—roads have been terrible. Mile after mile, especially along the detours, heavy dragging does not conceal the fact that at a time not far in the past there were two ruts zigzagging back and forth across the right of way, and there is nothing to show that anyone ever got out of them. We sailed along over very good dirt roads at 35 to 45 miles an hour, where immediately following a rain, even with chains one would not be safe in running 20 and where after two or three days of rain it would be impossible to run with any load.

Conditions are improving rapidly; a great deal of road is being surfaced this year, and while next year the traveler may find about as much detouring as this year, there will be much more finished road between the detours. The last 40 or 50 miles of this day's run was over roads generally ready for surfacing, or the last touches of preparation were being given, and considerable unfavorable criticism may justly be offered as to the plans for the road. There are entirely too many sharp curves. Quite commonly they follow the lines of the Government surveys, although the hills near the river sometimes prevent that, and there seems to have been a lot of poor surveyors here in early days. Every little while there will be a jog of from 50 to 200 feet, involving two right angled turns, each made in the width of the road. Occasionally there is a wide turn around with a comfortable swing which can be negotiated at a 30-mile gait, but ordinarily they require slowing down and a violent twist at the wheel to prevent taking all the road and infringing on the territory of the car coming from the other way.

Illinois had one feature not yet seen elsewhere which seemed worth general adoption: On the sign board which greets the motorist at the limit of every town there is the name of the town in large letters, its population in figures large enough to be seen plainly, the next town in the same direction, and the first city of consequence on the road ahead.

One almost universal feature worthy only of condemnation, is a notice of speed limit, usually of from 8 to 15 miles an hour. Such a thing is an absurdity, and is always ignored. There is a general exhibition of common sense on the part of the traveling public, and cars running through towns hold to a speed of 15 to 22 miles an hour, and because of the danger from cross streets keep their cars under control. They have as much at stake as the town and know that there will be no punishment for running at such speeds. Let the word go out once that the posted speed limits were being insisted on in a certain town, and there would be an immediate falling off in tourist traffic to an extent which would make business men sit up and take notice. The only enforceable law is one which has common sense back of it.

In the same way, Indiana and Missouri fix a speed limit on their roads of 25 miles an hour, and officers of the law watch the tourists and home people alike skim along at 35 miles where traffic is fairly heavy and 45 to 50 where there is a clear road. The man who runs considerably faster than other traffic on the same road is the speedster and becomes a menace to others. On certain roads where traffic is heavy the drivers are encouraged to make time in order to get them out of the way.

The hundreds and thousands of signs of something to sell to the tourist or service to render him, which line a big highway, show only too plainly that to the people who live there he is a necessity, and only by fair treatment can he be held. Thus far we have found better conditions—more consideration and fewer attempts to gouge—on this trip than on our journeys east. There has been a good deal of what is known as the Western spirit, but we know full well that the West has to live as well as the East, and all who live there are not qualified to enter the pearly gates. The western people are no more angelic but they are better advertisers, and have learned that the best advertisement is a satisfied customer.

Measured in that way, we are an asset to the country through which we have passed, for we are willing to recommend their treatment practically without exception.

⁂

Three strenuous days made all hands feel the need of a rest and it was taken under ideal conditions. The cousin who lives at Buckner took perfect care of us, and with pleasant converse most of the time was passed. In the afternoon we drove about the neighborhood for a time meeting some of the people, including some relatives of friends we had known in southern Missouri years ago. One object of interest was a well near town being drilled for oil. It has been under way for 16 months and is now down over 3,300 feet. Geological experts pronounce the chance for oil favorable, but with no producing wells in the state, it would seem to be wildcatting with a capital W.

A fairly early start was made Friday morning. A south wind all day Thursday was pronounced a harbinger of rain, and just after daylight two light showers passed over. The sky was not particularly threatening when we started after waiting to get the morning mail, but the clouds became heavier as we approached Kansas City—a run of 24 miles—in accord with the weather man's prediction of "increasing cloudiness and probable thunder showers." Independence, 19 miles short of Kansas, is the county seat of Jackson county, of which Kansas City is the larger part, is a place of some 10,000 to 15,000 and is the headquarters of the anti–Brigham Young branch of the Mormon Church; and in that town there are 14 Mormon churches, their membership including a majority of the people in the town. It is almost as great a peculiarity in that way as Zion City, Ill., where the followers of Dowie make up the whole population.

We were crossing the viaduct over the valley of Kaw or Kansas river when it began raining. This was also the state line, so we feel that Kansas owes us a vote of thanks for a badly needed rain. We certainly brought it and the Kansans admit that it was badly needed—worth several million dollars to them, in fact. Even the city needed the rain, for purposes of purification, as was evident from the smells—odors—arising from the stockyards and nearby places.

At the outer edge of Kansas City, Kans., the rain began falling in torrents and we ran under the shelter of a friendly filling station to wait for the shower to pass. (The weather report the next morning said the temperature fell 13 degrees and .59 of an inch of water fell in

9 minutes.) Two wide paved streets converged at the station where we were, each running up the hill for two or three or four blocks, and the water coming down them and meeting just below us reminded us of when the bear trap is open at the dam. Cars passing through it ran two or three rods with water up to the hubs.

After waiting 15 or 20 minutes we decided that it was to be more than a shower, so put on the curtains and started on. Our assumption was correct. It rained for hours and hours, sometimes hard and sometimes gently, but without a letup. Over an inch and a half of water fell during the day, as we ran ahead. The road was good, all hard surfaced, but we had ample evidence that the road was not without its perils. Climbing a long hill—and we were surprised to find how many hills Kansas has—we came to a new Dodge sedan headed east where the road ran north and south, its front wheels in the bottom of a ditch about four feet deep and the bumpers buried in the wall on the farther side. It seemed to be full of people, although we supposed one had gone for help, for until expert help arrived it was doomed to stay there. A few miles farther along was a bus off the road and in the ditch, which fortunately was shallow there. A Garford truck was hitched to it, and pulled it back onto the pavement in a few minutes. The road was lined with buses, we meeting or being passed by one at short intervals from Lexington, Mo., to Topeka, Kans., and we went but a short distance before meeting another one. A Ford was parked near the side of the road and in order to get around it, the bus came near running into us, we slowing up to prevent a collision. A few rods behind it was another Ford, and its driver attempted to do the same thing. Realizing that it was impossible, without attempting to stop—which he could easily have done—he ran to the right of the parked car, having to leave the pavement, and glided gracefully into a deep ditch. The car remained right side up, but it was destined to remain there until some much more powerful machine than Lena came to the rescue. All these tended to make us drive carefully, but other reckless drivers approaching or passing sometimes caused uneasy feelings.

The Long Oil Company service station in Wamego, Kansas. Hiram Long, brother of A. W. Long and station manager, stands next to the gasoline pump on the right. *Collection of David Dary.*

At Lawrence we stopped for lunch. This town is rich in historical memories, but there was too much rain to hunt for anything, so we went on. Topeka was not as large a place as we had pictured it, and we had to content ourselves with a passing glance at the state capitol, seen from street crossings. The earlier part of the day had been mainly through a hilly country, but beyond Topeka we entered the Kaw valley to remain. This is called the garden spot of Kansas, and it is well named. A garden spot it is, rich in wheat, oats, clover and alfalfa. The product which made Kansas famous and gave the state its nickname we have not yet seen—probably too early. (We refer to the gorgeous sunflower.)

At St. Marys we came to our first station of the Long Oil Company and received unpleasant intelligence. We had traveled a gravel road all the way from Topeka but were told that it was at an end. From there to Wamego, 15 miles, was a dirt road, but with chains we could "probably get through." We did. It took about an hour and a half, but we did not want to repeat it. So after a run of 155 miles (included in which were a few miles driving about Buckner the previous day) we slept beneath the hospitable roof of Hi Long at Wamego.[1]

⁖

Really this [Leap VII in original] was not a leap, but merely a cathop and should be so recorded. We spent the night at the home of Hi Long, and the next morning visited a number of the business places in Wamego, winding up with a tour of the park. A town about the size of Ravenswood, it has a park whose tourists' camp is noted from ocean to ocean, and perhaps has no equal in a town of corresponding size.

Beautifully shaded by trees now of goodly size—and remember that every mature tree in that part of Kansas not on a stream is where some man has planted and protected it—there are winding driveways, a large swimming pool, two life-sized statues and various other decorations. Several of these deserve special mention.

What probably is the piece de resistance of the decorative objects is an old Holland wind mill. This originally stood several miles out in the country. It was built of stone about the size and height of a large silo. That was taken down, each stone numbered and rebuilt in the park exactly as it had stood in the country. Thousands of yards of dirt had been removed in excavating for the swimming pool which really is a considerable lake—and these had been deposited in a pile similar to the pile of gravel near the Ravenswood House when we started on our trip, and on top of that pile the mill has been erected. The tower is rebuilt, but the arms of the mill are not yet in place.

Another decoration is a large fountain, perhaps 20 feet high, surmounted by a stork from whose bill the water flows, and the basin at the base, some 15 feet across, is stocked with gold fish. Until recently there had been 2,700 of them but some had been sold. For some reason—perhaps Kansas climate—they were unusually large, six or seven inches long.

Here and there on the plains of Kansas is a boulder of different composition from any of the stone of Kansas. Two such which had been near Wamego had been hauled in and deposited in the park where the tourist could stumble over them if he were not careful when he wandered about in the dark.

One of them weighed two tons and had been brought in entire, the other weighed 14 tons, and had been split before hauling, and then replaced in its original position. Geologists who have examined them say that these boulders were brought down by a glacier, perhaps some 3,000,000 years ago, from the vicinity of Sioux Falls, S.D., where the same kind of rock is to be found. The larger rock having been split and damaged, we declined to have anything to do with it, but as we were going direct to Sioux Falls we offered to load the other one into Leaping Lena and take it back, but the Wamegans felt they had possessed it so long that they had some "vested rights" in it.

Anyhow Sioux Falls has given up all claim to it by this time, for even some of the claims against the United States Government will probably be abandoned in 3,000,000 years. Still it would have been a fine thing to take it home, and it would have been a wonderful illustration of the progress that has been made in the years that have elapsed since the Ice King wrenched it from its native bed. We would have taken it home—up grade—in less than a week, whereas its southward trip down the hill probably occupied several thousand years, during little of which time it moved more than 50 feet during the annual course of the sun.

But as we said, Wamego was not willing to let go, and all we can do is to tell Sioux Falls where her property is and let her go after it.

While we had been looking at the beauties of the park and getting a number of pictures there the roads had been drying, and vastly improving their condition thereby. We had no desire to repeat the horrors of that 15 miles drive from St. Marys, but knowing that there was a warm welcome and a hot meal waiting us at Manhattan, we bade adieu to Wamego about 11 o'clock and reached Manhattan, 18 miles, a little before noon, where we were rapturously received by Arch Long, his wife and daughter, the latter no longer "Little Ruth."

Anderson Hall, the administration building of Kansas State Agricultural College (now Kansas State University), with period auto, circa 1925. *Courtesy Special Collections, Hal Library, Kansas State University.*

Manhattan, seat of Kansas State Agricultural College, and for 30 years the home of Arch Long—twice mayor of the city—deserves a more carefully written article than I can prepare sitting on a camp stool with my typewriter resting on Lena's front bumper while waiting for breakfast at Council Bluffs, Ia., so it must wait until home is reached, but the royal reception accorded the visitors must be told here as well as possible.

Just as soon as it was definitely known that the Clarks were going the Manhattan way, the Longs began to plan for their reception, and their planning was as intensive as that of the Clarks for their trip. First must be the means of locomotion, so a new Buick sedan was bought some months earlier than had been intended in order that it might be properly broken in and got in readiness to show the visitors as much of Kansas as their length of stay would permit. Apparently, too, the expected arrival was advertised, for everywhere we went and were introduced there came the inquiry: "These are the people you were talking about?"

The K.S.A.C. as the biggest thing in town was naturally first to be considered, so we were promptly taken there for lunch at the cafeteria. The school year ended a few days before, but summer school was on, and there were hundreds of people eating there, mostly students, but also many of the town people who wanted a good meal at a reasonable price. The afternoon was spent in going through some of the college buildings, visiting the Masonic Temple, Mr. Long being one of the past masters of the Masonic Lodge there, visiting the country club grounds, the sightliest spot in eastern Kansas, and driving about the city.

At the close of the day Mrs. Long placed us in what she called the attic, where we enjoyed a good night's sleep, warned to be ready for a strenuous day to follow. Our original plan had been to drive to Iowa that day but in view of the preparations made to entertain us in Kansas we had to remain there one more day. It was "Children's Day" at the First Presbyterian Church, following which all hands got into the Buick to "see Kansas."

As a preliminary and time saver we went to the leading hotel for the midday meal, and then with Miss Ruth at the wheel we sped westward at 40 and 50 miles an hour, the road fully restored since the rain two days before. Camp Funston, Fort Riley, the first capitol of Kansas, monuments commemorating the days when the trapper, trader, settler and soldier combated with the Indian for the possession of Kansas. On and on to Abilene, the end of the old cattle trail in the days of "North of 36" and those which followed, where Bill Hickok became Wild Bill and the most famous city marshal in the world.

Put away out of sight, but not forgotten, there are many old six shooters in Abilene that have notches cut in their handles. But they are not even mentioned nowadays, for Abilene is a modern city, and we got a glass of root beer at a place where once nothing was sold which did not carry a fight in every spoonful.

Back to Manhattan by a different route, and then out in another direction to the Watsons, West Virginia folks, Mr. Watson being a

While visiting Abilene, the Clarks drove by the downtown Long Oil Company station. *Collection of David Dary.*

cousin of ex-Senator Clarence Watson, while Mrs. Watson is an aunt of the cashier of the Jackson County Bank.

All this made a full day and no one was in a hurry to begin the next day when the Clarks were to resume their journey. Dark clouds had gathered the evening before, and about 9 o'clock there had been heavy lightning to the northwest, and there was a possibility of mud the next day.

CHAPTER TWO

Kansas to South Dakota

[AFTER WE K]ISS[ED] THE LONGS GOODBYE AT 9 O'CLOCK MONDAY morning, Lena turned his nose northward. Heretofore our journey had been westward along the Old National Road, and tourists had been the most common of sights, but here we were running "across lots" and they immediately became a rarity, only an occasional one miles apart. We were out into the "wheat belt" of Kansas, which any son of the state will tell you is the greatest one in the world, and occasionally a binder was seen at work that morning, although the bulk of the crop was not quite ready to cut. Relics of Friday's storm were seen in mud covered gardens and fields, and at one place we saw evidence of one of those things which loyal Kansans seldom mention—a twister. A house situated in a large grove had lost a large segment out of its roof and a lot of the trees were twisted off. This had occurred some 10 days before.

As we continued northward crops became greener and soon all harvesting ceased. Throughout the whole day, however, wheat continued to be the leading crop, its acreage exceeding that of corn, with alfalfa a good third. There was no longer any red clover, that having disappeared back near the Missouri line, and potatoes, which had occupied thousands of acres in the Kaw valley, especially back near Lawrence and Topeka, were to be found only in gardens.

Just short of the state line we met the first evidences of the storm the previous night, and as we went into Nebraska it became more and more in evidence. The wheel tracks were generally dry, but in all low ground, if one had to leave the track, the mud was deep. All along, the road was being dragged, both Kansas and Nebraska taking such action promptly following a storm.

A few miles short of Lincoln we struck a beautiful gravel road, wide and smooth as a floor, the only limit to speed on it being the capacity of the car. This led us to the pavement of the city, and in the heart of Nebraska's capital we turned east for the run to the Missouri river. There we once more turned north, crossing it by ferry at Platts-mouth, the earliest home of which I have any memory and within a half-dozen miles of the spot where I was born. The river was even muddier than ever, well up, but not as high as it had been a few days before, and very swift. The ferry was a flat boat scarcely as large as that at Ravenswood, operated on the trolley system, the river being considerably narrower than our own Ohio, although so much swifter that it may carry more water.

Eight miles farther, largely through mud as it was across the river bottom and up a small creek, and we arrived at Glenwood, Ia., the day's objective, 224 miles from Manhattan.

⚜

Glenwood is the home of one of our few remaining cousins, Miss Emma Barnes, whose declining years are being spent in the county seat of the county in which she was born nearly three-quarters of a century ago. Two weeks before our arrival she had the misfortune to receive a fall which seriously injured one hip, and was confined to her bed. This interfered seriously with the visit here.

In the afternoon of Tuesday we drove out to the old family church, in the cemetery of which four generations of Clarks lie buried, including my grandfather and my father, with many uncles, aunts and cousins. Some pictures in the cemetery and church and we returned to Glenwood, bade Cousin Emma goodbye and ran over the hill road to Council Bluffs, and what is said to be the prettiest tourist camp in Iowa, arriving a little after 6 o'clock, among the first of some 25 cars, mostly east bound. Day's run 32 miles.

The river road would have been nearly impassable. Eight inches of rain fell in Glenwood Sunday—four inches in four hours—and nearly two inches more Monday night. Tourists were held up all over Iowa. Tuesday night a great storm passed north of us—about Sioux City—and prospects ahead were not good.

⁜

The same [Leap X] being another cathop.

Tuesday was calling day, and as it would not be fair to drop in on ladies too early in the morning when we were not expected, we tarried at the camp ground. That Council Bluffs tourist camp is on the very tip top of the bluff for which the city is named. From end to end of the Missouri river is that bluff on either side, and for ages untold the river maintained its claim to all the land between the bluffs. In time of flood it wandered at will, eating into the bottom at one side until it reached the bluff, and then mayhap hugging its new wall for years, or without provocation suddenly forsaking it and eating its way back again, always building up one side as it ate into the other.[1]

But why it stopped at the bluff is a mystery to the unlearned. Those bluffs are nothing but sand! Merely a bluff! Years ago the river on a higher level deposited the sand there, in hills hundreds of feet high, and so majestic do they appear that even the river which made them does not attempt to destroy them. For scores of miles today we drove along the base of the bluff, and it was always merely sand. The peculiar thing about them is that they can be cut down as straight as the side of a house and they will stand that way through rain, freeze and whatever destructive agency Nature has to bring against them. This afternoon we passed two places where farmers had cut down a bluff to make room for a house and yard. At one of them the old bluff stood perpendicularly to a height of 40 or 50 feet but not more than half as far from the house. Should it cave down, the house would be ruined, but the house has stood there for years. The one thing which cuts these bluffs is running water, and if a little stream find its way over the edge of one of those artificial precipices there is soon a deep groove cut.

CUSTER BATTLEFIELD HIWAY
THE MOST SCENIC AND BEST MARKED HIWAY IN THE WEST

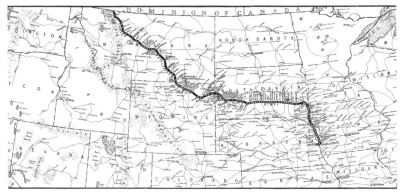

The Custer Battlefield Highway between Omaha, Council Bluffs, and Glacier National Park. *Courtesy South Dakota State Historical Society.*

But this was calling day. In Council Bluffs lives one of my cousins, many years widowed, with her daughter, while over in Omaha is another cousin with her husband and children. Through carelessly regarding the passing years, I was surprised to find that the little children were both grown up and married, and one of the grand-children was at home when we called. Another cousin of a more remote degree was also on the calling list, and after the social obligations were paid we ran down to Ft. Crook. Just below there was home at one time, and I wanted a picture of a house my father built in 1868. Unfortunately it was burned some years ago, so the trip was a disappointment. However, we got to see a lot more of the way land is saved along the Missouri. We crossed a lot of the old creeks on one side of the river or the other in the last two days, and no longer are they permitted to take their own way about reaching the Missouri, but in deep, straight channels, with high enclosing walls on either side, they are carefully and expeditiously conducted in a way to do the least damage. Late in the day we saw one new channel being cut for a stream whose room was worth more than its company.

At 4:30 we left Council Bluffs headed north on the Custer Battlefield Highway which for the first 25 miles is also the Lincoln Highway, making camp later than usual at Onawa, 70 miles out. Total run for the day, 127 miles.[2]

A beautiful sunset gave promise of a good tomorrow.

⁂

In many ways this [Leap XI] was the most interesting leap of all so far. Our camp at Onawa made us think of the "great open spaces." We were in a park [with] just Nile-like loam which makes the valley so rich. There from Denver [was someone] whose car was broken down and who was repairing it by sheer ingenuity rather than wait the three days it would require to get parts for that particular kind of car. The town was situated in the valley of the Missouri river opposite where the Big Sioux debouches into the valley, with the result that the valley was 16 miles wide, and the bluffs on either the Iowa or Nebraska side could scarcely be seen, and one could readily imagine himself out on "the great plains."

The road had been splendid from Council Bluffs up, and we had bowled merrily along. Part of the time it had been on the hillside, made of that bluff sand already referred to, and at other times out in the valley proper where there is nothing except the well, while the missing wheat was partly replaced[,. tThere] was no limit to the speed of the car except such as the driver might impose, and incidentally, we got a lesson in railroading. Heretofore we have occasionally run alongside moving railroad trains, and usually we have distanced them in the race if the road was fair. So when a locomotive gave a few snorts just behind, and the roads were parallel, there was a prompt stepping on the gas, although the car was already running a good 35 miles an hour. The speedometer ran up to 45, which Mrs. Clark had set as a limit, and that locomotive steadily glided ahead, followed by a long string of freight cars! Just a measly old freight train, but it was running an easy 50 miles an hour.

The character of the country had changed greatly in the last hundred miles' run. Our northern progress had taken us out of the wheat belt, and while there was still considerable of it grown, it had dropped into a subordinate place, and corn was king. That difference became more marked as we kept northward today. Corn was perceptibly shorter, but looking in that territory except sweet clover, which was pop-by oats, the latter becoming the second crop in importance, if one does not consider grass, which is much in evidence especially on the uplands. Alfalfa still remained quite common, but red clover had practically disappeared. A man at Onawa with whom I had a short talk told me that there was little clover in that territory except sweet clover, which was popular because it was such a wonderful land restorer, although it was admittedly hard to get rid of after a man was done with it.

Before reaching Sioux City this morning we were surprised to see a Mongolian pheasant in the road ahead. This was the first one we had seen since leaving Oregon, and did not know they had been introduced into any of the more eastern states. One of the most beautiful birds grown, rather larger than bantam chickens, the cock we saw was a magnificent specimen. He stood calmly in the road until we were almost upon him, then walked slowly to the edge of the road, turned his head slightly and looked to see how Leaping Lena was equipped as we passed within five feet of him. Another old friend appeared later in the day in the form of the western meadowlark, the bird whose assurance that "laziness will kill you" is almost as well known as the "bob white" of our own land. We heard no lark until today, but before the day's drive was over it became a common sound.

Out of Sioux City we were directed onto a wrong road, the King's Trail instead of the Custer Battlefield Highway which we had planned to follow, and it carried us over 15 miles of road under construction. A fine road it will be when done, but now it is not all graded, some being but partly filled in, all rough, with a number of short detours around bridges and culverts under construction. Added to the delay thus caused was more due to a blowout when running 45 miles an hour. The tire went off into a ditch a complete wreck, and Lena came near following.

Just before entering Sioux Falls, S.D., we came into the Custer Battle-field Highway, and on that road turned west. Ever since getting fairly away from Council Bluffs, a noticeable thing had been the long-straight stretches of road, and twice this morning there had been runs of about 15 miles without a curve. The would come a long turn at right angles, for here all roads follow the lines of the Government survey. But as we started out of Sioux Falls and consulted the *Blue Book,* we made some allowance for its instructions to "run west 46 miles." But really the road followed one continuous section line for that distance and only once varied from it, one hill being high enough and sufficiently steep that to get a good grade down, there was a swing out possibly 200 feet from the line established by Uncle Sam. Otherwise it was as straight as the flight of an arrow.

Another thing we learned here which will be of interest to some of our friends in Kansas. Sioux Falls will make no demand for the return of those stones which were taken to Wamego so many years ago. She has plenty of her own acquired in a similar manner, and the question once raised might become embarrassing should word of it reach Manitoba and points north. The southern part of this state is one vast deposit of glacial till, and on some fields there are so many of these stones—from a few tons weight to mere gravel—that they are a detriment. It is a common theory in all countries so afflicted that they make excellent fertilizer when they rot, but often the process of decay is no more rapid than the progress they made on their journey south in the days Bryan contends never were.

Out of Sioux Falls was a rolling country. A West Virginian might call it flat, but there was generally no question of the direction of its drainage. But there were occasional slight depressions, which by the aid of the storm two nights before produced a number of small lakes. Perhaps a number of them were continuous affairs, and we saw one which covered several acres and may have been quite deep. Some-times these temporary lakes were in fields planted to corn, and one of the most peculiar sights we saw was a man cultivating corn, and running his cultivator through one of those lakes. It was so deep that it came up over his feet as he sat on the cultivator—almost to the horses' bellies—while for fifty yards the only way to direct his course was by the rows of corn ahead where they came up out of the water. But the corn had to be cultivated and it would not do to turn around except at the end of the field. Riding cultivators exclusively were used, drawn by four horses hitched abreast and cultivating two rows at a time. Just once we saw a cultivator drawn by a tractor, the latter evidently made for that purpose, its wheels being very high, but apparently not very heavy.

One of the first things to attract the attention of the visitor in this region is the timber. Evidently when this region was settled there was not a tree in miles, and evidently also the first winter that a white man spent here he realized the need of timber for a windbreak. Just fancy the thermometer down a few jumps below where the mercury freezes up and quits work; then add a gentle gale from the north pole hurrying south at about Lena's best gait, and you can understand why man should desire to have something to hide behind. So trees were planted; every house and barn is surrounded by them. Not just a widely scattered row, but one row after another planted close together and only cut out as they become too close together. And the stumps do not die then. Some varieties of trees die when the body is cut down, and others spring up again from the root, but the latter seem to be the only kinds known to South Dakota. Evidently ever-greens do not prosper in this state, for we did not see them even in the cemeteries, and it takes a forest of naked limbs to ward off the winds of winter, so the homes are in the middle of a veritable forest. Apparently if a South Dakotan would marry and move onto virgin soil he must take several years for preparation that his windbreak may grow large enough to make life possible there.

As the Ohio rises on the very edge of Lake Erie, so on the north bank of the Missouri rises the James river, the maker and protector of the "Jim river valley," the garden spot of North Dakota, which goes contrary to all the streams of its part of the country and runs due north, finally reaching the Arctic ocean.³ That river we crossed about 6 o'clock and entered the town of Mitchell, one of South Dakota's thriving second-class cities—about the size of Morgantown or Fairmont. It was a little early to camp, but a wonderfully pleasant camping place with several cars already there, so we turned in, pitched the tent and started to tell our readers what we had seen in the 226 miles driven since morning. This has only been partly done in this effort, for there are others features which will be told later as they may be recalled when there is more time. The clouds which for several hours promised rain for tonight are far to the east ready to pour their floods upon the country we passed over earlier in the day, and even the wind, that almost constant companion of the prairie states, has quieted down and a peaceful night is in prospect, the most exciting exercise being the questions and answers as to roads by those who have just passed over them and those who are due to do so in the immediate future.

"How did you find the roads?" is the regular means of introduction in the tourist camp.

❧

This [Leap XII] was intended for an ordinary broad jump, but turned out to be a hop, skip and a jump, with almost a little fudging at the end, the reason for which will appear in due course as the tale unfolds. There are a number of things heretofore unnoted which belong one place as much as another, and as the present time is unusually favorable for writing, they may as well be put in here.

Perhaps first among them in the economic life of the nation, and especially of the region traversed, comes the cattle and other live stock seen along the way. After leaving the valley of the Kaw in Kansas, all the time, except in the immediate neighborhood of the larger cities, there has been a surprisingly large number of cattle, a good many hogs and only occasionally any considerable number of horses. Even where the latter were plentiful, the colts were scarce. Most of the horses were large draft

The Corn Palace in Mitchell, South Dakota, circa 1925, when W. C. Clark and family visited. *Courtesy South Dakota State Historical Society.*

animals, but if the number on the farms is to be maintained there must be a horse factory somewhere that we did not see. Very rarely was a mule colt seen, but the north has never taken to the mule like the south, and their origin has been mainly regions to the south of our course.

In one day in Ohio, one can see more evidence of hog raising than in all our travels since we crossed the Mississippi. Scarce once a day on an average has there been a farm on which there were family hog houses such as are so common in the Buckeye state. Nor has there been such evidence of breeding for anything more than just pigs. Perhaps there was more Poland China blood than any other, with the Duroc second, but there was evidence of much mixture of breeds, and Sam Ball has a better lot of pigs any day in the year than we have seen in three of the great corn states.

Of the cattle, 90 per cent have been Holsteins or Herefords, with occasional Durhams, now and then a Jersey, and in Nebraska we passed the farm carrying the finest herd of Ayrshires west of the Mississippi, the property of the president of the national Ayrshire Association.

Next on my notes comes chickens. We have seen two hatcheries, neither as large as the Diamond Hatchery, and the nearest we have come to a purely chicken establishment was one in Omaha which carries 350 or 400 hens, selling eggs and fryers at the door. One of the hatcheries also offered fryers. The breeds have invariably been one of the larger varieties, perhaps the reds and buffs predominating, with more white rocks than barred. It has been so long since we saw a leghorn, either white or brown, that one would be somewhat of a curiosity.

Getting back more particularly to the events of Friday, the beginning of our third week, the first thing after loading up in the Mitchell camp ground was to hunt for the corn palace. This had been called to our attention long before with the statement that it was the only one in the world. Being there we went to see it, even if it was in a state of decadence, and very passé.

The corn palace is an annual event in Mitchell, held the latter part of September. As a foundation for it there is a brick building about 150x175 feet, higher than an ordinary two-story building, built with a series of large panels on the cuter walls, but without windows. Those panels are adorned with pictures of scenes both modern and ancient—that is, ancient for that region—each with some special significance, the whole picture of each panel being made of ears of com, placed solidly together and attached to the building, red, white and yellow com enabling the delineator to make his picture complete. It is surprising how faithfully a scene can be depicted in that way. Between the panels and appearing as festooned draping are solid thatching of oats or flax, so that the two sides of the building seen from the street are one continuous picture except for the entrances, and when fresh must be worth a long journey to see.

The decorations put on last September at a cost of $10,000 are still in good shape, in spite of the weather, birds and squirrels. The latter, both animals and birds, were busy clearing away for the new artist next September. The wonder to us was that all the English sparrows, squirrels and rats in the world did not hear about the free eats and go to Mitchell, where the table is always spread.

A change we noticed shortly after leaving the valley of the Missouri shortly after Sioux City was the absence of silos. We have now crossed the full width of agricultural South Dakota, this being written in the Black Hills, and only one or two silos have been noticed.

For more than a day we have been seeing a strange animal. A man at Mitchell to whom we described it said he thought it was a young gopher. Almost as slim as a weasel, with a squirrel-like tail, head held high, as it rushes across the road at a glance it appears like a lizard, only close approach disclosing its hairy covering. If his surmise is correct, only young ones have been seen.

Out of Mitchell there was little change in the country until we reached the top of the Missouri bluff near Chamberlain, at which town we crossed the river on a steam ferry. Just east of Chamberlain was what is called a coal mine, the product being a cross between bituminous coal and lignite, the local paper proudly calling it "semi bituminous coal." Only a little is mined for local use, but we saw the waste on the hillside at several places, its color speaking plainly of coal. On the other side of the river we ran down five or six miles and then up the bluff over a long winding grade, and on the way up there were several places where the same black slaty croppings appeared, as also down the river in sight from the summit. Evidently the deposit covers considerable country.

Once west of the river there was a marked change in everything. There were no old settled farm houses, and few new ones. We drove mile after mile through lanes or fields without seeing a single tree. Not even a bush was to be seen except here and there by a house. Great fields were without any sign of a building, and the houses were widely scattered. Once we saw a school house where the whole country could be seen for miles. There were only five houses within a radius of a mile and a half, one of which was deserted, and the children in two of them, if any, would apparently have gone to school in a little village which was nearer by.

Towns which had been six or eight miles apart became 12 and 15, and usually the cemetery showed but few people buried there. Far less than half the land was under the plow, and a great deal of that had just been broken up for the first time and was not yet seeded, the sod needing to rot first. It was all so new we thought it must have been an Indian reservation recently opened to settlement, but were told that it was not, but had only recently passed from pasture land to farms.

Snow sheds began to appear along the railroad wherever there was a cut. A fence six feet high, boards put on horizontal with spaces between about as wide as the boards, stood back of the cut about 100 feet from the track. It checks the gales of winter enough that the snow will fall on that quieter place instead of going on as it had been doing.

Ever since leaving St. Louis there had been a constant stream of birds, many of them strangers to West Virginia. The English sparrow seemed to disappear with Mitchell, but the larks, killdeer, yellow hammer, magpie, blue jay, curlew and others appeared in ever increasing numbers. Still there was one which belonged to the plains and desert places which was still missing. A little stunted sage brush appeared in the evening and we knew that other bird was not far ahead. Soon he came, darting along as easily as though blown by the wind; apparently touching the ground occasionally, but so lightly as not to disturb a leaf. He was the same carefree fellow as of old—the same old jack rabbit.

Kadoka had been selected for the camping place that night, where this letter was to have been written. Consequently we must camp early. We arrived at 5 o'clock, the park in which was the camp, having a nice lake, a lot of shade trees—not seen before since morning—alongside and pretty fair grass in the park. Jumping out of the car, the women started to prepare camp, while I went for groceries. By the time I got to the street my clothes were covered with mosquitoes, and when I got back I found both the women fighting them and not a thing done. The grass was alive with them, and our arrival not only awoke them but reminded them that it was time to eat. There was a hasty decision to move on. Consultation with the natives as to the best locality to escape them brought the surprising information that it was just the same way for miles in all directions. A tourist traveling east said they had had a blow out on the top of a hill a few miles back and the mosquitoes nearly ate them up while they were changing tires. The natives added that they only came the day before (result of a recent rain) and that old familiar statement that they had never been so bad before.

We argued that conditions must be better somewhere, but no hope was held out to us short of Rapid City 122 miles away. The road was good, and we thought we could make it by midnight, even driving over a strange road. So we started for it. Philip was 19 miles, and slapping was pretty continuous, Florence claiming to have killed six at one lucky slap, each of which was dining on her face, while both the women found silk hosiery a poor extension for their knickers. While a resident of Philip was directing us to Cottonwood he kept both hands in motion and admitted that they were pretty bad, but had been there only one day. At a car in a tourist camp a man killed mosquitoes on his wife and himself while she did the cooking. At a farm house all hands were armed with towels except the baby and all were in constant motion.

At 11 o'clock we drew up at Wasta. One man who had not gone to bed said the mosquitoes had been pretty bad, but since it had grown cooler he did not notice them. We listened; there was none of the hated music; the tourist camp was a half block away, while Rapid City was 46 miles in the distance. By a vote of 2 to 1 we decided to stay, and pitching the tent and killing a mosquito or two each, we were soon fast asleep.

❧

At sunrise I rose to write this report of the previous day, the women having demanded that we make a late start. No sooner was I out of the tent that I was met by hundreds of the enemies of the night before. I then understood why another camper had started so early, his car having waked me when he cranked it. Writing was out of the question, neither could I remain with that ravenous host, and to go back into the tent would be to take a lot of the foe with me. So I called to wife and daughter; we broke camp in record time and ran 35 miles to Box Elder before stopping to cook breakfast.

It was a beautiful drive, graveled road nearly all the way, and the rest smooth and dry. Jackrabbits were plentiful and we saw one sage hen, a bird so nearly extinct that I was doubtful if we would see any. That pretty nearly completes the fauna of the plains as we will see it now. The buffalo we will not see unless specimens in captivity; the antelope is even more nearly all gone; the only bear we are likely to see will be tame ones in Yellowstone. The coyote has not appeared yet, but I am not in doubt as to him. We will travel several thousand miles yet through his habitat, and he certainly will be much in evidence, and we will see the fresh workings of the badger, even though we do not catch a glimpse of him. He is a "night bloomer" and with years in his home land I never saw but a few. The prairie dog is not yet quite due and the prairie chickens will appear in due season, although rarely.

At Rapid City we stopped long enough to take gas and were told that there were a good many mosquitoes there last night. On the way up here we stopped for a time and watched South Dakotans put up hay. When we were in Kansas, the first cutting of alfalfa was already sold and the second almost ready to cut, but by the time we had come this far north the first crop was just ready for cutting and we have seen considerable of it along. This was one of the most active scenes we had seen. Mowing, raking, hauling and stacking were all in progress. Part of this was new to us. No wagon hauled in the hay, but a sort of "go-devil" on wheels, 15 or 20 feet wide, mounted on wheels, with a horse hitched to each end and long teeth out in front just clearing the ground, the driver would run those projecting teeth under four of five cocks of hay, push it up to the stack and onto the teeth of the stacker, when a team of horses would cause the latter to rise in the air and turn over, dumping the whole load onto the top of the stack. When a man wanted to go up he just went up with the load of hay and was landed safely on top.

At Sturgis we went down to the tourist camp, one of the finest groves imaginable, doubly welcome after so long without a tree any-where in sight. Being among the first we had choice of location, and plan to visit Fort Meade this evening, attend the Presbyterian church in the morning and then run down to the state park at Custer. The women are doing a little laundry work while I write my reports, and all hands are recovering from the strenuous battle of yesterday. There may be a few of the singers show up tonight, but the worst is presum-ably over, and Jersey at its worst has no longer any terrors for us.

Day's run 81 miles, with a few yet to be added for the trip to Fort Meade and going up town after supplies. Total since leaving home, 2,017.

By sunrise the clouds were broken and fleeing before a delightsome breeze. I took the daily picture of the camp by mounting some mam-moth tanks of an oil company, and by the time breakfast was ready the sun was out. We spread the bedding to dry and made deliberate prepa-rations for continuing the journey. Mrs. Clark and Florence went to a store in the village and bought some traveling hats. Up to that point Florence had worn a straw hat—a most unsatisfactory head dress for touring, and Mrs. Clark thought she had lost her hat in Sturgis—(It later was found in the tool box!)—so by the time we started clouds were threatening again, but we moved on south through a very scenic region. Away off to the left rose Harney Peak, only visible at times, its summit more than 8,000 feet above sea level, but entirely free from snow, a sufficient proof that the snow fall had been light the previ-ous winter, for we afterward found deep snow on ground considerably lower. We drove a little out of our way to visit Sylvan Lake and spent an hour or two there. It is quite a local summer resort, the season not yet being really open. Just then it was enlivened by the presence of one of the troops of cavalry from Fort Meade, out on a hike, the soldiers arriving just before we did and not yet having made camp.

The country was very rugged, rocks forming a common feature of the landscape. We were out of the known mineral bearing part of the Black Hills, but not beyond the range of the prospector, that hopeful specimen of the genus homo who has done so much to conquer the West. Their dreams were familiar to me, being the same I had known years before in regions far removed. At Hill City we had been shown some specimens from a nearby "prospect," with the assurance that it was "on the same lead as the Homestake." O, the thousands of hearts that have been cheered by the certainty that their owners had discovered the extension of some famous wealth producing vein! The fact that the country was traversed by a multitude of veins, crossing and recrossing each other, in and out, appearing and disappearing, changing their characteristics with every few yards of extension, made no difference to the prospector. The famous vein might be 10 miles, or 50 miles away, nevertheless he could recognize it just as certainly as the oil operator knows that the rich pool best known in his section has at least a large bay reaching out under the land on which he holds a lease!

We were barely started from Sylvan Lake when rain began falling again, continuing quite steadily several hours. We were in a great game preserve, the most attractive feature of which was "The Needles," a region where granite monoliths 100, 200 and even 300 or more feet high rose from bases no larger than the tent and so many of them that we did not attempt to count them.

By noon we reached a game camp, where there were some forest rangers, and at a lunch counter we bought some sandwiches and other eatables together with coffee, and ate our lunch. The memorable part of the lunch was the sandwiches. I only recall having seen that kind twice before, once a few years ago at a restaurant in Ohio while we were detouring between New Matamoras and Caldwell, and once when Ashton Lodge had been enjoying a little feed and I took home some of the surplus sandwiches. On the latter occasion the women of the household would take one of the sandwiches as the brethren had prepared it and transform it into a half-dozen or more of the kind the ladies feed each other on those occasions when "everybody reports a pleasant occasion." These were evidently intended for prospectors and hunters who had been gone from their base of supplies for some time.

Following down one of the creeks which rise in the Black Hills we passed a big state game farm, there seeing our first buffalo calf on the trip.

A few miles down that creek and we were fairly out into the moat which surrounds the Black Hills, and the rain ceased. That moat is one of the curiosities of that region. Get one of the excellent maps of the Geological Survey and examine it. You will see that tributaries of the Belle Fourche river head about directly west of Harney Peak, and after flowing northwesterly until they empty into the Belle Fourche, swing with that stream around a half circle until after hundreds of miles of wandering they meet the Cheyenne away out east of Harney, the Cheyenne head waters having been but a few feet on the other side of the ridge from the Belle Fourche. Each follows an irregular half circle, and united they make a valley completely around the Black Hills, which lie within the area embraced within those two half circles. Not only is there that one great valley, but between it and the high lands are a succession of little valleys, each running not away from the mountain peaks, but around and parallel with their bases until they have accumulated sufficient force to break through the little ridge which confines them on the lower side, as at Rapid, Sturgis, Spearfish and other points. No wonder geologists work cheerfully year after year in that mysterious region. It was hard for us to tear ourselves away, for it is one of the most unique mysteries of the Creator.

We had not had a flat tire until after we passed Rapid City, from which place we ran again over the road to Sturgis, having finished a complete circle embracing rather more than the northeast quarter of the Black Hills. At Sturgis we got the tire repaired, took gas, bought supplies—so the notes tell me—and went over a road new to us to

Spearfish where we camped in a municipal tourist camp with a charge of 50 cents and shower baths extra. That latter was unusual.

Aside from having seen the lark and enjoyed his song all day, we saw a huge eagle sitting calmly on top of a telephone pole.

The speedometer showed 123 miles for the day, which included some bad roads, many miles traveled in the rain and an unusual amount of loitering along the way to look at the beautiful scenery. Once during the day the road ran through a tunnel under a sharp point of rock, but it was only a few feet long.

꧁꧂

Sunday morning was a lazy time about camp. The night had been rather strenuous. At the community house in the park—in the very center of the campers, there had been an old style dance. I did not learn the causes back of it, but in some of the stores circulars were displayed announcing a public dance in Sturgis "June 20, 1898," and I inferred that it was an annual event since. We were told that it was to consist of quadrilles and similar dances exclusively, all round dances being barred. The dancing did not bother us, we being at some distance from the hall, but there was a great deal of noise from the people who were coming and going until a late hour. Their cars all seemed to be the noisy kind, just like those which come or go about a Chautauqua tent during the performance.

I was one of the early risers, and armed with the camera, started out to see where the road went which passed the camp ground. By a long, easy grade it ascended the hill which formed the north bank of the creek on which we were camped, and which there broke through the encircling hills, and from the rim rock which formed the top of the hill I had a splendid view of the town and the valley in which it was situated. Passing the last few feet of rise which lay beyond the rim rock, and there lay the plains. Just under me was Fort Meade, which claims to have the finest situation of any military post in the West. To the northeast per-haps five, possibly 10, miles rose Bear Butte.[4] It is another Devil's Tower, only not so steep, as it can be climbed. Away to the north perhaps 40 to 50 miles was another, and 15 to 20 miles to the east of it was still another, the latter being twins. Evidently all these were alike in origin, and not dissimilar in appearance. Bear Butte covers more than a square mile of land, rises a thousand feet or so above its base by strenuous effort, as there are none of the difficulties which confront the climbers of Alpine heights. All else was just prairie—the land we had been traveling for a day or two, to which reference has already been made.

The morning's walk revealed a lot of wild flowers, some of varieties new to me, and I returned to camp with quite a bouquet.

Notices in the park invited us to the Presbyterian church at 11 o'clock, so an hour before we got in the car and ran first up the hill where I had been in the early morning, then back past the camp ground and on another road down the creek a mile to Fort Meade, where we drove for some time around the quarters and parade ground.

It is a three company post, now used strictly as a cavalry post. For the past year it has been occupied by Troops A, B and C of the Fourth cavalry. Once we stopped a young trooper and asked some questions. He was the temporary possessor of a bull snake about three feet long, which he was carrying in both hands when we met him. Florence was greatly interested in the snake, but had no desire for closer acquaintance than the width of the car. Just then the troopers were away on summer encampment duty, a mere "corporal's guard" remaining to care for the property, and it had a very deserted appearance. That was also increased by the fact that it had been built for a much larger force, accommodating eight or nine troops of cavalry in the old days when there were Indians to fight in this part of the world. In those days most of the duty on the plains fell to the cavalry, but in this age that branch of the service has fallen largely into disuse among all nations, mounted men being of little service under modern conditions, even the old object of rapid locomotion being surpassed by the auto truck, or "lorry" as our British cousins denominate them.

We were rather disappointed at church, the morning hour being given over to the Sunday school for its Children's Day services, and amateur performances of any kind are not very interesting when you do not know any of the participants. One or two features were of real interest, however, some others were unintentionally amusing, and there was more than the usual amount of prompting and urging the children to do their parts.

Two o'clock came before we broke camp, bade our neighbors farewell, and started for some other part of the Black Hills; we did not know just where except that it would be on a great circle which would embrace the more prominent features of South Dakota's "playground."

Up a very rugged canyon, much of the way its walls sheer rock for hundreds of feet, over one or two divides and down long hills, brought us to Deadwood, the pioneer town and commercial capital of the Black Hills, and county seat of one of the three counties covering South Dakota's mountain region. Planning to come back through there, we merely noted that it was a typical western mining town in its location, and passed on, up four miles, some quite steep but all good road, to Lead, site of the Home-stake, the greatest gold mine in the world. Some tramping to points of vantage, a number of snap shots of one of the largest holes in the ground ever made by man and of the mammoth mills where 4,000 tons of ore are daily ground to powder for sake of the dollar or two of gold that they each contain, and we were again on the road bound south.

Then for the first time Florence learned one of the optical illusions familiar to all mountaineers. We were going down a long gentle grade, not steep enough for the car to coast, and she found something wrong with the car. Where it should almost run itself she was compelled to step on the gas quite a bit. She tried to recall what she had heard of having to readjust carburetors for high altitude, and realized that it was a fact. Just then we came to where a mountain stream ran beside the road, and those waters were coming down with a rush to meet us—flowing rapidly up the hill we were descending.

Then a glance backward, and it became a surprise that we had been able to climb that hill on high.

Put a good-sized mountain in the background and on any grade easily negotiated by a car, one has a feeling that he is going downhill. The little pea under the walnut shell is not the only thing that deceives the eye!

Our fine highway finally came to an end in the forest reserve, and we came onto a road which made us homesick, it was so like West Virginia. Steep, rough and narrow, we could make little time on it and occasional meets were made with difficulty. A few miles of it and we came to the finished road again, and a few miles brought us to Hill City, a railroad station with a bank, high school, several stores, three filling stations and a dozen or twenty houses. Also a tourist camp on the public square, where several cars were parked beside a cooking house and abundant piles of wood.

All afternoon it had been evident that some part of the Black Hills would be dampened before morning, and by dark we could see that it was not far to the south of us, with dark clouds threatening where we were. As a precaution the tent was staked down more securely than usual and the curtains put on the car to protect its contents, and just at bed time the storm broke on us. For an hour we lay there and held the flapping walls of the tent as best we could while the rain pouring on the roof ran down them and was pretty evenly distributed between the ground and the edge of the bed. Then the wind lulled, the rain ceased and I went to sleep lying on a pile of wet bedding hoping morning would be dry and warm that it might be dried out before packing for another day's run.

The speedometer showed a run of 81 miles for the day, a total from home of 2,203.

⁕

Rain came at intervals throughout the night, and in the morning the tent was wet, although the bedding was dry, there having been no

The fish hatchery at Spearfish, South Dakota, that the Clarks visited. *Courtesy South Dakota State Historical Society.*

wind. But we waited a little for the tent to dry before packing it, and so were late in starting.

Spearfish is the site of one of Uncle Sam's fish hatcheries, trout of various kinds being supplied from there to the streams in that region. So our first act was to visit the hatchery, where the superintendent kindly showed us the various stages in the life of his stock. None were in the incubating stage then, as the roe is obtainable only at certain times of year and this was the off season. But he had several thousand young Rainbow trout only three weeks old—not yet ready to eat, the young fish like the young chicken, doing best when not fed too early. From those babies there were fish in all stages up to a foot and a half or two feet long, the latter of course, being their breeding stock.

On the superintendent's recommendation, we took the run up Spearfish canyon, and found it a sightly place. It offered thousands of ideal picnic sites, but the "features" mainly were its rocks; not equal to the Needle district down in the state park, but a very sightly place.

The Homestake Mining Company has a road up the canyon eight miles, but we turned back at six miles.

As we started out of Spearfish we passed an orchard of several acres, the first one we had seen since entering South Dakota. Indeed on only two or three occasions had we seen so much as a few trees about a home. We saw no apples on this one, and either it was an off year, or the fruit was still very small. A little farther on we saw another orchard of 40 or 50 trees. Apparently the pomologist of South Dakota is not overworked! Although we were now in a country where timber was not very scarce all the higher hills having more or less trees, the telephone poles were still of the kind we had seen so often out on the prairies—just a little pole wired to a fence post. Some of these South Dakota farmers work a hardship on the telephone people by using iron posts for their fences, but the spliced, joint ownership pole was very common.

Along here for the first time on the trip we saw lots of colts. There were no large droves of horses, but evidently it was a horse country, the main herds being off on range somewhere and we were seeing only the home places with the colts.

A peculiar formation was observable here. The lower lands were intensely red, not a clay as our road showed, but a rock which in places clearly showed strata, yet readily dissolved into earth, and the occasional farm showed that it was prolific soil. Looking off across the valleys one could see that everywhere at a certain level the red was capped with a rock almost white, which of course made light colored soil. Scarcely ever was there timber below the red line, while the light soil and rock quite uniformly bore pine trees, the larger ones having been cut.

CHAPTER THREE

South Dakota to Yellowstone

TWELVE MILES OUT OF SPEARFISH WE CROSSED THE STATE LINE, A large sign bidding us to "Quit roaming and try Wyoming." We did not look back quick enough to see what South Dakota had to say to the person entering that commonwealth.

Sundance was a mail point for us, and we got there a few minutes after noon, only to find that the post office was not open between 12 and 1. It struck us that we had found a post office with less accommodation than at Ravenswood. So we waited until the office opened, and not getting all the mail due, we waited awhile longer for the day's mail to arrive from Spearfish. That was a fruitless wait, but it gave a chance to have a long talk with the local newspaper man. There had been two papers in this county seat of 200 people, but the opposition was being moved to Buffalo, and the *Times* man had it all his own way. Also we found that little town was waiting for its Chautauqua, which would begin in a few days. Where the audiences came from we could not see, as there was far short of a house for each square mile in the surrounding country.

Twenty miles out of Sundance, a square turn to the right took us onto a road leading to the Devil's Tower, 12 miles away by the road, which was not ideal, but quite passable. Rain had fallen through all that country the night before, and some of the road was over gumbo which is impassable at a certain stage following rain. Also we had to ford the Belle Fourche river, and if it was swollen by rain it was not fordable by cars, so there was some uncertainty about getting through, and if we did cross the river and rain came, we might not get back. But Devil's Tower was one of the objectives of the trip, and while storm

The Clarks visited Devils Tower, which stands 1,267 feet above the surrounding terrain in the Bear Lodge Mountains of the Black Hills. President Theodore Roosevelt declared Devils Tower a national monument in 1906. Lakota Indians on the Belle Fourche River in Creek County, northeast Wyoming, call Devils Tower "Bear Lodge" and "Brown Buffalo Horn." This photo was made by George A. Grant about 1925, the year the Clarks made their visit. *Courtesy American Heritage Center, University of Wyoming.*

clouds were forming to the south, and one was even letting go its rain far off across the prairie, we took the side road and started to see that wonder.

It had been in sight occasionally for several miles, and as we reached the top of one hill after another it appeared ever larger. A new store was being built near the fording of the Belle Fourche, where we learned that the ford was all right, and heedless of approaching rain we went on. Beyond the river the road winds around for two miles, slowly climbing the base of the monolith, until we arrived at the camp site at the very edge of the talus at the foot of the tower proper.

A 1925 street scene in Sheridan, Wyoming, the year the Clarks visited the city. *Courtesy American Heritage Center, University of Wyoming.*

While we were examining the wonder, another car arrived, and two more before dark, so we had a fine camp. We took pictures in every conceivable condition, and after supper had a big camp fire around which Ave and some of our neighbors sat until nearly midnight. The Devil's Tower deserves a description beyond what can be given on the road, and, with other monoliths of similar origin (although not similar appearance, for it is the only one of its kind), will be treated in a special article at a more favorable time.

With a cold wind blowing apparently down off the Tower we went to sleep after a rather lazy day, the speedometer showing only 88 miles for the day, 2,414 from home.

One of the neighbors and his wife made an effort to climb the tower this morning and he went up a surprising distance. It is claimed, on what authority I know not, that there have been two men and one woman on the top of the tower; that a ladder was constructed by driving wooden pins into the crevices of the rock and nailing a wooden strip to the outer ends to sustain any which might not be firmly attached.

Our friend went to where he could see some of the pins, but he had heard that the outer strip had been removed to prevent anyone else repeating the performance. This was on the east side, where part of the tower has a slight lean to the west. This tale may be true, but I did not have the faith in it that the other fellow had.

It is noticeable that there is much less talus on the east than on the other sides. Also it is evident that at no far distant date in the past there has been a heavy fall of stone from both the west and south sides, as a large part of the stone at the foot on those sides is fresh, not yet sufficiently weathered to have any lichens on, while the older stones are at least thickly specked with them. Of course such thoughts come the most frequently when one is climbing over rocks as big as a house, where he moves with difficulty, with the tower looming hundreds of feet in the air above him.

Two or three more snap shots at it from favorable appearing spots and we were off. The day was uneventful. We were running through one of the poorest parts of Wyoming; the farms were all ranches and far apart, as were also the towns. Moorcroft, Gillette and Sheridan were the three principal points of the day, with some names for places between, the towns themselves not yet being built.

Water was to be found only at long intervals. Sage brush became very common, two flocks of sage hens were seen and one or two jack rabbits. A new bird appeared in the form of a black bird with white spots on its wings, similar to the red on the blackbird, but the bird itself was quite small. I had never seen them before and did not learn its name.

Late in the afternoon we overtook a band of 2,000 sheep being driven along the road, and it took some time to work our way through them, even with the aid of the herder and his dog.

Shortly before 7 we rolled into the tourist's camp at Sheridan, to meet with disappointment. It had been advertised as the prettiest camp in the West, but we found it bare of grass, not very smooth and quite small. Fortunately we got a small house to sleep in, although for once we were not afraid of rain. The threat the night before had brought no rain, but on the contrary was followed by one of the pleasantest nights of the trip, and there was nothing particularly threatening this time as we went to bed.

Speedometer showed 202 miles for the day, 2,616 from home.

———

One of the party required some dental work the morning after arriving at Sheridan, so we did not get away until after noon, the forenoon being used to write letters and send cards to a lot of friends who are still remembered in spite of the distance separating us. In the vicinity of Sheridan are a number of sightly places, but all too far away for us to spare time to see them. Sheridan is the site of a beet sugar factory, which turns out some 17,000,000 pounds of sweetness each year, and of a flouring mill with a daily capacity of 1,000 barrels. The same company owns other mills in other towns in this part of the world. Aside from these there is little manufacturing of any kind in the state.

At 1:15 we started again, all with teeth in shape for duty, finding a road of quite indifferent quality for many miles. It was very crooked and quite rough; many short heavy grades and frequent railroad crossings. At the Burlington crossing the standard warning to the automobilist reads: "Seven automobiles are struck by trains each day, and 13 passengers killed or injured. Common sense demands that you be careful." Railroad companies are all anxious to devise some means of preventing the automobilist from disputing the right of way with the trains, but none has yet been found.

Shortly before entering Sheridan the evening before we had seen some coal mines, and soon after leaving they became quite numerous, some of them of no mean caliber, judging from the villages of company houses surrounding them. But they were closed down or only running with a partial force, as shown by the many barred windows. Farther south along the Burlington there is considerable coal mining, Newcastle being quite a mining center. But Wyoming is destined to always rank far down the line as a coal producer because of quality. It is all lignite of varying grades, although usually fair, and while it burns well it will not last long, slacking rapidly when exposed to air and light. On that account its market must always be local, and high freights practically exclude higher grade coals from a distance. This combination may eventually result in establishing manufacturing industries here with comparatively cheap fuel. Of all the mountain states Wyoming has the least water power, her streams all being small, she being one of the few states with no navigable water. Her mining industry—coal and metal—is small, her tillable areas where there is moisture enough for a crop are limited, but as a stock country she will always take high rank. She claims first place in sheep and wool today, and in horses and cattle she ranks high.

Thirty-five miles from Sheridan we crossed the state line and entered Montana. This put us onto the Crow reservation. When the writer crossed it 25 years ago there was little evidence of occupancy by anyone but since then the Indians, who now number only about 1,700, have been given lands in severalty and the remainder mostly sold or leased. Irrigation ditches parallel the Little Big Horn river down which we travel, and the bottom is nearly all in grain or alfalfa, while as we go farther down the amount of "dry land" farming increases, and the outlook for a crop seems to be good. Last year these dry lands produced tremendous crops, the profits more than making up for the losses of the two previous years. The Montana Farming Corporation operates largely here, having one tract of 10,000 acres and another of 7,000 on the reservation, and for the three years have obtained a profit after paying rent for their lands. In most countries successful farming by a corporation would be impossible.

One village of Indian teepees was seen and photographed, and there were several fair villages of whites, sometimes with Indian mixtures either externally or internally, that is with pure blooded Indians and whites or mixed breeds containing both bloods in the same individual.

The 7th U.S. Cavalry on parade during the fiftieth anniversary celebration at the Custer Battlefield in 1926, the year after the Clarks visited the site. *Photo by L. A. Huffman, courtesy Montana Historical Society Research.*

Finally we came to signs commemorative of the tragedy of long ago, that event which had caused us to come this route instead of one farther south which had been strenuously recommended to us all along the way. For it was here 49 years ago today, June 25, 1876, that the Seventh Cavalry met the combined forces of the Sioux and Cheyenne, several times their number, and General Custer with five troops of his regiment were killed to a man—263 men—the only survivors being an Indian scout and a horse, while the other seven troops met losses which in ordinary battle would be considered very heavy. The Indians state their losses to have been about 700, but to this day no white man knows where they were buried.

We drove up to the battlefield, now a national cemetery and took a number of photographs, but this event, with its accompaniments in a way historical deserves a separate article, and will be written hereafter.

We drove on to the little village at Crow Agency and camped in a beautiful place where we had things all to ourselves, and I could but muse over the difference the 49 years had brought; or even the 25 years since I first was there.[1]

One thing in the afternoon had started a train of thinking along a different line which the reader is privileged to continue. We overtook

A crowd stands before the fence that surrounded the Custer Monument at the Custer Battlefield in 1926. Had the Clarks made their western trip a year later they might have been in the photo. *Photo by L. A. Huffman, courtesy Montana Historical Society Research.*

a wagon drawn by two horses—an unusual sight on the road—and as we passed I noticed its high bed was filled with bones. Now after the Indian in this country came the hide hunter to kill the buffalo, and after the buffalo were gone came the cattle with hard winters occasionally slaying them by the thousand, so that by the time the farmers began to drift in the prairies were covered with the accumulated bones of ages. Then it was found that those old bones could be ground into fertilizer, highly prized by eastern farmers, and they were gathered and shipped away by the carload, just as those in the wagon were destined to be.

That is one leg of the triangle.

The second leg began with my trip through here 25 years ago while it was strictly Indian. The hide hunter had gone and the farmer and bone hunter had not yet come. The Crow Indians had not yet adopted the customs of the whites to any considerable extent, and their dead were buried in their ancient manner, being wrapped in blankets and hoisted into a tree beyond the reach of prowling beast, there to dissolve into elemental dust, or remain as long as the tree stood. Now I could see, as I had been informed before getting this far, that the old corpses had all disappeared from the trees. Those of later years had been buried after the custom of the whites, but the old aboriginal remains had vanished.

That is the second leg of the triangle, and the reader can supply the third as well as I can, for it extends beyond the reach of facts known.

⁘

The same [Leap XVIII] being a short one made June 26.

We missed a rare opportunity last night. As we approached the scene of Custer's last battle there were a lot of autos loaded with Indians coming down the hill from the plateau on the west, scattering in three directions as they came onto the bottom land, and we decided it was a funeral occasion. At the battle ground we met some other tourists who had spent the day at some Indian races, the race track being in sight two or three miles to the southwest, and we knew it was a race instead of a funeral which had drawn the crowd we saw. So it was a time of jollification with the Indians, many of whom were at the race track. That night they had a dance. Not one of the modern fox trotting affairs—which doubtless they can do as well as anyone—but the kind of dance the Crows held in the days when the world first heard of the Little Big Horn. And we slept through the night not knowing that such rare scenes were being enacted only six miles away! Certain Indians nowadays put on what is said to be their old time dances for the gratification of tourists at so much per grat. But a gen-u-ine Indian dance given solely to please themselves is something worth going a good many times six miles to see, but like Vice President Dawes at a critical time, we slept peacefully on ignorant of the greatness of the hour.

After breakfast we visited a curio store, with a stock of Indian goods. The agency school across the street has been there some two score years teaching the children of the Crows the arts and sciences of the white man, and their own arts have been forgotten. So this kind of goods have become scarce, only a few of the old ones now being able to make them. And while the Indian has been acquiring the white man's art and science he has largely held onto his own superstition.

I think it was back during the presidency of Grant that the Indians were transferred from the War Department to that of the Interior, and instead of trying to civilize the Indians by overawing them with physical force, the plan was to reach them and convert them by the methods of modern Christianity. In order to do this the different reservations were parceled out among the different churches, only one to a reservation, in order that the savage might not be confused by having to select from a multiplicity of faiths. Either that policy was changed in later years or else this was an exception, for both Catholics and the Baptists are here, each with its church and teacher of the faith. I asked the garage man which had the greater following and he said it shifted a good deal, the most popular being the one which had the most to eat. Then he added that there were some who were Catholics all the time.

As long as the road kept down the Little Big Horn it was a fine highway, but later it took to the hills, after which it became sadly deficient, being rough all the time, sharp turns at short intervals and much of the way with an up and down direction like the surface of the sea. It made one almost seasick to ride over it. The variation to that kind of surface was long hills, two of our descents being the longest and heaviest of the trip so far. All of which things related kept us from reaching Billings until 12:30. This metropolis of Eastern Montana is a thriving city of 15,000 to 20,000. Like others noted, its manufactories are mainly beet sugar and flour.[2]

We entered the valley of the Yellowstone only a short distance below Billings, where it is very narrow, but above the city it widens to a width of two or three miles, with irrigating ditches carrying water onto every foot of it, and there it is a wonderfully rich country. Alfalfa, wheat, sugar beets and beans are the leading crops. Of the latter we saw one field of 40 acres with many "patches" of from five to 20 acres. At Billings the first cutting of alfalfa had been made some time ago, occasionally the second crop showing blooms, but farther up the valley cutting was in full blast, practically all of it being harvested and stacked by the methods heretofore described.

The difference in the time of harvesting indicated our climb upward. At Billings we were a little over 3,000 feet high, our camping place tonight, Warren, Mont., is some 4,500 or 5,000 feet. Even the cactus tells this story. All the morning hours it was in full bloom. Then came the Yellowstone valley where cultivation had eradicated it, and when we were once above the ditch and back to natural conditions there was only an occasional blossom, and at camp only buds were to be seen. But the sunflower was ever the same. From Kansas northward and upward it has shown a steady increase in blossoms, fully as much as the passing time would warrant.

During the afternoon the sun was hot and hot waves of air met us at frequent intervals. Especially was this noticeable when we picked up our usual nail and had to stop while five patches were put on the tube and the tire pumped by hand. And all the time straight ahead in the very direction from which that wind was coming, loomed the Rocky Mountains, covered with snow far down their sides!

A desolate looking land it is above the ditch, although in spite of its apparent worthlessness there were many farms—dry farms—where there was an abundant promise of a bountiful yield of wheat, now just well headed—and here and there a fine field of alfalfa.

We were due to reach Cody for camp, but bad roads and tire trouble delayed us so that we camped at Warren near the state line. This is a station on the Cody branch of the Burlington. The railroad company bought a spring in the mountains several miles away and piped it down here, and the 12 houses in town haul or carry water from the tank. They are well scattered, some being near a half mile away, the water problem is not settled to what one might call perfection.

With a "water system" this is an important point. The last town we passed before getting here was Bowler, where there was but one house in which was a store and a post office. I don't know where the water came from, but some of it was from the melting of the ice hauled from Bridger 16 miles away with a two-mile hill to climb. For the store carries cold drinks at only 100 per cent, advance above prices down in the valley.

The speedometer showed 152 miles for the day, making us 2,862 miles from home.

We were up and off early Saturday morning, June 27, for on that day we expected to enter Yellowstone Park, one of the great objectives of the trip. Between Warren, Mont., where we camped, and the next station on the Burlington lay the state line where we would again enter Wyoming and then all roads, would lead to the Park.

They did. But unfortunately we took one that was very deliberate about its entrance. We should have gone to Frannie, the next station and there turned southeast to Cody but instead we followed a routing from Frannie to Greybull and did not discover our error until we came to the bridge across Shoshone river and decided with a good road ahead it was better to keep on than to turn back. Routings in that section sometimes are not very full in their detail. For instance where we then were we were told to keep on through an irrigated district and at a certain mileage turn off across the desert. The next remark was that in 25 miles we would come to a railroad track.

It worked just that way. That desert would have delighted the heart of Zane Grey, but the most delightful thing we found about it was the road. It was as good as a paved street. Sometimes from the top of a hill we could see it far ahead. Once at the top of a hill we three guessed how far it would be to the top of the next one across the valley. The scribe's experience in desert land gave him an advantage and he made the best guess, putting it at 4 1/2 miles, while Mrs. Clark said 6 and Florence held to 3 1/2. The speedometer said it was 4.8. And it was generally a sure enough desert. Even sage brush would not grow except in occasional spots and cactus was very rare.

We followed that railroad which appeared out of the desert until it showed irrigated and cultivated land ahead, and coming to the very first house in Greybull turned sharp round and headed for Cody on a new route. The road continued good and 10 miles out we came to another irrigated tract, running through it for several miles. Then out onto barren land. This was not desert, but fertile soil only lacking water to make it fruitful, and many ditches had been made ready to carry the water which was to come from we knew not where. Here and there could be seen the house of a settler, usually about the size of our tent, and in which no human being could live with any comfort but which was sufficient to comply with the requirements of the land laws. The land perhaps was already sold to some speculator, for the papers that very day reported a speech by Secretary Work saying the Government was considering abandoning its reclamation projects in the northwestern states because it was not working satisfactorily, the lands passing too much into the hands of a few men instead of making homes for many people.

It was out in that arid region that the motometer began showing too much heat. An examination showed the oil low, although it had been alright late the evening before. An emergency can then on the fourth year of its touring was put into the engine and we went ahead. But the meter continued to show heat and frequent stops were made to cool it, with occasionally a long coast downhill. Finally we came to an irrigating ditch and a gallon of water in the radiator—which had been filled that morning—ended the trouble and we soon went down a long steep hill and as we turned onto the main street of Cody the engine stopped.

It was only four blocks to a garage and I walked down and carried back enough gasoline to run us in!

We ate lunch in Cody and laid in supplies for the stay in the Park. The banks of that village are very citified and close at noon on Saturday, but the grocer from whom we bought provisions had no hesitancy about accepting one of my cashier's checks from home. How to carry funds for a long journey is a problem to the tourist, who usually does not care to carry much cash. "Traveler's checks" are the usual means chosen, they being quite universally accepted, although I had one turned down by a garage man up in Maine. But this year I am using cashier's checks from the home banks, and have had no difficulty as yet.

With Leaping Lena full of oil, gas and water and an extra "grub" box full of provisions, we left Cody in mid afternoon, the snow clad mountains of Yellowstone in plain view. Four miles out we entered Shoshone canyon and the camera came into use, although it was not overworked until we reached Shoshone dam. Wedged in between two rock walls reaching far above it, that structure at first appears small. With a width of 40 feet on the bottom, the walls are but 200 feet apart at the top of the dam, 238 feet above the bed of the river.

While we were viewing the dam the busses carrying the regular tourists arrived, 18 of them with only one vacant seat. Florence was in charge of Lena at the time, when a bus stopped beside her and the driver said: "Hello there, Ravenswood. Do you know Beulah Gillaspie?" He had known her during her summer at the park a few years ago, and seeing our Ravenswood plate on the car was almost like meeting an old acquaintance.

The road was wonderful. Through three tunnels it ran to reach the dam and three or four above there, beside the lake formed by the dam or beside the river above, for we followed the Shoshone river closely from Cody 55 miles to the park entrance and two miles beyond where we camped beside a 40-year-old native of Wyoming now living in California, on his way home after a visit to the land of his boyhood. The desert has faded away, we are in the midst of a forest of pine trees, and our sleep will be deepened by the sound of the rushing river. The women are a little fearful of bears making a raid on the provisions during the night, but the Californian says there will be none until we get into the park proper.

Speedometer record for the day, 182 miles, making us 3,044 miles from home.

※

It was not our intention to travel any distance June 28, it being Sunday, but after a leisurely breakfast we broke camp and started for the camp ground on Yellowstone Lake, 25 miles away where we would be in the

The original Fishing Bridge in Yellowstone National Park, constructed of rough-hewn corduroy logs in 1901. The Clarks saw this bridge in 1925; it was replaced in 1937. *Courtesy National Park Service, Yellowstone National Park, YEL 171144.*

park proper and ready to begin the grand tour the following morning. The hill up to Sylvan Pass was to begin only a little ahead, and we had been told it was pretty steep and narrow; negotiable in second gear generally but with the last quarter mile demanding low gear in all cars. It proved much less trying than represented. Fully one-half the distance was made in high, including much of the way after it became necessary to go into intermediate, but the last quarter-mile was a heavy climb. There was never a time when there was not a meet in sight, although much of the road was too narrow for cars to pass.

We only went a short distance until we began to see snow nearby and by the time we reached the summit we could reach out a hand and touch it, some of the drifts being 10 feet or more deep. Mrs. Clark and Florence snowballed for a time while I took pictures of them.

From the summit to Yellowstone Lake the descent is much less than on the east side, little of the distance requiring brakes, while considerable gas is burned going down.

Approaching Lake Junction camp we crossed "fishing bridge," where the usual line of people were trying to catch fish in the outlet of the lake and some of them had the goods to show that they were succeeding.

Camp is a large grove of pine and spruce trees, with probably 50 cars in it, although they are coming and going all the time, so that an accurate count cannot be made. Near the edge of the timber, looking out over the lake we are bathing, washing, cleaning up and writing letters, occasionally slapping a mosquito. We cannot do much else, for the sign says we are forbidden to feed the bear.

Speedometer says 29 miles today, making us 3,073 miles from home.

❧

On June 29 we reached Mammoth Hot Springs.

Cars had been coming and going Sunday, but more coming than going, and by night there were probably 75 cars in camp. Most were regular tourists but a few were from nearby points there only for the fishing. One of our near neighbors was a fisher, and presented us with three fine trout weighing about a pound and a half each. It taxed the capacity of the family to dispose of them at one meal, but we succeeded. Except Columbia River salmon I do not think I ever saw fish so red, but I did not learn the name of the Variety. There are some half-dozen in the park waters.

At the permanent camps in the park it is the custom to have some sort of social gathering or amusement each evening during the season. Quite commonly that takes the form of dancing, unless there is some entertainer of note who will contribute to the public enjoyment. But there is never dancing on Sunday evenings. People traveling in their own cars are welcome to these entertainments, so we went. The program was largely musical, with some instrumental music and a reader of no mean ability. It reminded us very much of an evening at Chautauqua.

One of the features not on the announced program was the constant slapping of mosquitoes, but there seemed less of that before the end of the hour, and when we came out of the camp dining room where the

Many roads in and around Yellowstone National Park were poorly maintained during the 1920s, like these rutted roads in Lamar Valley. *Photo by C. A. Lord, courtesy National Park Service, Yellowstone National Park, YEL 39992.01.*

program was given, the air was much cooler and the mosquitoes had disappeared. All day they had been present in camp, quiescent during the occasional brief times in which the sun shone, but beginning depredations promptly when a cloud gave the appearance of evening.

We started in due season this morning, this being our first day of sightseeing in the park, knowing that the time spent in traveling would be interspersed with many stops to see things of which we had heard for years.

The first stop was out a half-dozen miles from camp where we met our first specimen of the geyser family. It was not a sure enough geyser but a not far distant relative. First there were pools with bubbles rising through them, the water all quite muddy, and as we climbed higher the bubbles took on the form of boiling water. In the midst of the bare ground which marked the place, there would be holes not large enough for a chipmunk to get into, but the hand held over them told that it was hot down below. Just a little farther was the Dragon's Mouth, and well named we considered it. From a hole in the side of the hill just about the size of a hogshead, there came ejections of

This 1920s auto camp in Yellowstone National Park is much like the ones used by the Clarks during their 1925 visit. Photo by W. J. Cribbs, but the location of the camp is not known. *Courtesy National Park Service, Yellowstone National Park, YEL 32622.*

water about once a second. Several spurts would be small, possibly not more than two or three gallons, and then would come an extra large one throwing twice as much water. The dragon was not spouting fire, but it was spouting water which had been very near fire, for it was boiling hot. The throw was horizontal and the water spurted from five to ten feet, with splashes considerably farther.

These two specimens were far from any other geysers, and by the time we have made the rounds they may not seem worth mentioning, but for "curtain raisers" they were not so bad.

There are perils of the road which no amount of prudence could have prevented. Thus today we saw the aftermath of such. The ranger told us the day before that a man and his wife had been driving when a telephone pole fell just in time to hit the hood, and they were pretty badly hurt. We saw men resetting the pole. The ranger added that it was not a Government pole but one in a line belonging to the transportation company, and while it seemed to him that the company should be responsible, it was claimed to be merely an act of God that the pole rotted and fell. I do not think that plea has occurred to the attorneys for Ravenswood in its damage suit over the broken light wire. It might pay them to watch the outcome of this matter.

It is not my purpose in these daily reports of the contortions and peregrinations of Leaping Lena to tell of all the wonders seen in Yellowstone Park. They have been told time and again by abler writers. This is to be more a relation of personal experiences. The day will come when there will be an article dealing with the Park as a whole, which may go into a good deal of detail, and there may even be one on the parks we will see this summer, taken all together. Therefore I will not attempt a description of the falls of the Yellowstone, its wonderful canyon, the gorge, pinnacles, nor any of its details.

We debated whether or not to go over Mt. Washburn, the highest point in the park accessible to autos, or to continue on from the summit of Dunraven Pass with no farther climb. But our discussion was wasted breath. When we reached the Dunraven summit, 8,800 feet above sea level, we found deep drifts of snow. Some were not less than 20 feet deep, and on the summit of Washburn nearly 1,500 feet higher they may have been 50. The road was not open, and will not be for some time, even with the help of many men to take the snow from the roads.

We had an earthquake in camp last night. Nobody felt it, but they did in Norris Geyser Basin, just a few miles away, so of course we had it, too. But when we arrived at Mammoth Hot Springs at 4 P.M. the northern entrance of Yellowstone was still receiving all sorts of tourists, even though all Montana was sitting up waiting for further shocks, and counting back to determine how many shocks there had been, and the story was that Santa Barbara, one of California's beautiful cities, had been ruined by the trembler.

What with starting rather late, climbing many mountains, stopping to see much and ending the day early, the run was only 65 miles as reported by the speedometer, making a total since leaving home of 3,138.

༺ஜ༻

The same being a short one made on the last day of June, the tourists walking a considerable part of the time.

Mammoth Hot Springs is the principal entrance to Yellowstone Park. For many years it was the only one, the Northern Pacific with its line to Gardiner having a monopoly of the Park business, which was then small, no private conveyances being permitted in the park. Finally other railroad companies succeeded in showing how absurd it was that the people should not be allowed on their own playground unless they patronized certain corporation, and other entrances were opened and the park opened to the public, whose property it was. Now there are good highways leading into the Park from each point of the compass, but being first, and possibly best—at least it is the shortest run from civilization on the outside—it still is the popular approach.

The great tour of the Park is an automobile road running around it with one cutting across the center. Besides these there are many trails leading into the wilder part of the park, either by hikers or on horseback. But by far the larger portion of the visitors see only the road around the Park, and that is all we had planned. Because we entered on the east and were to leave on the north we got more than a complete circuit, and while we had run from Lake Camp up to Mammoth Hot Springs, some of the "sights" had been passed by unseen because we were to go over that part of the road again. But beginning here we were to "make a clean sweep" as we went.

So we began with the terraces of the hot springs, the one great feature of the north end. We made the complete circuit of the Terrace Trail, learning when too late that we might have gone all the way around with Lena, saving ourselves a lot of hard climbing. We also learned that we could have looked at Minerva Terrace at the beginning of the trail and at Jupiter Terrace at its end 300 yards away and seen all that was worth seeing. All between, with the exception of the Devil's Kitchen, was merely a repetition of these on a smaller scale. The exception noted is a crack in the earth, apparently once occupied by hot water but now empty, down which a stairway permits one to go to a depth unknown to us, as we did not explore it. Perhaps nowhere else on earth is there so large a tract over which hot springs issue, and the water discharged makes a considerable stream.

The entire walk must have been four or five miles, and when we returned to Lena we were getting tired and it was almost noon. We ran out a few miles and stopped to eat beside a sprinkler filling station. When the weather is dry the road all seems to be sprinkled, and at very short intervals there are tanks from which the sprinkling carts can be filled. Probably the great purpose of this is to help fight fire in the timber, for fire is the greatest menace to the park.

In Norris Basin we came to our first genuine geysers—not counting the Dragon's Mouth—two or three of them being of note, and besides the Black Growler, where steam makes a hoarse whistle all the time, we saw two very good geysers in action, one repeating about once a minute and the other having a show for our benefit, although it performs but seldom.

A rain began about the same time which was not for our benefit nor at our request. There had been rain regularly every day and night since we entered the park. Three or four showers during the day and one or two in the night, all light, or at least not continuing long, and usually with more or less lightning, and it seemed to have commenced to continue indefinitely. So we passed up the Lower Geyser Basin with the intention of coming back the next day to see it. Some of the road around the park is for one way traffic only, some may be traversed in the opposite direction at certain hours only, but this was a two way road, so we could come back at any time.

At Old Faithful camp the ranger told us the transportation company had some tents to rent to transients, and after some trouble we found them—six, count them, six—and of course all filled long ago. So we had to camp. But just then the rain ceased, the sun came out and by bed time the ground was getting pretty dry, there was not a cloud in sight, we had seen Old Faithful perform twice, once by daylight and once under searchlight. Also we had gone to see the bears eat their supper, stayed long enough to see them eat, left the crowd to watch the other three that came for the second table, saw the speedometer read 53 more miles for the day, making 3,195 from home, and just as we were dropping off to sleep it began to rain gently on the tent!

❧

Which [Leap XXIII] really was too short to be worth reporting, but is given to keep the balance straight.

At this camp there are really only two things worthwhile—watching Old Faithful squirt water through her teeth and taking stock of the people in the camp. This is the fourth year that the Clarks have been camping along the automobile highways, and in that time there have been a number of noticeable changes. The first year a majority of the cars were of one of the cheapest varieties, while this year higher priced cars of all makes are common. Only a few minutes before this letter was commenced a Lincoln drew up within three or four rods of Lena, and the average car in the camp cost from $1,000 to $1,500. The style of tent is as various as the makes of cars, but the old preference for a tent attached to the side of the car is passing. The separate tent is more and more common, and the umbrella tent is rapidly growing in favor.

No matter what the kind of car, it is usually loaded, inside and out. We saw a flivver today carrying four people, no door of which could be opened, ingress and egress being only by climbing over. One man had a bath tub hung on the side of his car. It was the baby's tub, a bright red one, but probably there were times when papa and mama used it also, although at most of the regular tourist camps there are shower baths, free to the campers.

The free municipal camping places also are disappearing. A nominal charge of 50 cents a car per day is common, and with water, fuel and police protection added to the baths there is no objection to paying it.

All kinds of people are on the road, but in most cases they are all there also, father, mother and all the children. Babies at the breast and little fellows who enjoy a lot of running are all out together on the highway.

This is a big camp, the largest we have been in yet. In fact it is so big that a woman got lost in it this morning. Shortly after I began the day's activities an elderly woman came along carrying a towel. I supposed her on the way to the bath house, but to a woman at the next car she confided that she was lost. She was as helpless as a child lost in a strange city, except that she knew her name and that she belonged to an Idaho car. A number of questions were asked and answered without doing any good, and the suggestion that her people would soon be looking for her brought no consolation. A number of neighbors became interested, and soon one located an Idaho car which was the one wanted.

Watching Old Faithful is the other occupation, and we attended to it pretty steadily, making one run down to the Lower Basin and out through the Black Sand Basin to look at a lot of the lesser lights, having some laundry done in the Handkerchief Pool the last thing before returning, just in time to see Old Faithful perform again. Twelve outbursts in 13 hours is her regular gait, and each performance only increases the desire to see another. As an attraction it is easily equal to all the other geysers put together, and its time of performance is carefully noted. Each time among the spectators will be seen several loads of people who are ready to go, but line up to see it once more, and as soon as the eruption is over their journeys are resumed.

We think it may be the altitude which affects us, for we all notice that exercise wearies us quickly, and at night we are tired. Since we entered the Park Sunday morning we have been from 7,000 to 8,444 feet above sea level, and exercise "takes one's wind."

Watching the bears eat is on just now, but none of us went tonight, once being enough, so we are patiently waiting for the next appearance of O.F. [Old Faithful] when it will be dark enough for the searchlight to be in use.

The speedometer says Lena ran 26 miles today, or 3,221 since leaving home.

No rain today, but threatening tonight.

⁘

[Leap XXI] being that of the second day of July and our last one in Yellowstone Park.

With Old Faithful ejecting thousands of gallons of water per minute, while in eruption, through a narrow orifice, forced out by a steam pressure of hundreds of pounds per square inch—a pressure which no boiler ever made would bear—one would expect a noise which could be heard a long way, and in the immediate locality would be deafening. We were camped about three blocks from the geyser, and even in the stillness of night never heard it, and if put on oath I could not swear that there was a single sound audible from it when as close as I dared to be—just beyond the reach of the hot water, which went straight up unless blown a little by the wind.

So we had to depend on what mariners call dead reckoning for the time of the next performance, and sometimes we went too early. Also there is not the regularity to its eruptions that there is to a well performing watch. From its eruptions the first night we figured that its allowance between outbursts was 68 minutes, and on that basis we determined on the time of the first display we would see next morning, and shortly before that time I went to the curio store, leaving the women in camp to meet me at the "ring side." We allowed a little too much, and those who "abode with the stuff" came sauntering back just after the show was over. So this morning we disregarded our estimates, accepted that of the gas man instead, and waited nearly a half hour after we were ready to go, for the gas man wasn't on the inside either.

At the conclusion of the show we ran down to the hotel where the saddle horses were waiting for their riders, to get a picture of them as one of the features of the place. That let the rest of the string of cars which had waited that last spasm get ahead of us, but Lena takes nobody's dust long when Florence's foot controls the gas, and in a little while he was in the lead up the mountain, a run of less than five miles taking us to the continental divide, or summit of the Rocky Mountains, and for the next four miles we were on the Pacific Coast, crossing back again when we reached the pass wherein lies the divide between the two great oceans. In that first pass lies Lake Asa, which plays no favorites but in the spring debouches its flood waters both ways.

"It's a bear," exclaimed Florence, and slammed on the brakes as a fairly large animal dressed in black rose from the road and ambled toward the timber to one side. In the shade of a tree it stopped and sat down just as the car stopped. There was a frantic effort to get the camera in readiness, but Florence feared the shade was too dense, and said no picture could be taken there. Then with a bow the bear—it was evidently a yearling and a pretty well reared boy—stepped out of the shade four or five steps toward the car and sat down in the sunshine with as pleasant a smile as one could wish. The camera clicked, Lena began to leap ahead, and the bear's smile changed to a feeling of disgust. He had performed to perfection, even inconveniencing himself, and those West Virginia pikers never offered him a bite to eat.

At that time we were ignorant of bear etiquette but were soon to get a lesson, for we had gone hardly more than a mile when we came to two cars parked and six or eight people out in the road. We asked if it was a bear, bears being fresh in mind, and were told that it was, it being just behind the bushes, and they wanted it to come out and get its picture taken. One woman in the party had visited Yellowstone before and knew what to do so she got a sack of cookies out of the lunch box, shook the paper toward the bush and the bear came out and rose with his front feet on the car while she gave him a cookie and the cameras all clicked.

Then Florence must try it, so when the first cookie was eaten she got a cookie and "shook a paper sack," when the fierce beast came out

Many Yellowstone visitors, including the Clarks, enjoyed seeing the bears. Two years before the Clarks made their visit, Stephen Mather, head of the National Park Service, interacts with a bear to entertain a busful of tourists near the cabins at Camp Roosevelt. *Photo by H. W. Frantz, courtesy National Park Service, Yellowstone National Park, YEL 213470.*

and got a cookie. She was advised to hold it high and make the bear reach for it, but feared it would put its paws on her shoulders, which would be too much for her nerves.

Later in the day we saw another one at West Thumb, which evidently had lain around there and had been fed indigestible knickknacks by the tourists until it was suffering from indigestion. Coming along the rim of the canyon of the Yellowstone still later in the day we found a very large one leaning against a tree beside the road waiting for someone to "shake a paper sack," which is the bear equivalent of ringing a dinner bell, but we did not accept the implied invitation.

We looked at the wonderful canyon of the Yellowstone from various angles and on the way to Norris Junction passed a deer near the road. I got out and went back to get a "shot." It was a large doe standing with her head from me, and when I called gently to her she raised her head, looked at me long enough for the camera to click, and "turning on her heel," walked quietly away. I called to her again, hoping for another picture, but she would not look up any more. Still later at Mammoth

Hot Spring I used the camera on buffalo and picket pin gophers, which with a fine chance at a ground hog a few days before, should give me a good lot of animal pictures from the Park.

The whole day of July 1 without rain seemed too much of a strain and in the afternoon we had both hail and rain. There was little sightseeing except for the paint pots and geysers at West Thumb, things on which we were pretty well "fed up," and the grand canyon of the Yellowstone, part of which we had seen on our first round. So we traveled the larger part of the time, and late in the day passed under the archway at Gardiner, passing out of the Park, perhaps forever, but well satisfied with the five days we had spent therein.

Eight miles down the Yellowstone was Corwin Hot Spring, where we had been told there was a good camp ground and store at which we could get supplies. The camping place was as represented, but the store's stock of provisions was a can of condensed milk and two eggs. The women ran Lena down the river a mile and got a quart of cream and a dozen eggs at a ranch house, so we did not have to go hungry.

Speedometer showed 118 miles for the day, or 3,339 since leaving home.

CHAPTER FOUR

Montana and Idaho

[LEAP XXV] BEING MADE ON JULY 3 THROUGH A LAND OF NO HOPE or elsewhere hope has been blasted.

One part of the story of the West which has never been largely dwelt upon is that it is a land of blasted hopes. We were camped this morning at one scene of that kind. Almost the last thing we passed the evening before was a large tipple and a long row of coke furnaces. But it was idle, and falling into decay. We learned that it had been closed down for 15 years, and there was no expectation that it would ever start up again. For a time it had flourished; thousands of tons of coal of fair grade were taken from that mammoth mountain, and the coke furnaces glowed continuously in a land where coking coal is rare, and coke brings a high price. Then came troubles. Nobody here knows what. The story is that there were 1,800 persons who owned stock in the company, and the big fish decided it was time to eat the little ones. So a receiver was appointed, and as yet he has received nothing, and there is thought to be no hope that he ever will.

Even nearer by is another blasted hope, which like some of the dead geysers in the park still puts out a little steam, showing there is a spark of hope left. We are camped in a town once known all over the United States and even beyond her borders. A hot spring here was found to have wonderful curative powers for rheumatism. A three-story hotel nearly 200 feet long and correspondingly wide was built, with two bath houses, one with a pool about 50x100 where the water was only comfortably warm, for the ordinary cases and finishing up, and a smaller one where the water was only reduced in temperature to 120 degrees, for those so desperately afflicted that they were willing to be boiled if it promised any hope of relief. And for years that hotel was approximately full all the time. Men and women came from afar and were healed of their malady.

On the night of November 27, 1916, the hotel burned and for some reason has never been rebuilt. Work was started, one end was finished up so that the caretaker could live in it, and at rare intervals a little work is done on it. The frame is all up now, most of the siding is on, and the caretaker says once in a while a little lumber comes and is put on. But he has no hope that it will ever be completed. Transients and the sparse population for miles around come and enjoy the baths occasionally, possibly the patronage paying the caretaker's salary. But its glory is gone forever. Except for the tiny store across the river a quarter of a mile away the bath house is the only house in town. And it has an electric light system, hot and cold water running all over with spigots and drinking fountains galore! Where can you beat it?

And yet it is just as typically western as the big cities which have grown in a life time of the founder. We will reach another blasted hope at the end of this leap, and in a day or two will come to one in which I once had a vital interest, the history of which I can tell without once saying "they say."

Our road to Livingston, nearly 50 miles away, lay down the Yellowstone valley, and we hoped for good road and no grades. We were disappointed. The first 20 miles of the valley was made by a glacier in the long ago, and not only did it fail to shave off some of the projecting points of the mountain, but the intervals were filled with nothing but gravel, and that often quite coarse. I do not doubt but that in that 20 miles there is enough gravel to cover every road in the United States. And the valley is nowhere very wide. It made rough traveling because the larger stones had not all been removed from the road, and many hills were so long and steep that there was a good deal of shifting of gears.

A mile before reaching Livingston we had a little blowout, the first tire trouble in over a week, and it necessitated a wait of nearly four hours to have it vulcanized. This is a growing city. The valley for miles is wide and level, wonderful crops of alfalfa and grain are raised and the region is prosperous.

About 4 o'clock we turned westward again, following a small branch of the Yellowstone and the Northern Pacific railroad for several miles, then over a very low divide—which the railroad had to tunnel to a branch of the Gallatin, down it to the mouth, and out into the Gallatin valley, one of Montana's most fertile sections. For more than 30 miles we ran over a very good road, and on ground so level that for miles there was no bend in the road. Years ago I ran down this valley at the rate of 70 miles an hour, eating my breakfast in the dining car, and there was no discomfort. Today we were only running 30 miles an hour and the train behind us, which was operating the block signals just ahead of us all the time, finally overtook us, and it proved to be a long freight, mostly coal cars. So railroads can still make time there.

At camping time we arrived at Three Forks, one of the oldest towns in Montana, and the easiest to locate with certainty in the tales of early travelers. It is here that the Jefferson, Madison and Gallatin rivers come together, and by their junction to produce the Missouri. Lewis and Clark camped here on their famous expedition which clinched our title to "the Oregon country."

Here is another case of blasted hope, although it is far from being dead. For years Three Forks was an important trading center. Miner, stockman and farmer all came here. The two former were slowly vanishing, but the latter class were correspondingly increasing. Its one railroad was the Northern Pacific. Then came the Chicago, Milwaukee & St. Paul. It put on its experiment of a daylight train from Chicago to Puget Sound. At the end of each day's run was a town with great hotels, large enough to care for a trainload of transients from either direction. And Three Forks became one of those "one night stands."

Then the new company did still more—it located mammoth car shops at Three Forks. Miles of concrete walk were built, hundreds of houses went up, and a half-score of hotels and cafes prepared to house and feed the workmen. Three Forks "enjoyed a boom." A school building larger than Ravenswood's high school was built, the district issuing bonds to the limit to put up a fine building.

Then the Milwaukee discontinued its daylight train, and the car shops were moved to a new location. A town of 2,500 inhabitants and hotel room for 1,000 transients, dropped to a scant 1,000 people, with no transient visitors except the automobile tourists. Mining came to an end; cattle raising succeeded only on a smaller scale; for three years the farmers had small crops or poor prices.

Then came last Saturday's earthquake. The newspapers may have dropped the story early because of the much greater destruction a day later in Santa Barbara, but as a Californian suggested to me tonight, it is not certain that the California shake up was any more severe. There buildings towering high were numerous; here the town was mainly one story wooden shacks. Where they were two stories and built of brick they were ruined. In California a city of no mean size was the center of the disturbance; here were merely two small hamlets. We passed through the other, Manhattan, without stopping, but here we viewed the ruins well.

The school building lost the cornice and the top off its walls nearly the whole way around, and the walls are cracked to the very foundation, with occasionally a large section of the wall thrust square out an inch or two. Practically every brick must come down and the structure rebuilt entire. Being bonded to the limit—and even at a time of inflated values on which to base assessment—the school district is helpless.

The First Methodist Episcopal Church had a beautiful edifice. The bell tower on the corner lost its top and is cracked and wrenched outward down to the foundation. One gable end is gone down almost to the ground and much of another lies on the earth a mass of brick. Cleaning up the debris will cost more than the worth of the walls which can be salvaged. The Sunday School is meeting in the Odd Fellows' hall and the preaching is in the Presbyterian Church, those two structures being of wood and not remarkable for size.

The First National Bank building was badly damaged, the garage on whose ground we are camped tonight lost a lot of its front, where an imposing wall added beauty to the two story office and accessory department. Windows are broken and chimneys generally throughout town have lost their tops. Goods on the shelves of the stores were thrown to the floor, resulting in much loss, especially in the drug stores and in a somewhat lesser degree, in groceries. Had these business houses been tall brick and stone structures the loss of property—and perhaps of life also—would have been somewhat appalling.

The people like to tell how it happened—how the street seemed to rise up and dance, and how when one tried to run he had the feeling that he was making no progress. And through it all is no breath of complaint or discouragement.

Other calamities I have seen where a whole community was involved, but this was my first experience with an earthquake. Once before I felt one—and should have felt this as it was evident where we were at the time—but did not, but this was the first time to view the ruins while they were still fresh.

The scientist who talked to us at the community gathering at Mammoth Hot Springs the night after the quake told us that in this case the rocks where they had faulted somewhere in this part of the country had probably slipped as much as an inch, but there were faults in Montana where the movement had been 11,000 feet! However, his surmise was that only after hundreds—perhaps thousands—of movements was the displacement so much. Anyhow we can feel our own insignificance just as much if we believe the scientists as if we were strict "fundamentalists" and agreed in our ideas with William J. Bryan.

Some company looking for location where ground is cheap and quarters for workmen can be secured at low cost will do well to write to Three Forks.

Speedometer record for the day 117 miles, making 3,456 for the trip to date.

The same [Leap XXVI] occurring on the Nation's natal day.

The first thing which occurred to me this morning was a plain solution of one of the great problems of the day. Three Forks is the eastern end of the Chicago, Milwaukee & St. Paul's electrified road, the same extending from there to Malden, Wash., it being the longest electric railway in the world. At different points along the line the company owns water power rights in the neighboring mountains, and we saw a number of power lines coming in from them. That gives them the cheapest kind of power, and it is so used that instead of pulling a train up a hill with power and then using more power to put on brakes to keep it from going down the hill too fast, after an electric train has been pulled up a hill, the action of the braking force which restrains its motion generates more electricity which will help pull it up the next hill.

One of those engines was attached to a train of three cars at the depot nearby, and in order to get a picture of it I went over there with the camera. Just as I snapped the train started. Two people a block away began to shout and run; the conductor saw them and signaled the engineer. That mighty electric locomotive, more powerful apparently than any steam locomotive I ever saw, having six mammoth driving wheels on each rail, slowed down and stopped. The two flying figures arrived and climbed aboard; the conductor again signaled and the train was on its way to wherever it was scheduled to go.

Now that takes some time to tell, and it is not half of the story. By stopping to get those two people the passenger list of that train was doubled! I had an unobstructed view of the interior, and there were just four passengers.

That is half the story. The other half followed quickly. Across the street from the depot was a hotel in front of which a bus was taking on passengers to be carried out along that same line, and it had six of them. The electric train probably cost $125,000, perhaps more, and it ran on a track which cost half that much for each mile, which track it must keep up, and on which it must pay taxes. The bus cost perhaps $5,000 and ran on a road built and paid for by the public, including that railroad, and its rental for the use of that road was less than one per cent of its passenger fees. And yet it is expected that Congress will appoint a committee to find out why the C., M. & St. P. went into the hands of a receiver a few weeks ago!

The day's run was without any incident worthy of record. There was some trouble with the car, for which we stopped and had it examined by an expert at Phillipsburg, who found nothing wrong, but after which it troubled no more. It may have been due to bad gasoline, a thing tourists often mention but which we had never found before.

First and last it cost considerable time, and instead of reaching Missoula as we might have done we camped at Drummond in a very poor camp ground. The speedometer showed 181 miles for the day, or 3,537 from home.

⁓❦⁓

The same [Leap XXVII] taking the tourists to the old home in Idaho on July 5.

Drummond's was the poorest camp ground we have yet found, but was in a region where a good camping place would be hard to find, and the town was very small. A good stove and plenty of wood were furnished but the ground was very dirty, and only one or two of the half-dozen cars there were able to find even weeds on which to make their camping place.

The plan for the day was to make a short run so that Wallace could be reached early the next day, that town being the Clark home for seven years, but as time passed and everything ran smoothly, there was a growing impatience to get ahead and renew the acquaintances of bygone years, so Lena kept on leaping.[1]

Missoula had grown some during the almost a quarter century since I was there last, although the change there was not so marked as it had been at Butte the day before. In the old days Montana's metropolis had been an ideal picture of desolation. Naturally a barren hillside with little vegetation except sage brush, the discovery and recovery of the mineral wealth hidden in the mountain there had made conditions even worse than before, for the smelters had low smoke stacks from which belched forth a smoke poisonous to vegetation, and in the whole city there was no living vegetable matter. The housewives for a time imported house plants of various kinds, but they sickened and died so quickly and so certainly that the practice was soon abandoned, and there was not even the green of growing life in the windows. But the concentration of the smelting business under one head, and the improvement in methods brought about by further experience, and the melting of ores was all relegated to Anaconda, where one huge smelter was built on a high hill, above it towering a smoke stack 625 feet high, and the fumes which issue from it are so diffused by the time they reach the earth that vegetation, even in the immediate vicinity, is but little injured.[2] And at Butte young trees are growing all over town. In another quarter century it will be a beautifully shaded city.

Alongside us for the first 80 miles of the day's run was the double-tracked main line of the northern Pacific and the electrified main line of the Chicago, Milwaukee & St. Paul from Chicago to Puget Sound, and the remainder of the way was along a branch of the Northern Pacific and all but about 25 miles along the Milwaukee, and yet in all day we saw but one train, a dinky little affair of a baggage car and one passenger coach, just like Capt. Walker runs from Ripley! Not an ounce of freight appeared to be moving, and the passengers were waiting somewhere.

Two hard mountains to climb, the Camel's Hump and the Bitter Roots, the latter forming the boundary between Montana and Idaho, [at] an elevation which carried us into the immediate neighborhood of snow; the task even greater than climbing, of going down those same two mountains, and as we reached the foot of the last grade we were at Mullan, only seven miles from Wallace, and all thought of camping short of the old home was at an end. In the edge of Wallace we turned up a side street to see the site of the old home, then on to the tourist camping ground in a beautiful park which in the olden time was only a large bar of tailings from one of the crushing mills, and we prepared to clean up ready for church services in the evening, the speedometer reporting a run for the day of 198 miles, making 3,735 since leaving home.

This town of Wallace, commercial capital of the Coeur d'Alene mining district, the greatest silver-lead mining region on earth, was the Clark home for seven years, and although absent for nearly a quarter century, there were still a number of the friends of the long ago, and the day spent there was a very pleasant one. The town had grown substantially, not in any particular respect, but all over.

Membership in a fraternal order—charter members of the local organization—was made the occasion for a special meeting of the older members, resulting in a pleasant evening not ending until midnight.

A prosperous time the passing years have been for the Coeur d'Alene. Mines have been developed, yielded millions of dollars to their owners and been abandoned as worked out. The men who received the dividends have disposed of their suddenly acquired wealth as best pleased them. Some have helped their fellow-man—others have done little except injure themselves. There is plenty of evidence here as to the true value of money and whether it is a curse or a blessing.

One of the biggest improvements in the town was the paving of its streets and building roads to other parts of the country. Over one of those roads—not yet completed the entire distance but under construction—we left for the old home in Washington, where a sister of Mrs. Clark still lives. There was no stop until we reached Coeur d'Alene City, where we met a friend of our early years, now a leading lawyer of Idaho, and ex-member of her supreme court, Judge James F. Ailshie.[3]

From his office Mrs. Clark's sister was called over the phone and told that we would be there in three hours, and then Florence took the wheel, she having no regard for speed laws, and the 46 miles to Rockford were run in less than two hours. Here at the home of her sister, with another visiting her, we will spend a few days, driving about the scenes of early struggles. A few miles away lies her pioneer home, and about the same distance is the land which I homesteaded. In one direction lie her parents in their last sleep, and in another is the resting place of my mother and my oldest sister. All this country is hallowed in our memory, and here in the next few days we will live again the days when we were young people selecting life mates, and the spot upon which we plighted our troth.

The speedometer reports that we ran 117 miles for the day, making a total of 3,952 since leaving home.

AN INTERVAL

At Rockford the time from the 7th to the 13th of July quickly passed. The home of long ago, the scene of my first newspaper work on my own account was one of the early towns of the Palouse country, being a prosperous little town when I first saw it in 1884. In fact I think it was decidedly more prosperous then than it is today.

At the home of Mrs. Clark's sister, Lena was unpacked and we were at home for a few days. Old friends were getting widely scattered, and many were gone beyond recall. Many of the scenes of long ago were revisited and first and last a lot of the old friends were unearthed. Miles no longer counted. In the olden days a trip to Spokane was contemplated for days, and when undertaken meant two days of hard travel, one to go and the other to return. Now on a chance suggestion, a car will be filled in a moment, waiting only for the female members of the party to powder their noses afresh; the trip is made and the party is at home again in three or four hours.

In ways suggested by the foregoing, the days were passed, some of the journeying being done in Lena and some in the brother-in-law's car, but when the time came Monday morning for Lena to make another leap, his speedometer showed he had run up 132 more miles, making 4,084 since leaving home.

❧

Monday morning preparation for flight began early, but it was 10 o'clock before we were in actual motion. All the camping paraphernalia had been taken out to more readily use Lena for running about, and there were a lot of pictures to take and good byes to utter. Then we were off up the familiar valley of Rock Creek. Down that same road I had gone to town in the days when I was a homesteader, only it was a vastly different road—then merely the kind of a track made by repeated transits of horses and wagons; now graded smooth and broad and the surface protected by a coat of crushed rock well packed.

Five miles out a private road led from the highway to the house on top of the hill where my homestead days were spent. On one of the days we had gone there, and the house which I had built, mainly with my own hands, more than 40 years ago was still there except for the old kitchen addition, which had been removed and a different one built in its stead.

But the road today led not in that direction, but on up the creek crossing the state line into Idaho and at the same time entering the Coeur d'Alene Indian reservation three-quarters of a mile farther on. In ye olden time this had all been wild, uncultivated land, covered with bunch grass; now it was a pretty continuous wheat field. The country was beautiful. Given over mainly to growing fall wheat, the previous winter had been a hard one and much of the wheat had been frozen out, to be reseeded with a spring variety. This reseeding was in the full strength of its newly acquired heads of grain, as green as nature could paint it, while the fall sown was "ripe unto the harvest," but not with the gold of the poet, for the popular varieties grown here now are almost as red as blood.

Interspersed between these blocks of red and green were other squares—possibly only 10 acres but more likely 40 or more—of the newest entrant into the diversification of farming in this region, common garden peas. When someone inquired of a friend how many peas he had in this year and was told that he had 20 acres, the astonished stranger is said to have exclaimed: "Why, you certainly can't eat that many!" In the journeying during the interval I saw thousands of acres of peas, all the leading seeds men of the country being concerned in the crop here. For several years they have been grown, the amount increasing yearly. The farmer threshes them as he would wheat, and the seeds men run them through a fanning mill before accepting them, after which the peas are assorted by hand at the warehouses, this in part accounting for the fact that the $1.50 a bushel paid the farmer grows to about $8 by the time they reach the big eastern grower.

Some other seeds are also grown here—the turnip seed crop having been threshed only a week or two before we came—and a number of flower seeds have been raised here for many years. But the pea industry is the only one in which many men are concerned or to which many acres are devoted. Within 10 miles of Rockford there are probably 10,000 acres in peas, four-fifths of them being Alaskas. I don't know where the other varieties are grown, but here there are only the lower stalked varieties.

On across the reservation, now largely owned by white men who have persuaded the ex-savages to sell their lands, and of that still Indian owned but under cultivation, almost every acre is rented to a white man, for the Indian does not take kindly to farming. Then over a considerable mountain and down a long grade to the St. Joe, the railroad bridge across the river being plainly seen, a mile or so away. That bridge I had crossed scores of times, its principal reason for being remembered being that it is higher above sea level than any other draw bridge in the world, but away up here in the mountains is a regular line of steamboats running on Coeur d'Alene lake and the St. Joe river.

A few miles farther on and we were into St. Maries, a town just starting when we left Idaho 23 years ago, but now a town of 4,000 or more people, and the county seat of a newly created county of Idaho. Here we were greeted by Mr. and Mrs. H. M. Thostenson, friends of bygone years, whose children have so far advanced that it is their children who play about the home of the grandparents, although they are some on whom the passing years have fallen lightly.

The speedometer says we came 46 miles in the two hours run, making 4,130 miles over which Lena's wheels have rolled since they passed off Noah Stanley's ferry boat.

Although I had never been at St. Maries, the place was not entirely strange to me. The different mountain streams emptying into Coeur d'Alene lake are all similarly situated. In the dim past they ran their several courses into a deep canyon where their waters were united. Then came the upheaval which dammed them up and made a lake of what had been a deep gorge. Coeur d'Alene lake is some 30 miles long but scarcely ever as much as two miles wide, while a considerable part of it is 1,000 feet or more in depth, and its tributary streams are only continuations of the lake where the hillsides have washed down and filled up the valley except for the channel, through which the water scarcely moves but has sufficient depth to render it navigable for vessels of considerable size.

Consequently the St. Joe and St. Maries were streams quite like the Coeur d'Alene, and I was well acquainted with the latter. When the excitement over the white pine of Idaho began, there was a little town started at the junction of the St. Maries and the St. Joe which was christened St. Maries and for a time I listened to the call for a newspaper there—that being one of the first wails of the newly born western towns. There was no railroad and no promise of one, and the only means of inlet and outlet was the river, frozen solid for three or four months of the year, and even the assurance of a big "land office" business in the way of publishing final proof notices for settlers did not persuade me to locate there. Thus one of my financial mistakes. The

Milwaukee built its main line down the St. Joe, two mammoth milling companies put big plants there, the demand for more logs led to the building of a branch railroad some 75 miles long, old counties were divided and St. Maries blossomed out as the county seat and principal commercial center of Benewah county.

After an early supper the entire party in two cars ran for miles up the river—narrow mountain valleys with the road cut into the mountain side and occasional rich farms down on the bottom, and here and there a tiny lake of a few square rods or an acre or two, richly stocked with bass, and continually sought by fishermen. The river alongside was filled with lake trout, splendid fish in their way but too slow to excite the sporty fisher, who insisted on going farther up where there was swift water and the fish put up a harder fight when caught. Our host had made such a trip the previous day, and at supper we had been filled with the consequences of his trip, while the ice box contained enough [and] more for breakfast.

The return to town was made after dark, when we ran down to one of the mills and for an hour or two watched lumber being made at the rate of 10,000 feet an hour. The mill works two shifts of eight hours each. In the dreams of what is to come I see another mill even larger than this one, and well worthy of description as it is, I refrain from such an attempt now, feeling that the milling industry and the way in which it affects the country, together with its companion subject, forestry, is worth a special article.

Another illustration of the smallness of the world awaited us in the morning when a chance remark brought out the name of the resident pastor of the Methodist Church. He was the man who united us in marriage a third of a century ago, so before leaving we drove to the parsonage and I asked for the return of the money paid him on that occasion. He refused to pay it, contending that I had value received, but after he told his story of the intervening years, and showed the regular life of a Methodist preacher, how he had risen from one charge to another, each of more consequence than the other, until he had reached the top and with his declining years reversed his course and went down the hill like the setting sun; then I knew that he could no longer pay back the fees which he had collected on the upgrade.

Bidding the minister goodbye we were on the road for Garfield, Wash., arriving early in the afternoon. The first house we passed after entering the town was the one I built as a home for the bride to be, and in which both our children were born. The old friends remaining here will be few, but they will be very dear ones, and under such conditions we ran Lena down to the garage for an overhauling, with the speedometer showing a run for the day of 62 miles, or 4,192 for the journey.

ANOTHER INTERVAL

Wednesday, July 15, while the women enjoyed the hospitality of Garfield friends in general and Mrs. Guinn in particular, I drove down to Hay to see Jim Taggart. It had been 19 years since I had been through that country, and then it had been on a train, while now I was in an automobile with Mr. Guinn at the wheel, and therefore had a much better view. Except for better roads, better farm houses, a little more shade and an appearance of better tillage on the farms, there was little change in the first 30 miles. Then as now, wheat was the predominant crop, with now about one-third of the land in summer fallow. It is that method of summer fallowing the land at frequent intervals which has resulted in the near eradication of the wild oats, Chinese lettuce, Jim Hill mustard and other pests which worried the farmer and lessened the yield of his fields. Now they were quite clean generally, and the color of the landscape was that of the grain.

Beginning at Spokane and extending southward to an extent which we have not yet reached, there was a hard freeze at a critical time last winter and fall sown wheat was frozen out. About Spokane nearly a third of the ground was replanted in the spring—usually to the same grain. As we went farther south the condition was worse, and by the time we were well on the road this day, say 20 miles out, the destruction had been complete and every bit of the land was resown, and that in a region where spring wheat had been abandoned long ago as too uncertain to be profitable. But having been so hard to the farmer as to ruin his fall work, Providence became more kind, and the spring sown crop has met with perfect conditions. It seemed that even more than usual of the ground had been sown, for in that lower region, farther from the mountains and the cooler air which attaches to them, it is customary to crop the land only every other year, tilling it the off year to preserve the moisture and give two year's rainfall to one crop.

But this year certainly more than half the ground was in crop—wheat almost exclusively, with occasionally a little barley. It was now fully ripe, and harvesting apparently was to begin about the next day. To my disappointment it was not yet under way. Around all the fields a few swaths had been cut, and then other roadways had been cut around and over the hills to enable the harvesters to have access to the different parts, for on many of these hills the cutting machine has to run at the proper angle or it cannot be run at all, and it results in seeing fields with streaks and stripes running in all directions. Some of these strips were cut with a mowing machine and some with a binder, but the grain cut will be used as hay, there being no grass found which has proven very satisfactory as a hay producer in this semi-arid region. Some of the fields are immense, the largest we saw this day being one where there are 8,250 acres in wheat this year!

A little of this wheat will be bound, and we saw a few binders in the fields, but not one at work. They are on a new model, calculated for this country where much of the ground is so steep that an animal can scarcely stand on it. The tractor is helpless and all the work is done by horses and mules, the latter growing in favor because of the intense heat of harvest. But by far the larger part of it will be cut with a "combine," a machine which cuts and threshes the grain without letting go of it, the straw being scattered over the field, while the grain is run into sacks and then sewed and dropped in bunches on the field to be picked up later by wagons. A gasoline engine runs the separator and the cutting is done by a machine of the binder type—minus the binding apparatus—which hoists the grain directly to the cylinder. The length of cycle varies from 10 to 20 feet, and the amount of grain cut in a day varies accordingly—from 20 to 45 acres. From 20 to 30 horses pull the machine.

Into a region of that sort—with its possibilities as a producer of wheat still unknown, and then supposed to be merely a grazing region of doubtful worth—came J. B. Taggart with his wife and they opened a small store to sell goods to the sheep men and cattle growers. The country developed; the farmer came with his new ideas of "dry land farming" and values immensely increased. Like other merchants, Mr. Taggart had been compelled to take land in settlement of store accounts, and that land had risen in value from its nominal price of $1.25 an acre to $30 or $40, and in a brief time the Taggarts became one of the wealthy families of the county.

In his store, now of much larger proportions, I found Mr. Taggart, while in a neighboring town I saw one of his sons acting as cashier of the Taggart bank. Others of the children have married and gone, but back on those hills—barren except when the ingenuity of man conserves the scanty moisture which Nature supplies—remains the father, the principal factor in the life of his community. It is not all roses, for there are thorns in his life. The last two years have been hard on the farmers of that region, and the merchants and bankers have been left to mourn over many an account while a customer heretofore rated as solid has gone through the bankruptcy court and contributed little in the way of dividend to his creditors.

But the yellow fields all about give assurance of a harvest which will pay old debts, fill purses for the future and restore the sadly fallen values of farm lands. From 25 to 40 bushels will be the yield of each of these acres, and the price today is $1.33 per bushel. With fields ranging from 500 to 10,000 acres it can be seen that these farmers are going to have some money, and with that floating about the man who has been carrying a load for two or three years will probably "drag down" quite a pretty little sum.

✤

Which same [Leap XXXI] was a very short one made on July 16. In accordance with garage custom, the work on Lena was not done during the day allotted for it, but waited until the next morning when we were there watching to see that it was done, and it was afternoon before we started on the hop we intended to make in the morning. We retraced the routing of the last run as far as Farmington, and then out a few miles into the country to visit a nephew.

His family had all been acquired since we last saw him and unfortunately the three older boys were away from home helping to harvest the wheat crop of Eastern Washington, and we saw only the wife and three other children.

The speedometer reported only 17 miles for the day, making 4,209 since leaving home.

✤

Friday morning we left about the middle of the forenoon to make the run to Cottonwood, Idaho, where another nephew was to be found, the day promising one of the widest variety of conditions and scenery of any on the entire trip. Back through Garfield, and then on south through the Palouse country. Wheat, wheat everywhere. Little more than a fourth of the acreage was being "summer fallowed," and the other three-fourths was in wheat, only an occasional field of barley or oats being seen, and we were practically out of the pea country. The fall sown wheat had been badly damaged, and most of the crop was spring wheat, still entirely green and liable to damage from hot, dry weather, while the spots left from the fall sowing were thoroughly ripe, much of it cut and a little being threshed. Once we met a "combine" on the road, the cutting part being detached from the threshing section to accommodate it to the road, the combined machine when ready for action requiring a width of 30 feet or more, making it a bad thing to meet on the public highway.

Various towns once familiar were passed, each in turn presenting the picture which has become so familiar since we returned to this country, where the small towns have all improved considerably in the two score years since we left, but with practically no exception have not grown in population, and in many cases now number fewer inhabitants. The buildings are much better, the homes are better equipped and living is on a higher scale, but in both country and small town the number of people has steadily slumped.

All the better town houses and a great many of the farm homes are fitted up beyond the wildest dreams of the fathers of the present owners, who built those homes 30 or 40 years ago. The telephone is a matter of course, just as much as is rural mail delivery or the automobile in the garage, but it does not stop there. The water power company in Spokane has wires strung throughout the country to furnish lights and power for these small towns, and any farm home not too far from a line can have a wire run to the house and get anything wanted in the way of light and power. So you may stop at any of the better farm houses and you will find a bath room with hot and cold running water, an electric washing machine, probably an electric range for the family cooking—everything in fact except moving pictures and of course that lack is largely equalized by the radio.

All the principal highways have been graveled, and instead of either mud or dust according to the season, there is a fine road every day in the year. And speaking of dust, we of West Virginia do not understand the word in even its crudest sense. We were too early for dust here, but there were occasionally faint suggestions, which almost stifled us and made the natives admit that it was a little dusty. Our soil is usually either sand or clay, and disinclined to separate into "particles lighter than air," while the base of this soil is volcanic scoria ground by time or passing wheels into impalpable powder. In a road where there is much travel and no surfacing the dust now lies from four to eight inches deep, and after "wheat hauling begins" it will be more than twice as deep. The revolving rubber tire picks it up, a good sized pan full at each revolution, while an obliging wind seizes upon it with glee, transporting without charge in the general direction of the Rocky Mountains. As a matter of historic fact, dust storms from this country have been noticeable far beyond the Rockies, the dust laden air being plainly distinguishable clear through to Hudson's Bay.

I have endeavored to give you a picture of what the dust is now, but remember that it is a scant month since there was rain here, and it may not have any more for two months to come. In the mean time every wheel which passes along the road grinds more earth into dust that it lifts into the air, even with the addition of that which the wind takes of its own free will without assistance.

Surfacing roads so as to avoid that dust has cost an enormous sum, and run up the local tax rates to a degree which we would deem confiscatory, and yet there is no suggestion of going back to old conditions.

But getting back from these general conditions to the day's travel: About noon we suddenly shot out over the edge of the Palouse plateau, and for a moment it seemed that we were going to run out into the air above a bottomless abyss. Peering over the edge, guarded only by a fence at the side of the highway, we saw the city of Lewiston and the junction of the Snake and Clearwater rivers a scant two miles away as the bird flies, but some 2,000 feet below us. In the olden days men had built a wagon road down that barren slope, twisting and winding back and forth so that the descent was made in five miles. It was a wonderful road. Now Idaho has made it part of its "North and South" highway, and a new easy grade goes down the hill, the old five miles being transformed into eleven. Running east until a favorable projecting point is reached, it turns west to the next good point. The official count as we went down the hall was that it required 16 of these "switchbacks" to take us down. Each one carried us a good many feet farther down and into a climate perceptibly warmer.

At the bottom of the hill we ran across the bridge spanning the Clearwater river into Lewiston, and as I sought a barber shop for the improvement of my personal appearance, I was greeted with the information that the thermometer was registering 198, but with the acknowledgement that the 9 might have been a 0. The breeze was blowing at a lively gait, but we had found ere we reached the bottom of the hill that it was cooler with the wind shield closed than with it open!

Shortly after reaching Lewiston the nephew from Cottonwood joined us and ere long we were once more under way, running up the Clearwater to the site of the pioneer church of the Northwest, the old Lapwai mission among the Nez Perces, then up a hill quite like that we had gone down into Lewiston, the climb being made in eight miles, and on top was the mammoth wheat field of Camas Prairie, one of the granaries of the Northwest, rolling into Cottonwood about 7 o'clock, the speedometer reporting 155 miles for the day, increasing the run for the entire trip to 4,346.[4]

⚜

July 18 was spent at the home of the Cottonwood nephew, and after attending Sunday School and Church service the next morning—said nephew being superintendent of the former and lady preaching the sermon—in the afternoon the journey was resumed, we being accompanied as far as far as White Bird. This day's run over part of the "North and South" highway of Idaho, more notice of which will be taken later, and covered some historic ground. Besides the usual incidents of pioneer settlements generally, it was on the White Bird grade that the first fight of the Nez Perce war occurred, that being the real beginning of that remarkable retreat of Chief Joseph when for weeks he outwitted the whole United States army and almost succeeded in reaching the friendly realm of Canada, a few untutored savages opposed by the skill and ingenuity of the greatest nation on the continent.

Down near the foot of the grade is a spot marked by a peculiar circumstance. At the time of the White Bird battle one lieutenant disappeared and could not be accounted for afterward, the final entry opposite his name being "missing." When the North and South highway was being graded the plows and scrapers unearthed the bones of a man, and among the odds and ends therewith were army buttons and finally a lieutenant's epaulet, so after the lapse of nearly half a century the mystery of the missing lieutenant seemed cleared away. The monument erected there gives no name but merely recites that it is the last resting place of a soldier, but there is no reason to doubt his identity. How came he to his death? Presumably battling for the flag whose honor he had sworn to maintain. Who buried him in that lonesome spot? Quien sabe?[5]

Parting, perhaps for the last time, with the nephew, his wife and son, we journeyed on, first down White Bird creek, then up Salmon river to the mouth of Little Salmon and on up it through the mountains onto the meadows made long ago by the much sought beavers, we ran on late, with no desire for supper until at 8:30 we reached the village of New Meadows and camped on the stubble of a recently mown meadow, where an enterprising filling station had provided accommodations for tourists.

The afternoon's run was recorded at 111 miles, making a total of 4,475.

⁕

After breakfast we started on, the course changing from south to south-west, passing from the northward flowing Salmon waters to a tributary of the Boise, over a hill which seemed too small to be a watershed of any consequence.

I think I failed to mention heretofore that the personnel of the party had been increased at Rockford by the addition of Mrs. Clark's sister, Mrs. J. C. Lodge of Tacoma, who joined us at the home of the younger sister there, intending to accompany us on the way from there to her Puget Sound home.

Among the newer and therefore not yet well-known highways of the country is this North and South of Idaho, and in it may be found a lesson for West Virginia. Separated by mountain barriers almost insurmountable, Idaho was so thoroughly divided that there was real opposition within her borders to being admitted as a state into the Union, and a real effort was made at one time to create a state from the western part of Montana and the eastern of Washington, united by the "panhandle" of Idaho, leaving the southern part of the territory to be attached to Nevada, Utah, Wyoming or such other state or territory as might be willing to accept it.

The appearance of the automobile into American life, with the resulting advance of road building as a national and state policy, brought about the North and South project, and it is now practically completed to the point where it connects with the great lines in either part of the state and the remainder is merely the gathering together of various local roads mostly long in use. Having traversed that part of the road which presented the real engineering difficulties; the cost of which would have staggered any except the most determined people; and forming a feature which will attract the attention of tourist and scientist for ages to come, I take this occasion to roughly outline some of its salient features.

The Lewiston Hill already has been referred to in one of the former "leaps" of this narrative, so I will now say only enough to refresh the reader's memory and connect it with the latter description.

Adopting at the beginning a determination that no part of the road should exceed five per cent in steepness of grade, up which any car can go in high, and down which it can run without brakes, the Lewiston Hill was the greatest of the three mammoth mountains which had to be conquered by the steam shovel and scraper. Much of it as steep as a mansard roof, and nearly all of it too steep to be climbed by man or any domestic animal other than the goat, even steady heads are inclined to waver when they gaze over the edge of the grades, as already related, the road descends approximately 2,000 feet in 11 miles while from top to bottom in an air line is a scant two miles. Viewed from either top or bottom of the hill, that winding, twisting highway is a marvel.[6]

And to a tourist who is so fortunate as to be there at the proper time, one of the drawbacks of the scenery becomes a feature which will never be forgotten. We had that good fortune. When we reached the bottom of the hill and from the valley at Lewiston strained the backs of our necks looking at that marvelous hill, the elements which sought to keep us from seeing it made it all the more wonderful. Towering so high in the air that it would have hidden a winter midday sun had it been south instead of north, and reaching to the right and left miles beyond the range of vision it rose from the sandy valley, points and projections, canyons, gulches and recesses, like a deeply carved cameo, and ever of the dull grayish brown of mingled dead grass and almost dried up sage brush.

But over that monster Nature drew a veil in the form of air laden with smoke and dust until the heights were almost lost to view, and only by an effort could one locate the line separating land and sky. The result was ghostlike. It was an eerie thing, only half real and hazy as a dream. A weird thing it is, one of the unique things of earth of which some day poets and artists will rave, but which neither poem nor picture will reveal to man, only actual vision making that impression which never can be eradicated.

There is still another picture which will remain to man, denied to us by circumstances, and yet comprehendible in a way from a mere description. That comes on a dark night when automobiles come down that hill. Then the observer sees one bright star after another appear in the northern sky, high up in the heavens, and begin an erratic course, ever changing, but slowing working their way downward until they appear to teach terra firma just across the river. Rushing meteors we all have seen, but these things—not merely one meteor but whole schools of them, spaced at differences apart, pursuing the same courses but at varying rates of speed, passing and repassing each other, that is something reserved for the traveler on Idaho's great highway.

As already told, from Culdesac we had climbed just that same kind of a hill so far as its engineering difficulties were concerned, coming at the top onto Nez Perce prairie, thence down and across Lawyer canyon, not so great a depression but crossed by the Camas Prairie railroad on the highest railroad bridge in the world, and up onto Camas Prairie, one of Idaho's garden spots, these two prairies having once been the home of the Nez Perce Indians. Today they are merely two great wheat fields, the only exceptions being here and here a rocky protuberance, up to whose very edge the soil is rich and fruitful.

To the stranger one of the peculiar features of this country is that the top of the hills are productive, rich tillable land without artificial irrigation, while the slopes and the bottoms along the streams are so dry that only by pouring on water in immense quantities can anything be produced, sage brush alone excepted.

So that Sunday afternoon we had run rather more than 20 miles through Camas Prairie wheat fields, over a rather low ridge separating these waters from the Salmon river, and then down another of those remarkable "hills" 10 miles to White Bird, then by a gentle grade a mile farther to Salmon river.

There began a region which will be attractive to many a tourist, and which made me almost sick to run through without stopping. In the mining history of Idaho, Salmon river occupies a large place. Its gold was discovered early, and men are still hunting for more of it—not always successfully. Along the bars of the river, and up on the hillsides alike are the relics of those searches, where the gravels of both this and former ages have been sifted in rocker and sluice box and their golden particles removed. Along those same bars are hundreds of acres of other gravels which men have not disturbed, although doubtless they have dug deep enough into them to become satisfied that that magic substance "pay dirt" does not exist there. In other places, hidden away under the sliding rocks from far up the mountain sides are other gravels, once the bed of the Salmon or its predecessor, where the yellow metal lies thick. Here and there are tunnels where men have gone in and robbed these graves of a dead past.

The casual visitor who wants the experience of "washing" out a few "colors" may find the place at hand at any time. He has a reasonable assurance that the rewards will be light, for those old-time miners and prospectors missed few spots where gold in quantity was hidden, but at the same time he can have a reasonable assurance that his desire for "colors" will be gratified by almost every "pan" of gravel. I had bought a gold pan in Cottonwood, and would fain have washed a few pans of that attractive gravel, but arrangements had been made for certain connections farther on and there was no time. The gold pan is reserved for use in another spot which I know well, and there is still hope that there may be a sufficient addition to the world's visible gold supply this summer to make a stick pin or two.

Between White Bird and Weiser, the end of the North and South highway, there are a few sections uncompleted on which one must travel along the old country road, steep occasionally, rough frequently, narrow always, but there is but 16 miles of such all together, and they will soon be gone, and aside from them the highway is all that heart could desire. Wide, smooth, rock surfaced, protected by railings at all points where man's carelessness or timidity might lead to disastrous results, the cost has been enormous, but the consequence is as near perfection as one could reasonably ask, and as soon as it becomes known the travel over it will become enormous.

Out on the headwaters of the Weiser river a company is engaged in orcharding, and there are hundreds—possibly thousands—of acres of apple, plum and peach trees, nearly all of bearing age, although as far as seen from the road there will be no fruit this year.

Normally Weiser would have been the point of turning to the west, but a long lost brother of the two ladies on the back seat was reported to have been at Payette some time ago, so we ran the 15 additional miles up there hoping to secure some additional information. All that could be learned was that he was gone "to parts unknown" so we turned onto the "Old Oregon Trail," faced Lena's head westward, and before sundown were beneath the roof of my sister, Mrs. Lora Godsey, up

Catherine creek, eight miles east of Union, Ore., the speedometer reporting 242 miles for the day and making us 4,717 miles from home.

⁕

Really there was a break in the connection here which should appear as Interlude No. 3, which was represented by two days spent with my sister at her farm about eight miles east of Union, during which time we ran about to various places, gathering in the missing children, until all were at home, except one son-in-law, to the third genera-tion, and also in visiting a number of cousins in Union, whom I had seen little of and only heard from at long intervals since leaving Iowa more than half a century before. At the Catherine creek farm besides the mother there were four daughters, two sons, a son-in-law and three grandchildren, making quite a gathering with the addition of the visitors. It was a time of reminiscence and recounting of things of interest or concern; the running around added 79 miles to Lena's speedometer record. Also two flat tires to a total already distress-ingly large.

CHAPTER FIVE

Oregon to Washington State

THURSDAY MORNING, JULY 23, GOODBYES WERE SAID TO DEAR ONES who probably will never be seen again, and Lena headed for Portland. At Union we re-entered the Old Oregon Trail, one of the famous roads of the country—renowned both for its quality as a highway and for its historic interest. It was along that road that the early settlers of the Northwest took their wagons and their plows, and rescued an empire not only from the trapper and Indian trader, but from all claim of possession by the British Empire.

Across the Grand Ronde valley, straight as an arrow for miles at a time, covered with crushed rock, and as good a road as the heart of man could desire or his mind conceive, it flew past. Hay was the principal crop, no work in the fields being in progress because of the rain of the previous day but there were numerous new stacks, a multitude of windrows waiting to be bucked to the stackers and some alfalfa awaiting the mowing machine to cut the second crop of the season. I know not what old Frenchman named this the Grand valley, and then after looking at the encircling hills which enclose it as the walls of a bowl added Round to the name and made it Grande Ronde. But he named it well. No richer area is to be found in this, one of the richest of the states, and the most casual observer will note how beautifully the adjective of form suits it.

Beyond La Grande, a city which ranks a way down the scale in Oregon's list of towns, but which claims to have the second largest pay roll in the state, exceeded only by Portland, we began to climb the Blue Mountains. The valley is about 2,700 feet above sea level, but as one of the enclosing walls these mountains rise some 1,600 feet higher at the pass through which the road goes. To the weary pioneer, this was a terrible barrier, coming after months of toil which included the surmounting of the Rocky Mountains, and as a token of remembrance a monument was erected on the summit, which President Harding assisted in dedicating July 3, 1923. That part of the range traversed is mainly included in either national forest or the Umatilla Indian reservation, a number of the inhabitants of the latter being in evidence running their cars on the road.

A few miles of the road were being widened, and as a consequence we had a number of short detours, largely over pretty rough roads, but otherwise the road was a magnificent one. Although through a country of little value, the mountains being very barren and rocky, as we came down toward the valley the tilled land was giving promise of but a small crop. At the foot of the mountain we came to the Umatilla mission and shortly after to the reservation line, coming out into the Umatilla valley, generally irrigated with water from the river, and producing abundantly, the elevation of the valley being little more than 1,000 feet above sea level.

Pendleton, a few miles farther down, is the county seat of Umatilla, the largest wheat producing county in the United States, or at least it was so a few years ago. But for the fact that the Indian reservation takes up a large part of its area, and the land thereon is largely farmed but indifferently, its yield would be still much larger.

Pretty well down toward the mouth of the Umatilla is a dam by which the water is all taken from the river—no great amount at this time of year, and carried down onto the valley of the Columbia a score of miles away.

We came in sight of the "river of the west" for the first time as we entered the village of Umatilla, one of Oregon's oldest towns, and one of its smallest. Our course changed from northwest to southwest, and the country, which had been quite bare and rocky, became absolutely devoid of useful vegetation, and in places the rocks became practically the whole landscape. The hills rose ever higher on either side of the river as we went farther west, and at times even the sage brush disappeared, only greasewood and cactus remaining to represent the vegetable kingdom. Now and then some green spot would tell the tale of a water right which had been made effective, and whenever there was even a small amount of moisture the land proved its inherent worth.[1]

Once we passed what we supposed to be memorial trees on either side of the road, spaced at regular intervals for a distance of about a mile. They apparently had been set out last fall or early in the spring, and about each one of them had been thickly clustered a few score of cacti. They were being watered from a tank wagon as we passed, and the cacti showed that they prosper much better with water than without, all looking very healthy. For a time it was a mystery as to why one should set out cactus with the trees, but the reason soon became apparent.

That soil was sand, and if stirred up once, and left unprotected, it would take the wind but a few hours to remove the last particle of it. Great dunes of sand were to be seen in all directions, constantly moving—usually up river, as that is the direction of the prevailing wind—and there was only a normal breeze today. When it is at itself, a Columbia river wind could uproot a giant oak in a few hours, if the surface of its sandy bed was once broken. But that yard circle of closely set cactus would defy almost anything.

Off from the south came occasional streams, Willow creek, John Day's river and one or two lesser ones, their all too scanty waters having been used to the limit for irrigating farther upstream, some of them being perfectly dry where they debouch into the Columbia valley, and the best a mere trickle.

Although the hills which set a barrier to the Columbia are largely rock, and many places in the valley could never be plowed, still there are thousands upon thousands of acres all the way along which only need water to make them as productive as the valley of the Nile, and just below them and alongside flows one of the greatest rivers of the world. Some day the ingenuity of man will devise a way to lift that water at nominal cost and Oregon and Washington will be able to feed a hungry empire in addition to their present product.

Sage brush, which over so much of the journey has been dwarfed and starved looking, here grew to mammoth proportions, and alongside the road were the finest sunflowers we have seen on the entire trip. Even Kansas, which put that blossom on the map, must concede that the Columbia river sunflower is a daisy, a peach or whatever term may be used to express the superlative in excellence.

About every so often, a busy railroad must have a station that trains may meet, and so towns are spaced about in accordance with the business standing of the railroad which serves them, but here all towns fail. At intervals of six or eight miles are sidings, each with a section house and a name, but frequently nothing more, and only at rare intervals having any resemblance even to a village. The exceptions are at the mouth of some considerable canyon down which there is a road from the far interior, for once on top of these hills one would find a country made up in the main of vast wheat fields, the rougher, rockier portions furnishing pasturage for multitudes of cattle and sheep, all of which find an outlet down those canyon roads except the few occasions when railroads have replaced them. With few exceptions, even these sure enough towns have a dried up, deserted appearance. Two or three times we saw long wagons piled high with sacked wheat being unloaded at a warehouse—for if there was a road down from the interior there was certainly a long, high warehouse, and wheat was the one purpose of its existence.

The river was broad, deep and swift. Seldom less than a half-mile wide and frequently more than a mile, the water dark blue, changing to a brilliant green where the sun fell upon it and the beholder was in the shadow of an overhanging cliff, it everywhere showed a strong current with many swirls and cross currents which indicated the difficulties of navigation. With a swift current almost all the time, and rapids or falls at frequent intervals, the Columbia has never been of much value as an avenue of commerce. Before the coming of the railroad, a little wheat went down, with transfers around various rapids, but there was little actual commerce after the day of the Indian and the fur trader.

Still, such a river has an appeal—especially to the politician who is looking for a place to spend public money and must have a public demand to authorize it. The Columbia was an ideal thing for such a purpose, so from early times there was a constant demand from press and rostrum, in the debating club and around the grocery store fire, that the Government should build canals and locks around the rapids that transportation might be unfettered and the railroads be made to "quit robbing the people." For a generation the rapids at Celilo were the one bugbear, and the people of three states—for Idaho was also concerned—kept up an incessant demand for a canal around them, other rapids having already been put in shape that boats could get through or around them.

Finally the demands were heard at Washington, and after many surveys, reports and recommendations, appropriations were made through a series of years, and the Celilo canal was built, as we had ample proof this afternoon, when we came to that old fishing place— once the greatest in the world—and found a five mile canal cut through solid basalt, with numerous locks. The number of boats which have gone through that canal in the years since it was completed is negligible, and it had no effect in freight rates, but the people through their legislatures have done what they could have done in the beginning— regulated freight rates. Down the Columbia meant interstate traffic and was beyond the power of the legislature of any state—or any combination of them—but when the Washington legislature fixed the freight charge on a bushel of wheat from the eastern part of the state to Puget Sound, the roads down the Columbia had to make the same rate to Portland or go out of business. I wonder sometimes if the plan to "lock and dam" the Ohio will work out the same way.

"The Dalles," as the old French trappers called the rapids of the middle Columbia, must not be confused with the little city of the same name just below. The latter is merely a good sized town which may be duplicated thousands of times all over the world—the former is a thing rare if not unique in all the earth. This mighty river which I have been trying to describe suddenly contracts its width from the mile or more over which its water have formed their bed, and the whole volume of them is rushed in between volcanic ledges from one of which a mere child may throw a stone to the other—141 feet at the narrowest place, to be exact. How deep those tossing, surging waters may be no man knows. Long ago I read an estimate that they were 500 feet deep but no man knows and one guess is as good as another, for there is no seeing beneath the surface. It may widen out down in there—it may contract to a groove; that boiling current permits of no sounding.

This old town of The Dalles, the Wishram of Washington Irving, was once my home, for here 43 years ago I helped a railroad company make freight cars and cabooses, and tonight here we camp, the speedometer showing a run for the day of 235 miles, a total of 5,031 from Ravenswood.

⁂

[Leap XXXVI,] which was quite an easy one, both as to distance and nature of country, being from The Dalles to Portland, Ore., July 24.

That Columbia River Highway, which began at Pendleton and extends to Astoria at the mouth of the river, is in a class by itself as a scenic route, and the heart of it is between The Dalles and Portland. New York has her Storm King Highway, which she presents as the most wonderful thing extant in the way of an automobile road, and it may be good enough for the foreigners of the nation's metropolis but it is not in the same class as the Columbia River Highway.[2]

In the first place, here is the mighty Columbia as an accompanist instead of the puny Hudson. Then here is everything Storm King has in the way of embattled rock walls backed by mighty mountains, and here it is multiplied several times; and then here are a multitude of other things even more attractive. Storm King is a way cut out of the bare perpendicular rock at a height well above the highest tide of the

Sheppard's Dell Bridge on Oregon's Columbia Highway, west of Bridal Veil, as it appeared about the time the Clarks traveled the route. The reinforced concrete bridge with a 100-foot span was constructed in 1914 on land given to the state by George Sheppard. The bridge crosses Young's Creek and was the second bridge built on the Columbia Highway. *Courtesy Oregon Historical Society.*

Hudson—and that is all. The Columbia drive is also hewn from the living rock at the base of a mountain thousands of feet high—not a mere hill—and three times in its course the road runs up higher than the summit of the Palisades, each climb so gradual that any car goes up in high without a struggle or down without risk of running away or burning out brakes, and from those summits one may see the river up and down for miles and mountains in all directions, several of them with snowy summits that never disappear, crowned as they are with the slowly creeping ice rivers which man calls glaciers.

Here Indian tradition or fable says long ago there was a bridge such as no other part of the earth ever saw, beneath which the Columbia ran "in rayless gloom," and modern geologists admit that it is probable that such a bridge actually existed, the very abutments which supported its ends being still clearly distinguishable.

In the stream and on shore rise weird monoliths of massive size and enormous dimensions, some of which defy the efforts of man to scale, and all stand as reminders of the tremendous Power which placed the output of His workshop in such peculiar attitudes.

Many times and oft along the top of that lofty wall roams some stream born at the base of the still higher mountain which lies back of it, and arriving at the top of the precipice it plunges to the bottom at one sheer plunge. This scene of the lofty waterfall is repeated o'er and o'er, varying as to amount of water, from a tiny trickle to streams of real consequence, and from a series of cascades and short leaps to a breath-destroying plunge of more than 600 feet.

The Hudson has its attractions, and they are powerful—Storm King being the greatest of all, perhaps—but they are of a different character from these of the land "where rolls the Oregon."

Unfortunately we were not kindly received by the weather man. The morning was so cool as to call for wraps, especially on the back seat, while between clouds and smoke our vision was limited to objects at no great distance. Thus we lost the beauty of the mountain backgrounds to many of the scenes.

Because of these obstacles to sightseeing we spent less time on the road than had been planned, and arrived quite early in Portland at the home of one of my nieces, she and her sister with their husbands keeping us quite busy with sightseeing and visiting. The speedometer said 98 miles for the day, or 5,129 from home.

⁂

After a day in Portland, which included a visit to the old battleship *Oregon*, which went around the Horn without a stop and arrived off the coast of Cuba ready for the battle with Cervera's fleet, during which it sank two and captured two more of the Spanish vessels. Antiquated and obsolete now—as is the fate of every war vessel in a few years, so fast is the growth of constructive skill and knowledge—it lies in a berth in Portland harbor, there to remain until the tooth of time destroys it utterly, a reminder to the people of this part of the world of the prowess of American arms, as the frigate *Constitution*—"Old Ironsides"—does in the harbor at Boston. Her main shaft was cut in two by an acety-lene torch, and never again will she move by her own power. Before the battleship of today she would be as puny and helpless as would the *Constitution* in war with Cervera's fleet, but she served her day and time fully as well as the grandest ship afloat could do today and her place in history is secure.

Some of Portland's wonderful drives and parks, with a trip along the waterfront and through one of her great terminals, "where rail and river meet," finished the day, and the next morning we fixed the customary flat tire—just a leaky valve this time—and were off for Tacoma on the waters of Puget Sound, "the Mediterranean of the Pacific," crossing the Columbia on the Interstate bridge at Vancou-ver, a structure built since I left the west, as thousands of other great improvements have been.

This day's run was over the Pacific Highway, another of the great roads of the country, now practically all hard surfaced, from Vancou-ver, B.C., to Tia Juana, Mexico,[3] the only exception today being four miles between Chehalis and Centralia, the latter town being familiar to West Virginians as the point to which the Hatfields went several years ago.[4] A few miles of the way lie alongside the Columbia, a half dozen or more small rivers are crossed, a dozen prosperous towns of consequence passed through, including the state capital, Olympia, arid occasional glimpses of Puget Sound are obtained near the end of the day, the last scene of real interest en route being Camp Lewis, where so many thousands of our boys were turned into soldiers during the World War, and where there is still a considerable military encampment—the largest, if I mistake not, in the whole country.

Here in the residential part of Tacoma we turned Mrs. Lodge over to her lonesome husband, and here for the next 10 days we will be the guests of Mrs. Clark's sisters and brothers as they gather for a family reunion, and we will be filled to repletion with the sights and pleasures of "the sound country." Day's run 179 miles, total 5,308.

ANOTHER INTERVAL

The same occupying many days, covering various activities with much running around of circles.

Safely landed in Tacoma, time began to fly with even more than its usual celerity. Mr. Lodge had arranged to have his vacation begin the next morning, he being employed in the store department of the St. Paul and Tacoma Lumber Company. James Lodge, Jr., is a salesman, living but a short distance from the paternal home, and being in a position to practically fix his hours. James Cobb, Mrs. Clark's brother, is city salesman for Carnation Milk, and while he has to run his car and visit customers daily, the time could be greatly shortened. Edgar Cobb, another brother, lives at Puyallup, only a dozen miles away over one of the best highways in the country, Clark Belknap, a nephew of mine, although having an office in Seattle, lives about midway between the two rival cities of Puget Sound, and can run over in his car in 30 to 40 minutes any time; being an attorney with a specialty for consultations rather than court practice, his time is always at his own disposal. George Warren lives in Tacoma, is crier of the United States court here, which is in vacation; I worked with him in Idaho for several years; we were fellow members in several fraternities and warm personal friends, while he married a girl who had been a baby in a neighboring family when I was a small boy, the two families having continued friendly relations ever since. This much by way of explanation of the stage setting will show that there was no threat of idle moments in Tacoma.

Scheduled to occur during the 10 days we were to remain here were a boat trip to Victoria, B.C., an auto ride to Vancouver, B.C., and a camping trip up on Mt. Rainier. The two trips abroad had to be abandoned for lack of time, and the mountain trip will be treated in a separate letter, the other major events of the stay being as here set down, but told with no relation to their chronological sequence.

Chief among them was the trip to Seattle to view the parade at the triennial conclave of the Knights Templar. The three Clarks were accompanied by the elder Lodges, going over on the boat, the 30 mile run requiring nearly two hours. The Warrens were encountered on the boat and Nephew Belknap met us at the dock. With the forethought-edness that has made him a success in the practice of the law, he had arranged a private location for us to view the parade. The same being the roof of the Hoge building, in which his office is located, where either standing or sitting behind a railing which gave a sense of safety, we could look out over the city, at the 42-story L. C. Smith building, at other lofty structures in the business part of the city; at the beautiful residences on the hills on which Seattle is built; out onto Puget Sound with its fleets of merchant vessels moving hither and thither or the three United States war vessels moored in the harbor; across the Sound to the west at the Olympic mountains, usually considered quite inconsequential uplifts but still covered with snow; away to the south where Mt. Rainier, Mt. St. Helena and other peaks rise to heights where snow never melts; or down 20 stories to the streets whereon the knights were to display their uniforms and their graceful maneuvers.

The latter, of course, was the feature of the day, and received most of our attention. Down about Pioneer Square the various squadrons were formed, and as they swung into First avenue they came into our view. Up that thoroughfare they marched about 10 blocks, the latter part of the route being hidden from us by the buildings lining the avenue; then across to Second avenue, down which for eight blocks or more under the welcome arch they wended their way with us viewing their every movement; then across into Third avenue, where we could watch them for a time through a cross street if we desired, and then on to the grand stand on Fourth avenue. Our view point was much more advantageous than the grand stand. We saw the procession many times as far, and while our elevation of more than 200 feet from the sidewalk made close-ups and personal recognition out of the question, still good eyes could read the state names on the cars which headed each squadron in the line, as knights from each of the 48 states, Alaska and some of the island possessions, District of Columbia, Canadian provinces and a few from far off foreign lands tossed their plumes and with marching and countermarching in intricate figures made a display which many went hundreds and thousands of miles to witness.

All traffic on these four leading streets of the city had been suspended, and the sidewalks were so filled with spectators that it was impossible to get through them, the two rows of gay colored dresses and hats making it look from our elevated stand very like two rows of nasturtiums in full bloom beside a garden walk.

Police on motorcycles and horses headed the procession, and each division was headed by one or more automobiles with bands for each one with many in line, there being some 42 bands all told, and they were far enough apart not to interfere with each other, although at times we had our choice of the music from two or three of them by shifting our position on the top of the building. Divisions from states sparsely represented marched sedately along, stopping only as they were held up by others ahead, but the larger delegations would stop in each block and go through a series of evolutions which were wonderful, coming from men whose training is but an incident in lives usually fully occupied with business affairs.

The most widely advertised band of the occasion was from Chicago, and it was claimed that each member of it was a millionaire, their musical performances being strictly a matter of amusement and recreation. Several other bands were strictly professional, several of them being from the naval vessels in the harbor or military bands from Camp Lewis, while one which attracted much attention was a Scotch band, dressed in scarlet tunics and kilts from a British regiment stationed at Victoria, the capital of British Columbia.

Through seeing the beginning of the parade and not losing sight of it until it was half way along the line of march, we had it as our principal attraction from 10:15 A.M. to 2:15 P.M., our host arranging to serve lunch to us on the roof so we did not get hungry, and the novelty of the sights prevented us from getting tired.

One of the local papers estimated the number of marching knights at 8,000 and the spectators at 200,000 while the other journal made the figures 20,000 and 400,000 respectively. Either one seemed reasonable and I would not attempt to reconcile them.

The day was ideal for the occasion. There had been a fog in the morning—as there quite commonly is on Puget Sound—and it had been feared that behind the fog there might be rain—that being an occasional occurrence in the summers here—but almost at the very moment of starting the parade, the sun burst through, dissipating the fog in a few moments, and while some of the fat knights found the miles of marching rather warm with their heavy uniforms, up where we were, coats felt good all day, and down on the street but few were constrained to break ranks during the lulls in the march to get a drink at some nearby fountain.

In the evening the Clarks went down to the Belknap home at Three Tree Point, where the land juts out into the Sound, the beautiful home being on a knoll only a few feet above high tide, and through each of the 48 windows of the house one can gaze out over the water. After dark we drove back to the city to see the lighting on the streets, intending to merely drive about in the car, but so dense was the crowd, both in autos and on foot, that progress was slower than along the line of the day's parade, so the car was parked and we went on foot.

The two West Virginians had never before seen any such doing as those of either the day or night, and when we arrived at Three Tree Point again at midnight we had the feeling of a day very pleasantly spent, even though it did make us weary.

Driving, feasting, visiting—these made up the days spent in Tacoma. A few new acquaintances were formed, but in the main it was the intercourse of old friends met again after long separation, each with much to tell and eager to listen. One day there was a picnic in Point Defiance Park, the largest and most beautiful in Tacoma, where the whole day spent, watching the waves and the gulls, the rowboats, ferries and even ships which ply the seven seas, talking, talking and ever talking, and when it seemed time to replenish the internal fires of man, 37 of us sat down to one of the long tables of the park, the full tide beating against the seawall so near that one could almost dip his hand into the water. Not until the sun had disappeared in the ocean and darkness was stealing over the land did we load the remains of the feast into the automobiles and turn back to the city.

Another evening, the young Lodges, James Cobb, Mrs. Worley, the baby of the Cobb family who arrived from her home in Rockford early the first week of our visit to remain as long as we did or longer, Florence and the scribe went fishing. Two small boats were taken at Salmon Beach, and for the first time in a generation or more I rowed a boat. The work was somewhat novel, and for the first time in my life I had a practical lesson in "rowing against the tide," but I accomplished it successfully. Also it appeared that I chose a good course, for with the hook trolling behind Jim Cobb caught a beautiful salmon weighing an even four pounds, which next day when Mrs. Lodge had "done her prettiest" with it we found was one of the best ever taken from the Sound. My tally sheet showed that I rowed 63 miles to get it, but it was worth it, and besides it was the only one caught on that occasion by our party. When we landed at the dock and saw the catch of the man who had been ahead of us, something over 40 individual fish mostly about the same size as ours, we saw the advantage of being the early bird.

In such ways the days have gone by, and it was time to move on. July has passed into August, there are thousands of miles yet to be passed, friends ahead are clamoring for our promised appearance, and there is the ever present sense that it will be full late when we reach the Ravenswood ferry again. The speedometer has moved ahead 391 miles during these days at Tacoma, making a total of 5,699 since leaving home, so this 6th day of August, Lena is once more champing his bit with his nose pointed back toward the Columbia river, just beyond which will be the waters of the broad Pacific. There is still to write the wonderful trip to Mt. Rainier, with its miles of snow-clad rocks and ponderous glaciers, and another trip to the mills of the St. Paul and Tacoma Lumber Company. It may be that tonight we will camp at Longview, where the largest mill in the world is at work, which is also one of the newest and exhibits "the last word" in lumbering methods, and then I will write of saw mills with the fullest knowledge which can be gained by three visits to mammoth plants, one at St. Maries, one at Tacoma and the other at this new town of Longview which was created solely to be the home of a mill capable of cutting a full million feet of plank in a single day of 24 hours.

So the speedometer is set back to zero for the day's run, goodbyes are being said, and with promises of seeing each other again in the not too far distant future if possible, we will be off in a moment on another leap.

But before recording the events of that leap, let me tell of the wonderful trip to Mt. Rainier.

A SNOW CLAD MOUNTAIN WHERE
GLACIERS CREEP ALONG FOR CENTURIES

It was Monday morning, August 3, 1925, when the Moon car from Seattle, driven by Clark Belknap and carrying, besides his wife, her mother and two other ladies, and Leaping Lena, just then of Tacoma, carrying Mrs. Clark, Mr. and Mrs. Lodge and Mrs. Worley, with the News man at the wheel, started on their carefully planned trip to Mt. Rainier National Park, intent on seeing the wonder of high altitudes.

This is one of the numerous national parks of the West, its name indicating its chief feature, the third highest mountain in the United States. Due to its location near Seattle and Tacoma, and connected with all parts of "Vacation Land" by splendid roads, it is one of the most popular of them all. Last year there were more than 160,000 people visited it during the short season in which it is accessible, and this year 200,000 are expected. Monday and Tuesday had been selected for our visit because there would presumably be fewer people there than at other times in the week, and we had all the days of the week to select from. It turned out that our selection was a good one, for not only did we find no congestion of tourists as there had been the previous day, but the mountain was on its good behavior, which it frequently is not.

These lofty summits reach into a region where even the noonday sun brings but little heat, and the moisture which the air brings in from the Pacific Ocean often liquefies when it is forced up to that great height, and forms clouds which conceal the whole sky thereabouts. One of these monsters derives its name from that circumstance—Mt. Hood, which is so often capped with a cloud of fleece that its name seems peculiarly suitable. During the four days we were presumably in sight of Mt. Hood on this trip, we had just one fleeting glance at it, although some of our troubles may have been due to smoke as well as cloud.

Anyway, we left for Rainier with some doubts. The previous day the "week enders" had driven up to its very base at Paradise valley, the limit of automobile travel, and did not get a single view of the mountain, so when we started it was with talk of what we would and see "if the mountain is in sight."

Not only was it in sight after we got fairly under way, but it was in sight every minute from that time on, day and night, and even after we got back to Tacoma after 5 o'clock the following day, it was still holding up its head, for the first time appearing through the smoke which had concealed it ever since our arrival on Puget Sound.

Only a few miles out of Tacoma it burst upon our view, and except when some close-by hill concealed it for brief moments, from that time on we could judge our approach to the monarch by the way it continued to grow in majesty and grandeur.

At the park entrance we stopped to register and pay the $2.50 fee which Uncle Sam exacts from the driver of each car which enters the park, from which receipts a considerable part of the expenses of keeping up are met. It was there that the real climbing began, although the road from Tacoma, 56 miles, had been almost constantly upward. The road was decidedly worse after entering the park, indicating that the business is not paying very well, but with a speed limit of 20 miles per hour instead of the 30 which the laws of Washington permit, there was little trouble in making that rate, and some more reckless drivers—the balloon tire brigade—tore along considerably faster. One thing often noticed before on this tour was doubly apparent here. I refer to the speed of the Californians. They are always in a hurry! In the park Washington cars outnumbered those from all the other states put together, probably twice over, but nearly every car which passed us in the park bore a California license tag. People from other states jogged along and took in the sights as they rode, but the Californian rushed ahead as though there was but one day to see things in and the thing to be seen was far ahead.

At Longmire we stopped and cooked lunch on the tourist camp ground, and were not favorably impressed with the management. While all the camping places in Yellowstone Park there had been an abundance of dry wood, the tourist being only required to cut it into suitable length for his needs, here there was nothing but a small pile of well rotted logs a little larger than fence posts, which had not been suitable for fuel for several years. Beside the pile lay what had once been a double bitted ax, stuck carelessly onto the end of a once-upon-a-time ax handle, from which it would sever diplomatic and all other relations on the slightest provocation. The logs were not fit for fuel; the ax was not fit for anything. But prominently displayed on a post was a fine sign saying: "For cooking only." For miles around were dead and dying trees in the primeval forest which will fall and rot, but which are beyond the reach of the tourist.

Not only was the road from Longmire steadily upward, but it was traveling skyward at as rapid a rate as it is convenient for modern automobile to go on "high," but was wide enough for cars to meet at all points until we reached Narada Falls, from which point there are two roads for two or three miles, one ascending and the other descending traffic, each twisting and winding up the mountain side, sometimes far apart and at others only kept from coming together by a difference in elevation, one being well above the other.

Before that we had passed the Nisqually glacier, that huge river of ice which only the scientist comprehends, of which more anon, as it later came repeatedly under observation.

The two rival roads came together as we neared Paradise valley, another mile or so taking us to the end of the road where stands Paradise Inn, surrounded by numerous tents for tourist use, they being rented furnished or unfurnished as desired. Beyond lay the mountain.

For more than 75 miles we had come steadily upward, much of the time up steep grades, and were now at an elevation of 5,400 feet above the level of Puget Sound. Some of the ladies had been complaining of a queer tickling in their ears as a consequence of the rapid rise. But there beside us stood Mt. Rainier, covered with snow except where the rocks were too steep for it to remain, and we were but a little over one-third of the way up. The summit was a scant four and one-half miles away, "as the crow flies," but the crow might find it necessary to wind about some to gather altitude, for in those miles he would have to rise 9,008 feet above the floor of Paradise Inn, the summit being 14,408 feet above sea level, according to the Geological Survey.

Once comfortably located, the entire party took a stroll toward the center of attraction, the mountain, for it was only a half mile to the top of a ridge from which we could look down on Nisqually glacier. As we climbed the hill, an ascent much higher and steeper than it appeared because just ahead was that vastly greater one, we heard a roaring and looking backward a mile or more east of the inn, we saw a considerable river pouring over a high ridge, it being the melting water from Paradise glacier, an ice stream even greater than the Nisqually, but not so ready of access.

It had been about 4 o'clock, the very heat of the day here, when we made one of the numerous turns in the road and realized that before us was one of those curious things hard to accept as facts by those who never saw them, a stream of solid ice slowly moving down the side of a mountain, cutting and grinding its way, scraping off the surface of the living rock, and literally grinding the mountain to powder.

It was a long half mile from the road to the face of the glacier, but like all others who pass that way, we parked the cars, and wended our way up that boulder strewn valley. Cut deep where we were walking, on before us was a wall, apparently of rock, reaching high up the canyon on either side, beneath which came a considerable river, while from the sides of the canyon dropped numerous tiny waterfalls, and over the front of that dam in the valley trickled petty cascades.

It looked like a solid rock wall from a distance, but there was a peculiarity about the valley which told us that there was something different here. Up to a little above the level of the top of that dam the canyon walls were absolutely bare. They had a scraped and polished appearance. On the dam itself there was no color save that of rock until we were nearly to it, when there began to appear a whitish glint, increasing steadily as we approached, until when we came to the line beyond which we were forbidden to go for our own safety—for Uncle Sam is opposed to suicide and forbids us going where falling rock is a common occurrence—we could see ice down the whole face, especially near the center, while near the bottom where the river gushed forth there were great cracks and seams where the deep blue of massive ice was the prevailing hue. Over all lay rock, some as large as a table or larger, but mostly quite small, and protruding from the face were many of considerable size, shipped long ago by slow freight, and now after the lapse of centuries about to be delivered.

That night at the guide house we heard and saw a lecture—for it was illustrated—which threw a little further light on this matter of glaciers. A sign on our way up to the glacier marked the side of the face some 40 years ago, and conveyed the information that it was receding at the rate of 53 feet a year, a rate which if continued will wipe it out in two or three more generations. The lecturer told us that its rate of progress down the mountain was from 16 to 23 inches a day. Probably that is summer schedule, while in winter it likely goes slower because there is snow on the track which must be cleared away. Some idea of that snowy obstruction may be gathered by recalling the lecturer's statement that last winter—not a particularly snowy one—the snow fall at Paradise Inn, measured as it fell, while unpacked, was 108 feet! That is not an error of the machine in setting the figures—ONE HUNDRED AND EIGHT FEET!

Up on that mountain side there may be more or less, but whatever the fall there, to the resources of the glacier must be added the snow on the ridges alongside, practically all of which blows over into it, and the face of the glacier, or its front at the end is quite narrow compared with where it is formed up on the mountain side. The only publication issued by the Government giving the dimensions the Nisqually is several years old, when it extended considerably farther down the valley, and therein is the statement that the face is from 500 to 600 feet high. As we were looking at it from the danger line, some 200 yards away, the agreement among the observers was that the face was perhaps 200 feet high, and 600 feet from wall to wall of the canyon—offered as a conservative estimate. Farther up the depth of the ice is said to be 500 feet or more, and a mile above the front it seemed to be more than a half-mile wide.

In the center of the glacier face at the bottom is an arch 20 or 30 feet high, with breaks above it where large cracks in the ice show that the arch might soon be materially enlarged, and from that hole issued the Nisqually river. It tells another part of the story of the glacier, just as do other streams heading on Mt. Rainier under similar circumstances. Its water is milky white with the finely ground up rock which its mother has scraped from the mountain. Go to the harbor of Tacoma, and the milky water from the Puyallup river can be seen far out. In spite of its load of rock it is still lighter than the salty water of the sound, and so spreads out on top, there to remain, a white coat on a sea of blue, like cream on a pan of milk, until a passing boat's propeller churns it all up together and the white is lost in the immeasurably greater amount of blue supplied by the Pacific Ocean.

In our climbing the next morning we passed alongside some of the upper reaches of the glacier, and got a view of it entirely different from that down at the face. Half way up, or a mile above the face, and perhaps 1,500 feet higher in the air, it was a constant succession of that terror of glacier explorers, crevasses. Through the middle of the glacier, where there was but little rock fallen from the mountain sides, deep crevices could be seen as regularly spaced as the waves on the ocean, but unlike the waves, they appeared to be much deeper than they were in distance apart. Starting in cracks in the ice, bent in its slow movement down the mountain, water flowing along and down through them soon widen them to respectable proportions, and when the snow of another winter falls upon them it bridges them over. Then with the coming of the "season" the careless or unenlightened mountain climber attempts to work his way across the glacier, only to step upon come snow bridge weakened by the growing sun, going down to death or severe injury. Therefore Uncle Sam keeps reiterating the insistence—do not go upon the glacier without an experienced guide. But each season finds its crop of people too smart to listen to advice, and so there is an annual list of glacial accidents.

Here I have used up all this space on roads and glaciers when I started to tell about the mountain. Rainier stands among the great mountains of the world, and while not as inaccessible, or rather as hard to scale, as some of the Alps, it takes a mountain climber of at least the third class to reach its summit, and the number who do so is not great, and those who succeed fewer than those who make the attempt. Although some 1,300 feet lower than Mont Blanc, the snow line is lower, and its sides are sufficiently steep to make it a hard mountain to surmount. No white man ever climbed it until 1870—and so far as known no Indian ever climbed it—and while the ascent has been made from two or three directions only professional climbers have mounted it except by one route.

All this and much more being learned from the lecture of the evening, the men of our party went to bed with a firm resolve—or rather three firm resolves, one each—to surmount the mountain or bust a suspender buckle in the attempt. Only occasionally is the ascent made in one day, the usual custom being to go in the afternoon from Paradise Inn to Muir Shelter Cabin, a rock house high on the mountain side built by the Government for the shelter of climbers, and the next day going from there to the summit and back to the Inn.[5] The distance by this route is probably not more than nine miles each way or eighteen up and back, but mere distance becomes a matter of minor consideration.

A party had just returned, it being the one hundred and seventy-first trip for the guide in charge, covering a period of several years, and we decided to form a part of his convoy on the one hundred and seventy-second. Engagements had been made several days ahead, and the time on the mountain was limited, so we had to forego the days of preparation of hardening oneself by climbing lesser mountains as the guides recommend; neither could we wait until noon the next day to go to Muir cabin for the night. We were already 5,400 feet on the way up, that much achieved without effort and the remainder had to be accomplished on the morrow that we might be ready to return to Tacoma in time to meet our engagements.

To the Muir cabin was a climb of 4,600 feet, leaving the peak still 4,400 feet above, and the combined distances made less than two miles—a mere bagstel to old mountain climbers like us, although we were admittedly a little off form from lack of recent experience.

Midnight is the customary time of departure for those desiring to make the round trip in one day, but above all else we felt the need of a good night's sleep as a preliminary to such strenuous effort, so we selected daylight—itself rather an early hour in this latitude and season—and went to bed with the advice of the lecturer ringing in our ears. He said by all means take a guide who was acquainted with the mountain, and at another time he pronounced it an endurance test, only the strong and persevering succeeding. That sounded all right, but how did those guides learn the way? Somewhere back there a first man must have appeared to choose his own way from start to finish and yet went through to the top. The glory that was his could not be ours for we knew the way almost in its entirety. Up to McClure rock, the end of the first 2,000 feet of climbing, there was a broad trail, several of them, in fact most of the way all in plain sight from the Inn. A hogback extended from there up to the Cowlitz Cleaver, another 2,000 feet, and along a knife blade to the ranger signal station plainly visible from the Inn. From there the climb was but small to the Muir cabin, and the rest of it was merely following one's nose, remembering that the steeper the grade the faster one would go up. Exceedingly simple, and with no apparent need of guide or unduly early rising.

Daylight was to be the hour, but with a full moon in the heavens it was a little difficult to tell just when its glow was replaced by the stronger light of the day orb.

Each of the adventurers took the precaution of informing his wife where his life insurance policies were to be found in case of need, and investing her with all the spare cash carried in his pockets, for a man on that mountain has no more use for money than on a desert island, and there are men employed whose special duty it is to recover the bodies of such as perish on the mountain, without depending on picking the pockets of the victims as compensation for salvaging the remains.

That peak looked mighty cold and bleak as we gazed at it through the tent doors, but it also looked very close. However, on the debit side was the additional face that it appeared a long way up in the air. Two miles is not far when it is spread out level, but stand it up on end and it makes the back of your neck ache to look at it very long at a time. Incidentally I might add here that some of the party later decided that it appears to be a long way when one looks down it at an angle of slightly less than that of the side of a house!

That moon was rather a drawback, for it was shining so brightly that it was difficult to distinguish its efforts from those of the sun, and therefore it was 4:15 when the first man was out of bed and submitted a report that it was daylight on the summit and time for the party to be off. If the guide and other climbers had left at midnight the handicap was sufficient. In fact it was too much as far as overtaking them in time for breakfast at Muir station was concerned, so it was necessary to carry their own lunch, thus adding materially to the load.

Jumping into their clothes and climbing boots, eating a hasty bit and pocketing the supplies for the day, they were off at 4:30, alpenstocks in hand, moving not rapidly but steadily, determined to overtake the other party by the time it reached the summit. The larger the party the more slowly it moves, for at certain dangerous points only one man at a time is allowed to be ascending, the others all waiting above or below.

A half-mile up the mountain and we came to the first snow, just small patches in hollows, where an abundance had blown over the hill in the winter and a few feet of it in the lowest hollow was not yet melted. Beside these fragments were blooming flowers, millions of them on ground which had been buried by snow a week before, and yet a few feet farther from the snow were strips of desert, the ground so thoroughly parched that the least disturbance stirred up dust which looked as though it never had been damp. Occasionally there were spots of real soil, but in the main the surface was solid rock or finely powdered sand, the output of some glacier of bygone days, when the valleys on the mountainside were differently placed than those of today.

The rock in place was a gray granite, and a glance over onto the surface of the Nisqually glacier, 500 feet or more directly under us, showed that the rock which had fallen onto that gravel train was of the same variety. When we rose the moon seemed to be having some difficulties of its own. The papers recently had made no prediction of any unusual trouble in that quarter, but it looked as though something had knocked an immense hole in one side of it. A spirited discussion arose as to the cause of it, the prevailing opinion being that dazzled by the brightness of the snow on the mountain, the moon had collided with it in the night and had a big hole torn in its side. Soon it seemed to be recovering and it became evident that it was merely an unpredicted eclipse! Coming at such an unearthly hour in the morning, the papers had seen fit to make no reference to it, and we wasted a lot of sorely needed wind in discussing a matter which otherwise would have been passed in silence.

As the reincarnated moon was descending into the Pacific Ocean, the sun was peeping over the Rocky Mountains and casting its beams on the summit of Rainier. I had gone 5,000 miles to see that thing, and it was worth it. With the appearance of that light the sky, which had been as colorless as the snow on the summit, turned a deep blue, and the hazy mountain suddenly burst into form, its snow and rocks, either white or gray, standing out in strong contrast to the blue background, while the slowly descending fire made the summit gleam like a mighty bonfire, and the rocks sticking through the snow seemed more unassailable and unscalable than ever.

Swinging a little to the right, we crossed over to the foot of a ridge steeper than the ordinary, getting a few rods of almost level ground and then stopping to rest a moment at the end of the first pull up the steeper rocks, we looked to the south. From the camp of the previous night there had been a very pretty view in that direction, the Tatoosh range running nearly east and west a few miles to the south, separated from Rainier by a deep gorge, its peaks rising much higher than the camp, each as steep as a church steeple, spots of snow here and there where a flatter spot or crevice held the snow it was still white, but otherwise with no color except the solid gray of the rock. In ignorance of the name of the range a suggestion was made that it might be the Seven Devils, but Eleven Devils offered as an amendment seemed much more appropriate.

From the camp those jagged peaks appeared to overtop everything in that direction, and their altitude was second only to that of Rainier itself. But when we looked back at them now they had shrunk amazingly, appearing but little higher than the site of the camp. Beyond and high above them was another range, not so jagged, but still quite respectable mountains, covered almost entirely with snow.

But they were mere hills compared with what we saw still beyond. Off to the southeast rose Mt. St. Helens, just as beautiful as Rainier; with more snow apparently, for we were looking at the north side where the sun had not yet undone the work of last winter, and its sides were not so steep as Rainier's so there was little rock too steep to hold snow. Then to the east, apparently about the same distance from us and from St. Helens, the three forming a fair triangle 40 or 50 miles on each side, was the finest of all—Mt. Adams. Its sides apparently smooth and regular, its snowy crest appeared easy to surmount and whereas the top of both Rainier and St. Helens come to a sharp point, on which the climber might find it hard to stand in time of heavy wind, the summit of Adams is a nicely rounded dome. One who looks at it from that angle will know at once where a certain Detroit automobile manufacturer found the model for the cap of his radiators; the summit of Mt. Adams is exactly the same shape, even to the little ridges by which you take hold of it to unscrew it.

In the foreground as it were stood these two mammoths, each a beautiful sight, but lacking the grandeur of Rainier, because they were not so high, and instead of rising from almost sea level they stand on the summit of a mountain range. Back of them, occupying a minor place in the picture at this level but assuming a more commanding position as we climbed on up, was Oregon's most famous mountain, Mt. Hood, now vastly shrunk from the early day claim that it was the highest mountain in the world, but still one of the noted mountains of the earth, and one of no mean caliber. For days we had looked in vain for it when down in the region where it is the chief glory of the landscape and now when we were a hundred miles away it appeared to perfection, minus the cloud cap which so often halos it.

Off to the west lay the Olympics, many of their summits still crowned with snow, although they will be bare before winter again returns to rearrange their mantel. But a heavy smoke lay in that direction, hiding all these petty elevations of only a mile or so above sea level. Even in contour of the land nearby could be told but imperfectly because of the smoke, and east and north the whole country was still hidden by the mass of Rainier, still towering far above us, but growing perceptibly nearer at each time we stopped to rest.

It was along here somewhere that the gray granite began to disappear, being replaced with a similar rock of a deep red color, and among the "float" appeared many small pieces of pumice stone. Heavier than that found in some other regions, yet very fair specimens of the output of a volcano when it has "gas on its stomach" and its attempts to belch up what is disturbing it is but half successful. When the resultant expectoration cools it appears like ordinary rock to the eye, but in its best known form is so full of minute cells that when cast into water it floats high. The specimens here were of a heavier quality, being really merely scoria instead of pumice stone, although they were surprisingly light. Around the mountain side could be seen that layer of red granite in many places, and above that the lava, crystallized mostly in massive form, the direct output of the mountain in the day when it was making itself by vomiting up its inwards—sort of lifting itself by its own bootstraps as it were.

But we are tarrying too long; close as the summit appears, there are yet many weary steps to be taken before it is mounted. On ahead there in the air, cutting the sky like a knife, is the Cowlitz Cleaver, a good 2,000 feet higher than McClure rock. The view from it will be wider; the peaks to the south will appear in more glory, towering yet higher above their surroundings.

Once onto the Cowlitz Cleaver, for a time the climbing is not so severe, but the road is difficult, made naturally of huge clocks of basalt, many of which have to be laboriously and individually climbed over, each so sharp on top and lying on so frail foundations that the snow cannot lie on them, but is whisked away by the 100 and 125 mile breezes which kiss the cheeks of Rainier; as yet no improvement has been made on Nature's construction. It is what in the guidebooks would be marked "unimproved highway; too rough for fast travel."

But there is an end to that long, rocky upward slant, where we quit terra firma and for the first time take to the snow, creeping around the edge of a pinnacle, scalable on the opposite side and occupied as a ranger signal station. But on this side it does not appear to be satisfied with merely perpendicular, but sticks out over; it has a way of pushing you farther out onto that steep snow roof which is not pleasant, to say the least.

Once around the shoulder of that station we are on easier going; it is snow continually from there to the summit, and not nearly as steep as the side of a house; the fact that snow lies on it shows that. From that ridge we have an uninterrupted view to the north, but the peak still rises to the west and hides everything.

There is nothing to do now but pick them up, swing them forward and set them down, alternating from one to the other, which method will eventually bring us to the crater. We are near the summit now, and while still far from "home and mother," there is a coziness about it which much of the road behind lacked. The wind is less severe, for the very tip of the cone is shielding us from its full strength. To the mountain climber the wind is one of the real terrors; when it is near the earth friction restrains it so that it seldom attains a velocity of more than a hundred miles an hour, but up high like this there is no friction to speak of—the mountains which reach this height are rare—and once started it keeps going, occasionally getting an additional spurt, so there is really no limit to its rate of progress.

But as I said, here there is shelter behind the cone. Then, too, it is not so steep, there being only the slope the wind made as it swept across there when it consented to permit that snow to find a lodging place.

If we were really cold, there are the caverns around the edges, where the steam from the crater work their way up along the wall of the crater from internal fires below! It is quite consoling to realize that we need not freeze to death!

Up that gentle slope, around the last projection, and the summit is gained; the reward for the hours of labor is received. We can look in all directions—see the Pacific to the west, the Atlantic to the east—or it may be only the sage brush plains of eastern Washington, but it looks like the ocean. Beyond Mt. Hood to the south lie Mt. Jefferson and the Three Sisters, the former with his bald head shining the sun and the latter sisters with their noses freshly powdered. To the northward is Mt. Baker, the only real rival Rainier has in all these miles.

These distant mountains must be viewed rapidly, for it is about as far back to the Inn as it is reputed to have been to Tipperary, and the hour grows late. One final glance around and we are off for home.

This is simpler than the climb. The night before the lecturer said it was easier to come back than to go up, for in going one had only hands and feet to get up with, while coming down there were five points of contact.

So we promptly brought that fifth point in contact with the snow, firmly grasping the alpenstock, without which the climb could not have been made, and our troubles for the day were over.

Such in brief is the ascent of Mt. Rainier. In such a way we planned to make it, but when we reached McClure rock, three hours after leaving camp, we remembered that we had failed to register. That was a gross violation of regulations. All persons making the ascent of the mountain, either with or without guides, must register with the chief ranger, so that if you don't come back within a reasonable number of days he can go on the hunt of you. It is like these places where the occupation is dangerous [and] you are asked to give the name and address of your next of kin or other relative or friend who is to be notified IF ANYTHING HAPPENS!

But we had neglected to register; our whereabouts and purposes were unknown, and there would be no search for us IF ANYTHING HAPPENED, so we took the shortest route home. We had looked over millions of acres of Washington and Oregon without seeing a single one susceptible to cultivation; we had learned somewhat of mountain climbing in high altitudes, and in the years to come when we shall have told the story until it is thoroughly familiar we may remember how we stood on the very tip of Mt. Rainier and came back by sitting down and "letting Nature take its course." Really Belknap did come down one snow bank that way and found it a relief to muscles which otherwise would have been employed, but were then at rest.

We reached camp just as the midday meal as ready, and in a short time were packed up and on our way back to Tacoma, well pleased with our acquaintance with the King of the Northwest.

⁘

This [Leap XXXVIII] was made on the 6th day of August, being the first for some time while we were nominally sojourning at Tacoma, and really running about over the Puget Sound country. It was the beginning of the second leg of the triangle which makes up the journey, and was simply a return over part of the road traversed going from Portland to Tacoma.

The start was made in fair season considering that it was the first day after so long a stop, our friend Mrs. Warren being taken on board as a passenger to go with us to Tumwater, a suburb of Olympia, the state capital, to visit her sister, with whom we were also to dine.

The road passes through Camp Lewis, one of the white elephants Uncle Sam inherited from the war. Tacoma and Pierce county, in which it is situated, issued bonds and purchased 69,000 acres of land, with a long frontage on Hood's Canal, the southern part of Puget Sound, and gave it to Uncle Sam for war purposes. On that was located Camp Lewis, perhaps as much as 10 per cent of the land being used in some way. The 40,000 or 50,000 men of that day have been reduced to a mere handful, and the other numerous activities have entirely disappeared. The great flying field which was to have been established there was taken elsewhere, because other politicians had a pull, and other contractors wanted the job of clearing the field so it would be as good as that already cleared at Camp Lewis. There is not the slightest likelihood that any considerable part of this immense tract will ever be of any use to the Government, but having once taken it, of course it will hang onto it. In the meantime the people of Tacoma and Pierce county are paying for it in their taxes, and the land itself, which may have been worth the price paid, is escaping taxation entirely. If 50,000 acres of it could be returned to the donors the Government would be just as well off and it would relieve the taxpayers materially.

Olympia is unique among the state capitals in that wild land comes up to its very doors. To the northward along the road which leads to all the principal cities of the state, and some of them but a few miles away, the virgin forest comes up to the very gates of the city. Were it still pioneer days, the savages might lie in wait in the forest and shoot the legislators as they were assembling in the legislative halls.

The road for the day was part of the Pacific Highway, than which there is no better. When we went northward there was a detour over the four miles between Centralia and Chehalis, but the regular highway was opened up this week, making every foot of that highway through the state of Washington paved and in perfect condition. We will have the pleasure of traveling over a goodly lot of that road in Oregon and California, encountering it frequently in our zigzagging back and forth about those states, but we can find nothing better than what Washington has furnished.

That splendid Tumwater dinner had been disposed of, good byes said to friends, and a good many miles put behind us before the usual blow out came when near Castle Rock. Another tire went to the junk heap, the sixth since leaving home, and then Horror of Horrors—

The treasurer of the traveling company had left her purse at the home of her midday hostess, having taken it into the house to powder her nose and then forgotten it. Fortunately another member of the company had enough cash for present emergencies, but as the hostess is to visit Tacoma tomorrow, and does not know our mail schedule so cannot forward it until word can be got to her, there is a time approaching when we may not eat regularly—nor frequently.

We are camped tonight in the tourist park at Longview, the newest town in Washington and the only one strictly made to order. In three years it has changed from farms and fields to a city of 6,000 people and everything which might be expected to go therewith. Incidentally, I would add that among its industries is the largest lumber mill in the world. We have seen two large ones already, but planned to see this, the greatest and most modern of all, before attempting to tell the News readers how lumber is made and sent to market. Only the first section of this one is yet in running order, the second being under construction, but that first section cuts a million feet of lumber a day.

So we are camped here after a run of 125 miles today, or 5,824 from Ravenswood.

Chapter Six

Back to Oregon

On the 7th day of August.

Contrary to the experience of many days, there was no tire trouble this day but two other things helped to delay us. First on the program for the day was a visit to the mills of the Long Bell Lumber Company, the largest in the world, and we had been told that the first trip through in the morning, all visitors being conducted by guides at stated times, would be at 8:45. Therefore we took things easy and drove to the mill entrance only a moment before that time. Really the first trip was made at 8:15 and the second an hour later, so we waited there a half hour and started an hour later than was necessary, as we might easily have been there for the 8:15 trip, and so it was an hour later when we were through. That trip and what we saw will not be told of now, but must wait a more favorable time and be incorporated in an article on lumbering in the Northwest.

The second unlucky break was at the ferry, we arriving just as the boat slipped out of the landing and had to wait a half hour for the next boat. The result was that we did not land on the Oregon shore of the Columbia until noon, just then commencing our run to Tillamook.

On the ferry I had quite a lengthy talk with a doctor residing in Longview, and he gave me considerable information regarding that new city. In a little over two years it has assumed a position of real importance among the cities of Washington. Its daily paper will compare favorably with those of much large cities, although the doctor freely stated that it was run at a considerable loss, but was the only way of placing the town properly before the world. An Ohioan from Mt. Vernon, and for some years a practitioner in Spokane, he was enthusiastic over this place, pronouncing it the most wide-awake, progressive town he had ever known. That old familiar western method of boosting instead of knocking was much in evidence all the time after crossing the Mississippi, but nowhere more than in the state of Washington.

The doctor did admit one thing which was not perfect, but that was not at Longview nor even in the state of Washington. He said the Columbia River Highway from Portland to Astoria was not as good by far as it was along the upper river. The grade and surfacing were all right, but the route was necessarily crooked. Even where it might easily have been straight there would be a number of little curves back and forth.

That his criticism was not without foundation was evidenced later by our finding workmen in various places building new roads which would take a lot of petty curves or make others less abrupt.

But the road was a magnificent one, occasionally climbing to considerable heights—in one case over 700 feet above the river—but only in a very few places is the river to be seen and on account of the smoke those few were disappointing. On that highest point, Clatsop Crest, a few acres had been set aside as a park and presented to the county, and when the air is clear it must be a very popular place.

But there are beautiful roads which show neither mountains nor rivers among them, being that lower part of the Columbia River Highway. The mammoth fir and cedar trees which originally occupied the ground in all this region are gone except for an occasional small spot, and even the trees which sprang up their place after the lumberman had taken them have largely been killed by fires; still there is a world of growth, mostly firs with fern and bushes of various varieties for an undergrowth on the higher ground, and with alders on damper spots, and the eye of the traveler meets a constantly changing panorama—a series of scenes each more beautiful than its predecessors.

Astoria is the oldest town on the Northwest coast, and a city which has been the subject of diplomatic conferences, once taken in war and restored by treaty, the spot selected as the site of the metropolis of an empire. Once the center of the fur trade and now one of the greatest fish marts in the world, it is only in recent years that it has assumed the appearance of a city, and in many ways is still peculiar. Just above the mouth of the Columbia on Baker's Bay, all the business district stands on ground either filled in or else naturally but a few feet above high tide. We entered it over plank roads—bridges and full width of the streets, planks once nailed to stringers laid on piling, the nails half drawn by the warping and tilting of the planks until they were a constant menace to our tires. And after a few blocks over concrete pavement apparently on solid earth, we left the place on another long plank street, the only one running in that direction, beside which the city council had put a sign announcing that people traveling it did so at their own risk! In the heart of the city are some substantial buildings but none of particular note, unless it be the post office, a small building of Uncle Sam's popular style of construction which stands in the center of a block, with cement walks from each corner of the block to the corresponding corner of the building but with no entrance except on the river side.[1]

Because of its fishing—it being the heart of the Columbia river salmon business—Astoria has long had a large percentage of Greek, Italian and other southern Europe people. Some of these are now in the second and third generation and are thoroughly Americanized, but the names are still noticeably foreign to our thinking. The most peculiar that we saw on a sign was that of A. Haataja. He is a shoe repairer.

At Astoria I bade farewell for a time to familiar ground so far as actual observation is concerned, although as to some of it I once made a long distance study, as will hereafter appear. My impression had always been that after a short run out from Astoria we would come to the shore of the Pacific Ocean and follow along it to Seaside, the pioneer beach resort of Oregon. That ride alongside the ocean had been one of the reasons for coming this way—which really was a detour from our main route. But that idea had been erroneous. We promptly came out to where apparently an ocean was—at least there were immense deposits of sand laid in parallel ridges, but on one occasion through a cross road we could see to the westward through the cuts in four or five such ridges, and yet no ocean appeared. Into Seaside, still with no evidence of the briny until we arrived at the end of a street where there were no connecting streets, but only a concreted circular wall with a notice to all cars to keep moving, and there just over the wall was our w. k. [well-known?] connection with the Orient, its waves coming boisterously in over the beaches, upon which were scores of beautiful damsels and gay gallants in bathing suits as dry as those under the back seat of Lena which we have carried four years without even trying them on. The weather was too chilly for bathing by anyone except children, a few of whom were disporting in the water, although more were merely playing in the sand.

Lena kept moving until he had completed the circle and then sought a parking place to rest while Florence took her first honest to goodness look at the ocean.

The ocean gazing did not last long, for we were late and must make Tillamook to camp if possible. The road was described as bad for 10 miles and good the other 45, and the description proved accurate. Over several miles of the bad part contractors were busy making it into a good road—with a long way yet to go—and we passed over some of it with difficulty. Once we waited until a blast ahead was fired, and then until some of the rock thrown out was removed, and once a tree had been burned down, falling across the road just before quitting time and therefore remaining these. Three other cars were in the procession at the time, and it was soon found that by the aid of the two camp axes in the party a detour could be cut through the brush, so the delay was short.

It was nearly 8 o'clock when we arrived at Tillamook and began a hunt for its tourist camp. Back in 1888 when I decided to publish a newspaper of my own, among the points considered was Tillamook, county seat of a remote county in Oregon, then without a paper. My choice fell elsewhere, but naturally I have kept Tillamook in mind all these years, and came to it with a feeling of greater interest than I would an ordinary town of the same size.

The speedometer showed 150 miles for the day, making 5,964 as a total, the journey being about half done.

⁘

Covering the events of the 8th day of August, beginning on the shore of Tillamook Bay.

The coast of Oregon is indented by a number of bays, some of them of considerable magnitude, but all with outlets so shallow, or else the bays themselves are so shoal that they are but indifferent harbors, accessible only to vessels of light draft, the state's only real seaport being Astoria at the mouth of the Columbia, and because that river was of sufficient size to accommodate seagoing vessels of all sizes, the port was established far inland, it being cheaper to move goods up and down the river by water than by any other means.

One of those minor harbors is Tillamook Bay, now a scene of considerable activity because of lumbering, fishing and other industries peculiar to its situation, and in a more important way perhaps in the long run, because of the leading industry which has sprung up in the county. Above everything else Tillamook is a dairy county. The heavy dews and fogs from the ocean keep her pastures green all summer, and the winters are so mild that it is seldom there is weather which is so bad as to check growth. Clatsop, Tillamook, Lincoln, Lane, Coos and Curry, Oregon's coast counties, are all similarly situated as to opportunity, but Tillamook is far ahead of them all because of the action of her people in cooperation. With the beginning of the dairy industry there the people began to pull together instead of each trying to get more out of it than anyone else, and the result is that today the county proudly boasts that it manufactures more cheese than any other county in the United States, although but a small part of its area is cleared of timber and in grass. As we went out from Tillamook for several miles up Trask river, the country was cut up into small holdings of from two to five acres, most of these tracts having a house on, the owners raising a goodly part of their living on the fertile soil and working in dairies or mills to make up what they lacked of their seeds. These little tracts were valued at about $1,000 an acre, and yet they are too far from any city to make market gardening profitable. Really dairying is responsible for that sort of values.

It was 35 miles to the summit of the Coast Range, and so easy was the grade that we did not notice when we passed the divide, not realizing that we had reached the top until we came to a decided descent. The road was the best that can be made with gravel and in places was surfaced with tarvia or concrete.

By the time we were fairly down the mountain the temperature began to be noticeably higher, and once out into the Willamette Valley it proved to be a hot day. Hot and dusty. For more than 50 days there had not been a drop of rainfall.

The road reached the valley about the boundary line between Polk and Yamhill counties, in one of the oldest settled parts of Oregon, and now one of the most prosperous and best developed. While wheat and oats have always been the staple crops of this part of the world, it was this immediate locality which broke away from cereal production solely and branched out into various things, nuts finally becoming a staple. The English walnut takes the lead, with filberts second, and occasionally almonds. Hundreds of acres are in nut orchards, and once in bearing a few acres represent a living for a family. Experience shows that the best way to start the orchard is to plant black walnuts, grafting the English walnut onto them.

Still, cereals take most of the land, and it was now harvest time, several threshers being in operation. Wheat was all cut, but there were still some oats ready for the sickle. This crop is sown at all times, the fall sown being dead ripe, winter sown about ready to cut, and the spring sown still quite green.

The valley is from 20 to 30 miles wide—much farther than one can see through the smoke—at times quite level and at others with many hills, giving it a rolling appearance. It was prairie from the time of the first settlement except the larger hills, which were then covered with oak and along the creeks, where ash and willow were plentiful, the latter making a considerable tree.

In the mid afternoon we reached Monroe, in and about which village six years of my boyhood were spent and which I had visited three or four times since leaving it in 1877. The town has grown considerably, but is still the typical small town where few live except retired farmers. Most of the trading is done in larger towns, Corvallis, 17 miles north, or Eugene, 23 miles south, good roads having proved the ruination of the local small dealers except the garage and gasoline man. One exception here is the department store. Before the days of the automobile, Adam Wilhelm and his sons owned here one of the largest department stores in the state, and it still does a good business, although not so much as it did 25 years ago.[2]

The old one-room school house where I absorbed some of my knowledge has been replaced by a modern high school. All over the country the two big improvements have been in the roads and schools, and while many of the small towns have lost population and business they have wonderfully improved their schools, paved their streets and replaced the old wooden sidewalks with cement.

Three miles out of town on a side road, we reached the home of a nephew and brother-in-law of mine, in a neighborhood largely descended from the families living here when I was a school boy amongst them more than 50 years ago, with everything keyed up for a family picnic on the morrow which will bring together scores of the people whom I knew in that long ago.

The speedometer read 6,016 miles from home, or 141 for the day.

A FAMILY GATHERING

Among the pioneer families of Oregon were the Starrs, a number of whom settled in the vicinity of Monroe, the first post office there being called Starr's Point, and it being a prolific family, as were so many of them in that day, their descendants now number high up into the hundreds. On August 9 this year, for the third time there was a reunion of those descendants held at the old campground near Bellefountain, six or seven miles west of Monroe, it being the camp ground sacred in the annals of the Starrs for four or five generations, as the scene of many a wondrous revival. Methodists the family was in the beginning, and until this day to speak of "the Church" to a Starr means the Methodist Church and none other, for except in rare cases where they have intermarried with members of some other denomination or live where the Methodists are not organized, the Starrs are still true to the family traditions in matters religious—and in politics as well, there being few of them who do not vote the Republican ticket.

Among those Starrs and intermarried families, I had lived and gone to school several years in the long ago, and it was a rare bit of good fortune that made our visit coincide with that picnic. We went early, but found a lot of autos already on the ground, while the greeting of old friends was continuous. It had been 50 years since I had been on that particular ground, and almost as long since I had seen many of the people there. By noon and time for the picnic dinner there were about 300 people there, of whom I think at least 75 had been personal acquaintances—many of them school mates.

It was a great occasion for many, and among all who were there I doubt if any enjoyed it more than the man from West Virginia. Of course he was entitled to a prize for having come the farthest to attend the picnic, but there were many other contestants, Southern California in particular being well represented. There was some beautiful singing—this neighborhood and my family having long ago been noted for its musical ability—some speeches, the writer being privileged to make one of them, and as the country correspondent reports, "a good time was had by all."

Among the scenes of the day was the place where my father had operated a mill some 50 years ago, a more modern and much larger mill now occupying almost the same site, and the old house which was then the Clark home was still standing. It was almost night when we returned to the home of my nephew, the speedometer having rolled through 18 more miles, making a total of 6,155 since leaving home.

❧

It was noon on August 10 when we started south again from the old boyhood home, after bidding goodbye to the relatives there. The visit had been unusually pleasing because of the Starr reunion the day before we left. Contrary to usual meetings of friends separated by so many years, there was not the mournfulness caused by so many faces missing that might have been there. Among the immediate families there had been but few deaths, and there were so many friends coming all at once that there was no time to stop and check up to see who was missing.

The afternoon run was over ground once thoroughly familiar, passing through Monroe, Junction City, Eugene (site of the University of Oregon), Cottage Grove, Oakland and various other towns, including one or two which had come into existence since my day, due to the location of a saw mill or other industry. Forty-three years ago I went to Roseburg and helped build the railroad southward from there, my last work being a few miles beyond Myrtle Creek, in which village we spent the night at the home of John Jackson, a friend of my boyhood days, his wife having been my schoolmate for a time and also in the later time when I was helping to subdue the wilderness by farming on a homestead. Like myself they had wandered far in the meantime, from Canada to Arizona with many stops between, but he had located at last not so very far from where he was born, where we found them pleasantly situated and gliding gracefully down the last hill of life.

The country was not so much changed. The towns had grown, Eugene and Roseburg especially having blossomed out from mere country villages into quite cities. The greatest improvement was in the roads, but houses also were better, and somewhat more numerous, even in the country, for this is one region in which the number of farms is not decreasing. There had been a remarkable increase in orchards, and along the latter part of the journey there was much market gardening, the frequent stands along the road indicating that the tourist provided the principal market. The biggest mistake in orcharding was in apples, their growers seldom having found them profitable. The market is far away, so only the very choicest fruit will pay the cost of transportation, and the much greater amount of lower grade product is almost a total loss. There is a growing movement toward nut growing, and it is likely that in another generation they will find that business also overdone. It is ever the tendency of man to rush in where another has made a success rather than each mark out a line for himself. Now walnuts bring the grower about 30 cents a pound, but with European nuts bringing less than half that, it is evident that there can be a supply grown in this country that will exceed the demand at the higher price.

We saw something in the afternoon which we regarded as very curious and presenting a new animal trait. Shortly before we passed, a cat had killed a ground squirrel in the road. The body was still limp and the blood fresh when we came along, and another squirrel was dragging the body off the road. This squirrel is not a flesh eater so there can be no charge of possible cannibalism. Apparently it was only an act of saving the remains of a friend or mate from further mutilation. Our wheels passed within two feet of the rescuer, but it paid no attention to us, continuing to drag the corpse off the pavement where it would not be in the track of other cars. We would have liked to watch further proceedings but such a thing is impossible on the road. Before the car can be stopped and backed up the "show" is all over.

Dead animals are very common on the road, squirrels, rabbits and all the smaller animals of the country, that afternoon even showing two or three skunks—an animal the motorist avoids when possible—and occasionally a hawk loses his life while feasting on the victim of an auto without taking the precaution to move it from the highway first.

The speedometer showed a run of 135 miles for the afternoon, all over one of the finest roads in the United States, making a total run since leaving home of 6,268.

⁂

The spirit of adventure entered into the run of August 11 to a greater extent than usual, for it was to be into a country not only unknown to us but wild to a degree hard to find any more. We back-tracked down the South Fork to the Umpqua, a dozen miles, through a valley quite narrow generally, the immediate bottom of the stream being covered with sage brush, growing in gravel which is so devoid of soil that it will grow nothing else. The second bottom and sloping hills running down to it were largely covered with orchards, prunes leading, with peaches and some apples. Truck patches were common and some of them quite extensive, watermelons, cantaloupes and tomatoes taking the lead, and a roadside stand with vegetables and fruits on display were always in sight.

Then we turned westward up a tributary creek and were on our way to Coos Bay, one of the unique localities in Oregon which we had never seen. Aside from the mouth of the Columbia, Coos Bay is the best harbor on the Oregon coast, and it was settled at an early date. Lying just north of the gold region of California and Oregon, its early days lack the glamour of the mining districts, but it soon took a prominent place in feeding the gold digger, producing all the vegetables known to this region, the cereals in a small way, and fish in abundance. Later came the knowledge that the hills were underlain with coal of a fair quality—the only coal in western Oregon, and the best in the state. In that quite an industry sprang up, and there was the usual amount of lumbering, numerous mills being located in the towns which grew up around the bay.

The Umpqua river empties into the bay, being navigable as far up as the tide runs for small vessels and the bar at the outlet will not permit large ones to enter the bay.

A good gravel highway leads from the Pacific highway eight miles south of Roseburg, and on it we crossed the Coast Range through a low pass, there being no heavy climb, and so level was the summit that we did not know when we passed it, not being aware that we were on a stream running direct to the ocean until we came to one filled with logs. For miles as we followed down it the bed was liberally sprinkled with beautiful cedar and fir logs stranded on the rocks, the stream being a mere trickle after all these weeks of no rain. Sometimes there would be a pile of them, the remainder of a log jam last winter when they were being driven down to the mills on the bay. In other places other logs were being shot down the mountain side in chutes and either rolled into the channel or else yarded on the bank ready for the swollen stream when the wet season shall come again.

Cedar is becoming scarce in the Northwest, but in this section it evidently is still common, for sometimes nothing else would be seen in the river and all the logs being shot down were that kind. Such as are of proper size and quality are destined to be made into shingles, and when they go onto the market will be known as "Puget Sound" shingles without ever having been within 500 miles of the Sound, just as in former days all the red fir lumber went onto the market as "Oregon Pine."

We followed the river through Myrtle Point to Coquille, then by a sharp turn continuing on with it to "Bandon by the Sea," 20 miles farther. We had to take the word of the map for the by the sea part, for we did not see the sea at all, but turning southward continued on the gravel road, now part of the Roosevelt highway, to Port Orford, 30 miles farther.[3] At Bandon we had the sea smell quite strong, ran over some plank roads in the center of the street just like Astoria and yet did not catch a glimpse of a breaker until we drove into Port Orford and almost ran into the ocean before Florence could stop the car, her surprise and speed both contributing to the difficulty of stopping in time.

There were some beautiful rocks just out in the water there; seal rocks they would have been in other places, but there were no seals here. The larger rock, about as big as the largest building in small cities, was the scene of a battle in the early days, when nine white men were attacked by a large force of Indians and won out after a prolonged and bloody fight. These coast Indians along here were all enemies of the whites and were only defeated after several years of fighting.

A heavy fog was coming in from the sea, but we had several minutes of fine view before it arrived. Experience had taught us the advisability of buying supplies early, grocery stores in the West usually closing at 6 P.M. to the grief of the tourist who sometimes goes hungry to bed as a consequence, so we bought some provisions in Port Orford and set out for Gold Beach. For several miles we ran along the coast, looking down into the ocean often from considerable heights, but the fog was usually too heavy for us to see any distance out to sea.

It was literally a "rock bound coast," the sea breaking against solid cliffs most of the way, and the trees which grew from crevices in the rock showed the effect of a life of battling with the wind. Scarce one but had been broken at times in its life, and the broken top leaning landward would stiffen itself at the break and make another effort to rise only to have the disaster repeated. Many of them grew off on a long slope to landward, like a roof, as a consequence, and the limbs which naturally would have stuck out toward the sea bent inward, helping the illusion that it was a growing roof to shed the rainfall direct into the waiting ocean.

Halfway to Gold Beach we came to the end of the graveled road, the last 13 miles being the worst road we have encountered on the entire trip, barely wide enough for a car, twisting and winding around the hill side, meeting places often hundreds of feet apart and around so many turns that it was impossible to see from one meeting point to another, it was only by sheer luck that we got through. The road is a temporary one, and should by all means be made a one-way affair, with traffic regulated to certain hours in each direction. Elsewhere a broad highway is being built, and in a year or two more there will be only pleasure in making this trip, but now only the lucky can make it in comfort, and even they with little peace of mind.

Four miles out of Gold Beach we crossed Rogue river on a free ferry maintained by the county, following down that stream to Gold

The Oregon Coast Highway Bridge crossing the Rogue River. The Clarks crossed the river by ferry in 1925 before the bridge opened in 1931. *Courtesy Oregon Historical Society.*

Beach, county seat of Curry, the southwestern most county of Oregon, where we camped after a run of 168 miles, 6,436 from home.

August 12 proved one of the hard days of the trip, although little progress was made. The day opened with us in a historic spot, Gold Beach having been one of the early mining points of Oregon. It was in the early 50's that gold was discovered in the sand on the beach of southwestern Oregon, and there was the usual rush to get some of it, just as there was years later when that metal was found in the sands of the tundra at Nome, Alaska.

It was not the sand which the tides brought in or swept out daily, but an old deposit on a little higher ground, perhaps an old ocean level, and while there seemed abundant gold in the sand it proved very expensive in most cases to get the sand and Water to wash it into connection with each other. Still, a good deal of money was made by the more fortunate, and the work continued with more or less vigor. In later years came the discovery that the white metal which had long interfered by sticking closely to the gold was platinum, then worth a considerable sum, and now several times as valuable as gold. That gave a renewal to the industry, and ground which could not profitably be worked for gold alone was made to pay.

Then with the growth of quartz mining on the Pacific Coast and the establishment of smelters came the added value of the black sand which represents a considerable part of the total weight of the beach deposit. While this black sand is largely iron, like all iron coming from gold bearing ledges, it carries considerable gold—enough to make it worth shipping and smelting.

With these various items of value, the sands have been worked most of the time for upwards of 70 years, although just now there is nothing doing at Gold Beach, once the center of the work. At other places there is considerable work still in progress, the principal aim of which is to recover the black sand. The gold and platinum has been ground "exceeding fine," the particles being too small usually to be seen by the best of eyes unless there are a number of them together.

Ocean sands have drifted before the wind and covered the richer deposits of an older age, but with a record of having added millions of dollars to the world's gold supply, Gold Beach is an object of interest, and even in its faded condition there is yet something of the unique about it—not because of "the glory that was" but for its own picturesqueness. A casual stroll about the town failed to reveal a single foot of sidewalk, although I have since been told that had my feet carried me into the proper quarter I would have found a little. The county of which it is the capital has only 3,000 or 4,000 people, and has stood practically still for years. New industries have been opened up, dairying and milling, but they have merely taken the place of the mining, so the people only turned from one means of livelihood to another.

Until recently there were three papers in the county, one here at Gold Beach, another at Brookings under the same ownership, and a third at Port Orford. The latter was a losing venture and was sold some time ago to the county seat publishers, and when the mill at Brookings closed down a few weeks ago its paper was immediately suspended. So now there is but one.

The Roosevelt Highway down the coast of Oregon is going to bring some new life to Curry county, but we found that it is not yet completed. That is a mild way to state a tremendous fact. Merely saying it is not completed gives no idea of how much it lacks of being so. The previous day we had traveled over 13 miles of the uncompleted part as already related, and today there was added 25 or 30 miles more. Even that does not tell what I want the reader to know. It is not only not completed; it is not even begun! The road is perhaps the worst of equal length that has even been regularly used for automobile travel. Certainly it is by far the worst we have encountered.

In Yellowstone Park and elsewhere there have been harassing bits of "scenic highway," to quote the guide books, but they were comparatively smooth, reasonably direct, and wide enough for one car to go along with frequently places wide enough for passing. But this temporary road is different. Up and down, rough as it can be and still be used, crooks as short and regular as a negro's hair, its meeting places were far apart and then too narrow to be safe even with the most careful driving. Florence avers that some trees the road completely circled three times. But I think she became dizzy with the constant turning and miscounted; I doubt if there was a single tree that we circled more than twice!

Around point after point we ran where the road was not wide enough for the car to turn, the hind wheels scraping against the wall and shoving over into the same track the front wheels had made; these were not mere turnings of a corner, but almost complete circles, and it did fairly make one dizzy to go around them, there being the feeling that we were going around and around, and at any time by a moment's negligence in permitting the front wheels to run a few inches too far out the car would have plunged down the mountainside hundreds of feet, perhaps into the ocean. Lena has some dents in a rear door made by the passenger on the back seat gripping too hard and unconsciously leaving his finger prints in permanent form! One would be safer to part company with a car if it started down that mountain, but somehow I could not realize it just at the time, and persisted in hanging on tight.

Once we ran into a blockade. A Ford climbing the mountain had run short of gas and refused to go farther. Two other cars came up and the Studebaker man obligingly loaned the Ford a gallon or two but still it would do no more than spit a few times and stop. Then a small tree was cut and the Studebaker began pushing. We were hanging over the edge hoping the caravan would not push us off when it passed, and up at the next bend was a Dodge in an equally precarious situation.

Three more cars came struggling up the hill, so we who were hanging on "by the skin of our teeth" had to take six chances each of being "bumped off." The pushing arrangement did not work well, slipping frequently, but eventually the Ford disappeared around the turn behind the Dodge, all six were past up, and Lena slipped back into the road and we were again on the way. We had gone several miles before that Dodge overtook us, and we had about decided that it had been shoved over the bank.

Earlier in the day I had stopped and "panned" a few shovels full of that sand, that I might have a trifle of gold and platinum to add to my curio collection.

The gold seeking, added to a late start multiplied by the condition of the road, resulted in our reaching the home of my niece in Brookings at almost 6 o'clock, the speedometer showing 41 miles for the day—air line about 18—making a total of 6,477.

◦⁘◦

Brookings has the misfortune to be a town of one industry, the saw mill being the only thing in town employing labor, and in June it shut down. Various were the stories as to the cause of the suspension of operations, but it was not reasons the men wanted, but labor, so most of them had flown to other parts of the Northwest Coast to seek work in other mills which were still running. The closing was evidently done on short notice, the last log remaining on the carriage half sawed up, with two more logs on the way from the pond to the carriage.

Lumber in the yard at the time of suspension was said to have amounted to 25,000,000 feet, but one-third of it has been shipped since. One of the company's vessels was loading while we were there, which would account for about another million feet. Originally built to saw fir, by a little alteration, the mill had been transposed to a redwood mill. That famous California timber has to be handled like the proverbial baby, and to yank it about, drop it and handle it generally like fir and pine are handled would ruin a large amount of it. So it takes more care and time. But in spite of that the mill was rated as good for 120,000 feet of lumber for each eight-hour shift, and had run as high at 210,000. The latter was when running largely on "Australians," or merely cutting the logs into "cants" for export, to be cut up by mills in Australia. A great deal of Pacific Coast lumber goes out in that shape, saving freight on the slabs, adding to ease in handling and in some cases making a saving in tariffs at the other end of the voyage.

Fortunately for the people there, just as the mill closed down, work was begun on several contracts on the Roosevelt Highway, so there was work for all those willing to do that kind of work. But in timber as in other things, there are men who scorn to do other kinds of labor.

We went down to the wharf to watch them load lumber, and found one of the most up-to-date lumber handling plants on the coast. A traveling crane takes the lumber from the stacks in the yards, loads it onto cars, which a locomotive runs down onto the dock, when other cranes pick it up in bunches of about a four-horse load and bound with slings—heavy ropes—put them at any desired spot in the ship without misplacing a board and leaving the slings on so that at the end of the voyage they can be picked up and the cargo discharged without having to touch a board with human hands. It was an interesting operation.

Out in the harbor was another interesting sight; no less than an old whaler. One of those ships familiar to every reading boy of my day, when the sea still retained its fascination for American boys, and the whaler ranked next to the pirate ship in popularity. This was not merely a whaler returned from some long voyage with her tanks full of oil, or preparing for a venture of doubtful profit, but a whaler then and there in pursuit of whales. Brookings is not on a bay, but merely a small indentation of the coast, where vessels cannot dock to load or unload except in calm weather, and whales are frequently seen close in. So the old whaler had come into shallow water, anchored and from her crow's nest the lookout was continually watching the seas, while the crew listened every moment for the joyous cry of "A-a-ar blows." Indeed, while we were watching the lumber being swung on board, the captain of the lumbership spoke of the whaler, and said, "There's one spouting now." But it proved to be only a whitecap, or at least we so decided and there was no sign of activity on the whaler. But the next morning as we left she was already gone—possibly in pursuit of a whale which had gone out to sea, mayhap to the antipodes where whales were believed to be more plentiful. One never knows where a whaler or a pirate goes when it disappears.

When we left Friday morning the sky was clear, the sun shining brighter than any time since we crossed the continental divide onto the Pacific Coast. For about 30 miles our road ran south, crossing the state line and entering Del Norte county, California, a more progressive county than Curry. Because of her shortage of harbors the latter had been held back, and has made little progress until the coming of the Roosevelt Highway. There is not an incorporated town in the county—and in this part of the world some very small aggregations of people are incorporated as a city—and there are but four churches.

Our road to Crescent City, the capital of Del Norte, was all well graveled and most of the way along the sea, both in sight and hearing of the waves beating on the shore. That is a rugged coast, and ships usually give it a wide berth. We saw one in the morning, far out to sea, that seemed to be coming toward the shore, but after watching her for an hour she was no closer in and had seemed to be running with us, so we put her down as a liner from Portland to San Francisco.

We crossed several small rivers, the road leading through a country originally heavily timbered, but from which it had practically all been cut long ago. One exception was a quarter section of redwood, the first I had ever seen, although we were to travel through miles of it later in the day. I had seen big timber before. Eight to ten million feet of lumber on a square mile is no curiosity in the Pacific Northwest, but this would be easily twice as much as I had ever seen before. I have seen cedar trees on Puget Sound as large in diameter as any of the redwood, but this far surpassed in height anything I had ever seen in timber, and it was wonderfully thick on the ground. Its limbs are insignificant in size and only a few feet in spread, but the trunks grew so close together that only occasionally rays of sunlight stole down to the ground. And there were no "swelled butts" as in so many kinds of timber. Starting at the very surface of the ground the boles rose into the air straight as an arrow, with scarcely a perceptible taper until straggling limbs began to appear 75 or 100 feet up in the air, and it made the backs of our necks ache to look at the tops of the trees 150 feet still above the lowest limbs.

A peculiarity which added considerably to the density of the forest was its habit of growing in bunches. Two, three and even four trees grew as if from one root, each about the same size, giving one the impression that a tree had been cut and from its stump sprang up a number of sprouts, each of which developed into a tree. Wherever there was room and sunlight young trees were growing which we took to be redwoods although its leaves on the trees were too far away to be recognized with certainty.

The road from Crescent City to Grants Pass is a part of the Redwood Highway, and when completed will become a very popular way of reaching southwestern Oregon or the coast country of California. We found considerable of it still in the making—they really were working on it—and only a little of it done. South from Crescent City to Eureka we heard there was also considerable bad traveling on it, but in a year or two more there will be a fine road there for the tourist.[4]

The state line and the summit of the Coast Mountains come at the same place, the former being 36 degrees if my memory is right, and the latter 4,500 feet above sea level if the sign tells the truth. Some of the road was pretty bad—mostly on detours—but we did not find the Oregon side any worse than California's, even though one Californian told us it would be.

The return into Oregon was into Josephine county, one of the minor counties of the state, albeit an old one. In its earlier days its principal industry was gold mining, and it has yielded many millions in the precious metal, although not much of it has paid any great profit to the miners who devoted their lives to the business. Both in placer and quartz it is famous for being "pockety," producing immense sums from small areas and then following with a lot of territory just rich enough to keep the miner at work without paying expenses. The most famous mine, the Gold Hill, yielded $250,000 at a trifling cost, which its owners spent in mining rock which returned less than cost. But they never found another "pocket."

The usual flat tire delayed us but a short time occurring just as we stopped for lunch, and we reached a camp ground in Grants Pass about 5 o'clock. This was a mail point, with a lot of letters. It is also the home of a nephew of mine, who proved to be away from home, working at a mill we had passed 29 miles back, and it was uncertain when he would be in town. But we met his wife and two boys, all secured since I last saw him.

Speedometer record for the day 133 miles, making 6,610 for the trip.

※

In yesterday's letter I said that in its early day Josephine had been largely a mining county. Considerable is still done in that line, but when I first had a personal acquaintance with it nearly 50 years ago, live stock and farming furnished a livelihood for a large part of its people. The latter had no market except that provided by the miners, but the cattle could be driven out when fat and wool could be hauled to railroad and shipped. Forty years ago a railroad was built through the county, and since then the fruit industry has grown wonderfully.

All this information as to Josephine county applies equally to Jackson county, which we entered a few miles after we began our run on Saturday, August 15, and at Medford where we had a wait—the first flat tire of the day—I visited a fruit packing shed. An old friend lived in the country nearby and I had a considerable wait before he came in with his load of pears.

I had seen fruit packed in public packing sheds in the Ozarks and thought I knew something about it, but Medford soon showed me that what I had seen was as nothing.

This was only one of several packing sheds in the town, for experience has proven that no man can pack his own fruit, but there were 48 sorters at work there, and I know not how many packers. In the orchard the pears are put in boxes furnished by the packers, each holding a box of fruit, but built enough higher that one will sit on another without touching any fruit. Unloaded onto a platform they are stacked seven boxes high, the stack being wheeled away on a truck made expressly for that purpose, just fitting the box and letting go of it at the desire of the packer.

Inside the packing house these boxes are placed on a roller way with canvas belts running down between each two. On either side are eight sorters, who pick up each pear, put the well colored ones on one belt and the second grades on another, the selection being only as to quality, size not being considered. The culls are dropped onto another belt which carries them back and drops them into a box. The good ones are carried along and both first and second grades are divided into five sizes by passing under rotating brushes placed at different heights, the first only touching the largest and rolling them off into a bin, and each succeeding brush rolling the next size. By that method of grading the packer can say with a close degree of accuracy just how many pears a box contains after it is packed.

At these bins—20 for each set of 16 sorters, are the packers, who take up each pear separately, wrap it in a sheet of tissue paper which they remove from the stack at their left by means of a glove on one hand, packing them compactly in a box of regulation size for pears. (My recollection is that a box of pears contains 40 pounds and an apple box 50.)

Placed on another roller way the filled boxes—the pears standing high above the box all over—are carried to the men who put on the tops of the boxes, who place them under a clamp which forces them down even with the top of the box, nails on the top and the box is ready for the label which will indicate that the package so marked contains a certain number of pears of a certain variety and standard. That day they were working on Bartlett pears, but some other day it might be something else, although that region—the Rogue River Valley—is running more and more to pears to the exclusion of other fruits, its product ranking with the best.

The previous day we had stopped at a roadside market and bought as fine a box of peaches as ever man ate for 85 cents. The same day that kind of peaches were selling by jobbers in Portland for $1.50. I don't know what the consumer paid in that city, but evidently there are some problems of transportation and middle men to be settled there as well as nearer home.

It was noon when we bade our friend good bye and started for Crater Lake, arriving about 5 o'clock with only one more flat tire. Dust was the most prominent feature around the rim, but we finally found a spot fairly grassy and made our camp, intending to remain two nights at this remarkable spot. Some 75 or 100 other cars were parked here, even more including those belonging to guests at the Inn, and nearly all of them were from California. Only Lena was from east of the Mississippi, Washington and Missouri each had one and Oregon three in the first 25, the rest being Californians. Some of them are on the way home or we would expect to find that state deserted when we get back to it next week.

Speedometer reading for the day 127 miles, or 6,737 for the trip.

⁂

The Sunday at Crater Lake, August 16, was spent quietly. There were a large number of people there, the crowd beginning to arrive early and continuing until about noon. Many of these came in local cars, so the preponderance of Californians was overcome. Among the new arrivals were also several tourists including one car from Wheeling— the first from West Virginia in several weeks. Among the cars parked at the hotel was also one from Hawaii, the first we had seen from there, and with a license plate so like West Virginia's that we did not know the difference until close enough to read the name.

After a fairly early Sunday morning breakfast we started down to the lake, an excellent trail leading from the rim near the hotel. The sign board said it was a mile, but long before we got down there Florence demurred to the measurement, finally deciding it was about three miles. We walked down very deliberately, stopping frequently to view the lake or other scene, and were an hour in reaching the water.

My first impression on reaching the rim the previous evening— every car pulls up to the parking line and the occupants get out and look at the lake before hunting a camping place—was one of disappointment. It appeared too shallow a bowl. I had known of it for 50 years, and always heard that the lake was surrounded by a wall scalable at only one or two points, rising from 1,000 to 2,000 feet above the water. But looking out over it I could see no such depths. Long before we reached the water the next morning I could have accepted twice those figures as accurate. The trail starts from one of the lowest points in the rim, and the official figures give it elevation at 897 feet above the water, the highest point being 1,979. Incidentally I may mention that when the survey was made the soundings gave a depth of the lake in one place of 2,008 feet, which after due allowance for stretch of line and other corrections which deep sea scientists assure us must be made, the depth is given as 1,996. The surface elevation of the water at the time of the survey was 6,179. As the lake is fed only by direct precipitation and perhaps some subterranean springs and emptied only by evaporation and seepage, its elevation varies slightly from year to year. Its shape is nearly round, being five miles one way and seven the other, with no bays or indentations on its border. Its size is what gives the visitor the feeling that the walls are not very high. It looks like a saucer, but really it is a bowl so deep that it never freezes, even though the cold is intense here at times in the winter. (We had frost the first morning we were there.)[5]

The first thought of the visitor is of the intensity of its blue, becoming almost black in the shadow. That blueness seemed to even increase as we descended, until as we neared the bottom and came close enough to really see the spots where there was a little shelf below the water line, the edge was a vivid green. The next day as we were driving around the lake between Wizard Island and the shore, the water was shallow enough that it was green all the way across as seen from the rim, there 1,200 feet above the water, yet the shallowest point in that channel is 85 feet deep; the deepest perhaps 200.

At the foot of the trail was the boat landing, from which gasoline launches make regular trips around the lake, a 25 miles trip, and across to Wizard Island. This island is a cone rising so steep that it is climbed only with difficulty, rising about 780 feet above the water, in its top being a crater 600 feet across and 90 feet deep, in one side of which is a small lake.

Florence decided on a boat ride and chose the launch running over to and around the island. There are a number of row boats on the lake, but she did not care for rowing. The old folks returned to the rim and began writing letters. By mid afternoon the cars began leaving, and few came up the hill, so by night the camp ground had a rather deserted appearance. The soil is part of the vomiting of Mt. Mazama, which was the progenitor of Crater Lake, being mainly sand

and volcanic ash and as no rain had fallen for two months the rim was extremely dry, dust being everywhere. Still we were so fortunate as to find a little grass on which to make our camp.

There was no garage or service station on the rim, so it fell to me to patch the tube concerned in the last flat tire of the previous day and in putting it back on the wheel in place of the "spare" which had brought us in, and which is so poor it is used only in emergency, it was convenient to run the car ahead about a foot. In doing that something was encountered which rewarded us by giving another flat tire the next morning when we were otherwise ready to start. I think it holds the short run record for trouble!

Monday morning we were away as soon as that tire was in shape to run, starting on the "Rim Road" around the lake. Take a cone pointing upward, then beginning at the top, bore a conical hole point downward, and you have a miniature representation of Crater Lake, except that its walls are jagged and therefore irregular in height. But you can readily, see that into that inverted cone there would be no drainage from falling water. Neither is there into Crater Lake. The boat encircles the lake on the smaller circle of the cone 1,500 feet below the average height of the rim, and travels 25 miles in doing so, while around the rim is built a road, running back quite a distance at times, and frequently twisting, winding and zigzagging back and forth to go up or down the steep elevations; and yet it is only 35 miles around, even though in two places it is as much as two miles from the lake.

As we drove around frequent stops were made to use the camera. At one point a road led away to the north, running to Diamond Lake (a beautiful mountain lake covering several miles, well stocked with various kinds of trout). We could see the lake in the distance, and the road indicated that most of the tourists went that way, but we stuck to, the rim, winding our way about until about 2 o'clock we bade farewell to Crater Lake and a few miles farther on "checked out," the ranger telling us we had choice of two routes to Fort Klamath. Shutting our eyes to the noted beauties of Anna Creek canyon, famous even in the day when Crater Lake was known only to residents nearby, we chose the shorter and less hilly road by the Pinnacles. What we missed in Anna Creek canyon we probably will never know, but the wonders of the "Pinnacles" will never be forgotten.

Just to the left of the road was a narrow ravine, so steep that we could not see to the bottom, but apparently the home of a small stream and while it seemed to grow wider, and presumably deeper, it was not until we had followed it several miles that an abrupt turn in its course gave us an opportunity to see down into it. The walls were almost perpendicular and fantastically carved. A dark bluish gray rock, evidently a conglomerate, for all through it were pebbles from the size of marbles up to a wash tub, of harder material, some of them almost washed out from the softer material cementing them together. We followed down it for several miles, finally coming to where another stream similarly decorated flowed in, the wider ravine along there giving room for the water to get behind much of its wall rock, leaving scores of pinnacles from a few feet to 50 or 75 feet standing up in the air like totem poles.

The dust along there made the road almost impassible, the wheels of the car turning up great clouds of it, and the tracks were worn down so that the car dragged in the middle most of the time, but that center gave way so easily that it only added a little more to the dust.

Out of the dust we came onto a graveled highway, part of the Dalles-California Highway, and turned south on it. Two or three miles and we cut off the ignition, coasting down Sand Mountain for seven miles and landing almost on the site of Fort Klamath, a three-company post in my day in that country, but now abandoned and every one of the old buildings torn down. Nothing was recognizable. I could not even find the grave of Captain Jack of Modoc War fame, who was hung here at the close of that bloody struggle. Perhaps it forms part of some settler's meadow.[6]

Then came Klamath Agency, now little more than an Indian school, Modoc Point, Klamath Lake and finally the thriving city of Klamath Falls, the outgrowth of the old village of Linkville. There we camped in a tourist park alongside "Silent Smith," nephew of Jim Bridger, his name indicating his fame as the most talkative man in the United States army. Entering the army a boy in 1863, a protégé of General Custer, he gave us a history of the army and Indian from the Modoc War on. Many of his tales seemed unbelievable, and yet in many instances he got around to times and things with which I personally was familiar, and in every case his statements were absolutely correct. Packed away in his memory, and evidently carefully card indexed, are a multitude of thrilling tales of the days when the West was young,

Speedometer showed a run for the day of 96 miles, a total of 6,833.

※

The first one [Leap XLVII] of the trip occupying two days, August 18 and 19, but it seems to work out that way best.

Klamath Falls, where it begins and ends, is just now one of the most growing towns in Oregon, and bids fair to continue to grow for a good many years to come, although with its chief concern the production of lumber and timber products, it will decline rapidly after the summit is reached unless something else comes to take its place. But in any event it will continue the principal town of the southeastern quarter of Oregon. Just now it presents the unique spectacle of a town making efforts to prevent a railroad from building to it! When I knew it before, it was 200 miles to the nearest railroad, and the wildest dreamer did not entertain the possibility of one ever being nearer than about 50 miles. As soon as a few more miles of roadbed are completed, it will be on the main line of the Southern Pacific's San Francisco-Portland line, and a cross country road to Reno, Nev., connecting with the Union Pacific and the Western Pacific. Besides that the Oregon Trunk road, owned and operated jointly by the Northern Pacific and Great Northern, is proposing to extend its line from Bend to this place, and there are strenuous efforts being made to have the Interstate Commerce Commission deny the Oregon Trunk that privilege.

This is one of the instances of the working of "big politics" such as are frequent but seldom seen. Really the mills of this section are fearful of the competition of the mills of northern Oregon and Washington, which would have a new entrance into California markets over that extension, and the Southern Pacific would have a rival in territory exclusively its own. The fight is not being made by the people nor for the people, but it is none the less very real, as there are some influential people taking a hand in it.

Our camp is at the edge of town, over two miles from what was the town when I was on earth before, but it has not grown in all directions to that extent, and one way not at all. Still it presents a very thriving appearance, with some mills carrying a large payroll, and the claim is made that the 5,000 population of the last census has been doubtful since.

The irrigation project here is one of the largest in the country, was among the early ones and is often cited as an example of that way of making desert lands useful to man. It was one of the early projects developed and cost far less per acre than many, there being no expensive dam to build and no valuable rights to buy. A short tunnel took water from Klamath lake at an elevation which made it available for use on a large area, and the principal cost was for main ditch and laterals. Water rights were sold on long time, and yet there is much talk of it being difficult for farmers to meet their payments. The overhead or upkeep cost amounts to a considerable sum. In many cases it is much as though a farmer bought a farm, then paid for it again in the purchase of a water right, and then paid rent on the land in the shape of the upkeep charge.

On the other hand there are those who claim the farmer is making money and that the whole claim of not making farming pay is a game to get the Government to reduce the charge and give the water to the consumers on easier terms. What is the truth I do not know, but anyone can see that there are thousands of acres under the ditch which might be farmed and irrigated but are not, and also that the ditch does not carry near the water that it might, while the river flows on with its volume scarce diminished by the farmers' demands. The crops look well, but frost on the morning of the 19th cut down potatoes and other tender vegetation.

It was afternoon when we left town on the 18th for a run up to my old home at Bly. Roads were reported bad, and the report was not true—they were much worse than that. Twice the usual amount of tire trouble came to us, and it was dark when we arrived at the home of Harrison Brown, a Klamath Indian who had been my friend in the long ago. Naturally he failed to recognize me, but when I spoke to him in Klamath he recalled me instantly, and we were cheerfully furnished not only camping ground and fuel but hay for our beds as well. Incidentally I might say that my one query if he did not know me was the only Klamath sentence uttered during our long visit that evening or the much longer with him and his wife the next morning. That was one of the most marked changes I saw in the whole trip. In the old days the Indian men spoke English with difficulty, the women not at all. Now it is the language used in all conversations about their homes, and many of the smaller children I was told, do not speak Klamath at all and only understand a few words of it. A generation or two more and it will be a dead language. Of the Chinook, once the common language between white and Indian, or between different native tribes on the Pacific Coast, I heard not a word.

The Klamaths are disappearing; their death rate has been very high. The infant mortality is appalling. The old people live to be very old, but the children do not grow up. Our host for the night is an older man than I by several years—I think about 70—a brother and sister a little younger are living; also a brother older, the latter's wife having died a few days before, after a married life of nearly 50 years; another brother still older died only last spring, and the father of this family was burned to death only a few years ago. These four brothers and one sister were the parents of about 30 children, of whom only a half-dozen are now living.

There was ice in the water bucket when we woke in the morning, but an hour after sunrise it was growing uncomfortably warm. Everything on the farm was photographed and we bade good bye to these friends with an actual hope of seeing one of them again, and ran a dozen miles still farther east to Bly, now a little village. Some 45 years ago a post office was established there, my father being the first postmaster, with myself as deputy. The name was my suggestion, it being a Klamath word signifying up or the head of the valley, and as deputy under different postmasters I had practical charge of the office for several years—no difficult task in those days, except that all mail passing through to a dozen post offices to the east was all clumped indiscriminately into the same sacks and we went through it all and kept out our own. Under prevailing regulations, postmasters at way offices were allowed seven minutes to distribute the mail, but as the driver either dined or spent the night at practically every office, there was no difficulty because of the time allowance.

There are now perhaps twice as many houses in the valley as when I dished out their mail, and a larger part of them were occupied by families, bachelors then forming the bulk of the population, but there were only three men of the old days still there. One or two others I had known in other parts of the county. The valley today is worth less than then; the abundant grass of that day has been eaten out, tame grasses and grains do not do very well, and stock-raising, then an extremely profitable business, although affording few of the comforts of life, is now a hazardous business. Last year the hay crop was a failure and cattle had to be driven away at heavy cost and fed expensive hay. In the old time there was enough grass beneath the snow that the loss would not have been very heavy had there been no hay at all.

Choosing a different route back, including many miles over a road where there was not even a trail in that day, we passed Bonanza, now the residence of an old friend who betimes was a fellow reporter on the Klamath County Star—purely a thank you job, unless the editor forgot his manners—until recently editor of a paper in this town, and all these years the husband of one of my pupils in the days when I "kept school" and "boarded 'round." At the home I called for her by the maiden name she had not heard for two score years and she responded, but of course did not recognize the old teacher.

Back again in Klamath Falls early in the evening, with more mail, but not that most wanted, the speedometer reporting 169 more miles, putting us up to 7,002, assuring us that the journey was well more than half run so we were really on the way home.

⁂

[Leap XLVIII,] in which Lena carries his passengers across a state line on August 21.

Before bidding farewell to the relatives and friends in Klamath Falls, we spent an hour or so in a visit to one of the cities' box plants. More and more the lumber of the timbered regions is being put into shape for the use of the consumer before it leaves the place where the logs are sawed, thus materially reducing cost of delivery, both through saving in freight and in working it up in large quantities by skilled labor and machinery.

Thus it comes that with six large mills at Klamath Falls, all but one have a box factory. The one we visited is owned by two cousins of mine and a third man, and is probably typical of all. They own a mill by the side of the lake, and about one-half the output of the mill goes to the box factory. The lumber is principally pine, and so much of it as is clear is planed and shipped away, as is all fir, but the rest of the pine goes to the yards for seasoning and in due time is taken to the box factory. There is no specializing in boxes for any particular purpose, although a very large part of the output goes into fruit boxes, prepared for growers and packers all the way from home to Florida. Some are shipped to West Virginia. The boxes are all shipped "knocked down," the boards tied in packages. Two rotary presses were printing names on the ends of boxes that morning, one of them from a customer who takes 450 car loads a year.

It was a busy place, with planers, saws and many other machines whizzing and whirring. Much of the work is done by women and girls, and practically all work is by the day rather than piece work, as the machine sets a pace to which the operator must conform, and any one in that place will do the same work. There was a nice clean, wholesome smell to it all, the odor of new lumber, and while the operators must go home laden with sawdust, it is clean dust that they scatter.

I did not ask the number of employees in the box factory, but there at the mill and in the lumber woods combined there are 550 names on the payroll.

Just by way of giving a hint of what these factories mean to the town, all the fuel of Klamath Falls is waste from the box factories, the only cost to the consumer being that of delivery. The factories are only too glad to have it hauled away, as the excess must be removed at their own expense. In this one factory the amount of waste is 100 tons a day, or 60 to 70 truck loads! The waste from the mills is carried by machinery to incinerators and burned. People would not haul it away because it is wet and must be seasoned before it is fit for fuel. In olden days it went into the lake or river, but state laws have stopped that everywhere.

Once more on the road we followed a gravel highway over the Cascade mountains back once more into Rogue River Valley, going down to Ashland, only a dozen miles from Medford, where we had been a week before on our way to Crater Lake. This drive was one familiar to me, except as to the road, which was anything but familiar, the one I knew being all heavy grades, sidling, rocks, ruts and (most abominable of all) corduroy. That was the pioneer way of making a road across swamp ground—cut poles and make a road of them by laying them side by side. Sometimes notches were cut where the wheels would come, which helped until the pole turned over. Now the road has an even grade on hills, the mountains being all climbed in high gear, and except for the little dust that goes with a gravel road it is a perfect highway.

At Ashland we had an old friend, a fellow townsman in the days when we were young married people. Sixteen years ago he left Washington and bought a jewelry store in Ashland, and since then has served about half the time as mayor of the town. This happened to be one of the years he was in office so we drove in without fear.

An hour's chat with the mayor and off again headed southward over the Siskiyou mountains. For seven years I lived in that part of the country but never crossed the Siskiyous. Once I went south on the railroad but got off at Ashland, went over to Klamath Falls and then down the river to Ager, thus going around them. In the earlier day they had a bad name. Rising 2,500 feet above Rogue River Valley—their foot on the California side being lower—they were steep and rough, difficult to freight over. Then, too, there were undesirable citizens there at times even at a later day than mine it was no unusual thing for stages to be robbed on the Siskiyous, and occasionally travelers were held up there. Wells-Fargo messengers carried sawed-off shot guns and rode beside the stage driver. And at least on one occasion the gun was used and that robber retired permanently.

Now there is a beautiful road twisting and winding its way up, and the robber who would stand out in the road and attempt a holdup would be bumped off into the canyon by a passing automobile.

At the top a disappointment awaited us. We had expected a magnificent view of Mt. Shasta from there but it could not be seen. The Siskiyous extend east and west and Shasta was so nearly east that it was hidden by nearby peaks and spurs until we were nearly down the mountains. Then we were on the west side, from which the winds had driven the snow as it fell so that we merely had a tremendously high mountain rising out of the valley a few miles away, with some streaks of snow up toward its summit. From much of the Klamath country we had viewed its northern side where the snow we now could not see had lodged when the wind drove it into drifts last winter.

Once down the mountain we were into one of the old mining regions of California. Gold was discovered there in 1851 and men have been digging it ever since, although in smaller quantities in recent years. Yreka, the county seat of Siskiyou county, was all worked over in the early day, the site producing $10 000,000. It isn't worth half that now unless it is for the gold remaining under the houses and streets, some of which is being sought by a company dredging deeper than the old time miners went.

There we purchased some supplies and drove on until camping time brought us to a wayside tourist camp, a small hill to the east hiding Shasta, but in no wise interfering with the passage of cold air downward from its summit. The speedometer said 154 miles for the day, making 7,169 all told.

⁓

An account of the events and information gained on the 22nd day of August, when we journeyed from near Weed to the heart of Trinity county.

We had counted on one night in the shadow of Mt. Shasta, where we might see the lights and shadows play upon its brow, but we were disappointed in a number of ways. The principal, or most enduring one, was the fact that from our camping place Mt. Shasta could not be seen. This presumably was Shasta's own fault. Not that Northern California's pet exhibit is bashful—very much to the contrary. It not only is in evidence all the time, but the day has been when it was vastly more so. And that is the reason we could not see it.

Somewhere back in ancient times if the man in the moon was not otherwise engaged, and had a good glass, Shasta put on a show which must have amused that w. k. person greatly. Of course we cannot know what was the matter, but evidently something disagreeable had been eaten, and the mountain—then younger and perhaps smaller than now—proceeded to unload. There is ample evidence of the operation. For miles the plain—for Shasta rises from a plain which reaches far—is strewn with hillocks of lava, badly broken up but universally rounded in form. In size there is a wide diversity, all the way from the size of a large business block to a pretty respectable mountain. But each is round on its base, and rises like a dome. They may be touching each other or they may be far apart, but they are as much alike in everything but size as a Dutchman's growing children. All about is a level of rich tillable soil, but their domes are all of broken lava. There is only one answer to the problem—Shasta threw them there in a fit of anger or disgust. And one of those domes lay between us and its distinguished author, completely concealing the latter from our view.

Then another difficulty of studying the mountain at short range was the fact that it was cloudy. For two or three days a south wind had been blowing—a pretty good omen of rain—and that night at times it threatened to carry the tent away, even though it had been staked down with more than ordinary care. Just over that hill behind which lay Shasta was the Southern Pacific railroad, and it seemed that all night long it was occupied by a succession of double headed freight trains. Their noise added to the wind and a bed none too comfortable, plus the anxiety resulting from fear of rain, made the night quite unpleasant. So we were awake and off betimes the next morning, running down to Weed in a short time. There while the car was getting a supply of gas I went to the home of Nelson Wilson next door, and woke him, telling him it was a joke on him that a man could come from Ravenswood and catch him in bed. As the readers of the News already know, he lost his wife shortly after their return home from their Ravenswood visit in the spring. He was building some more houses in the growing town of Weed, where but for storm and cloud the people may daily see the mountain we had expected to see the previous night.

While the gas tank and tires were being filled it began raining, and although friend Wilson assured us that it would not amount to much, the prospect was not cheering as we started on.

Earlier in the trip we had seen the beginning of the Columbia river, and here we saw that of the Sacramento, the stream whose sands have been pouring out gold for three-quarters of a century. And they had been doing the same thing here. All along the way were old placer diggings, and some not so old, only lying idle now waiting the season of more plentiful water. Here had been great hydraulic plants in the days before the agriculturists won their long fought battle against the miners in California and stopped them from filling the channels of the streams with tailings.

Here were places famous in the history of California as recorded by Mark Twain, Bret Harte and their confreres. Here was Portuguese Flat, once the scene, of brilliant and boisterous life—now a hog lot. Here was Oak Bar, from which frantic toilers tore millions of dollars worth of gold—now a pile of barren gravel which will be an eyesore for centuries to come.

At Redding we bought some supplies and turned west, crossing the line into Trinity county, not only one of the pioneer regions of the state, but one of its leading producers to this day, and the one county above all others that has produced nothing but mineral. Its timber was either burned to get it out of the miners' way, used in mining, or is so far from market that it has no present value. The county is so mountainous that there is no land for agricultural purposes. It is doubtful if the entire crop of the county would feed its population for a day, certainly not for a week. Its river and creek valleys have been turned over one, two, three or four times on the hunt for gold, and high up its mountain sides— just as high as winter's rain can make water run in streams as large as a garden hose carries, the washing has gone on. For miles below Weaver- ville, its county seat, the broad valley is but a series of hills of piled gravel from which all the sand and soil has been washed.

It was too early to camp at Weaverville, but a merchant there—not the Chinaman from whom we had to purchase vegetables—told us we could probably get to Junction City before it was too late. His cousin was postmaster there and would tell us where we could camp. The dis- tance was only 10 miles but we found the usual allowance locally was an hour and a quarter to make it. The mountain was not so bad to climb, but a fright to go down. On its western slope was an old hydrau- lic mine that has lain idle for several years, but in its day was the largest mine of that kind in the United States—which I take it, is equivalent to saying the biggest in the world.

At first we thought Junction City was deserted. There was a store, a warehouse, and miraculous as it may seem, a church, all old, falling into decay and deserted long since. Then around a turn in the road, over a lot more tailings, and we met a man with a gold pan, a prospector returning from his day among the hills, who told us that the three houses just ahead made Junction City. The postmistress received us as a committee from the chamber of commerce, and told us we could find good camping facilities about a mile farther on under two apple trees beside the road.

We found the place already occupied by two Oregon prospectors, and pitched our tent beneath one of those trees—so far as we know the only fruit trees in Trinity county—after a run of 159 miles for the day, making 7,328 from home, and around the camp fire listened to the tales of those prospectors, one of whom was familiar with the local history in bygone days, and went to sleep to dream of finding gold in such vast quantities Lena sank and perished beneath the load. And yet the dreams did not come up to some of the prospectors' stories.

CHAPTER SEVEN

Northern California

[LEAP L,] BEING A SABBATH DAY'S JOURNEY MADE AUGUST 23 THROUGH the mountains of Northern California.

That rain which began at Weed the previous day was merely a shower, which we ran through in an hour or so, but it was followed by others at frequent intervals all day. We would come to places where there evidently had been no rain but some would begin falling, and when we were through that, the road would be dry again. Apparently we struck all of them, and went to bed that night in a narrow canyon where our vision was so circumscribed that we could get little idea of the prospect for the morrow. Another light shower fell in the night, but with the morning came clear skies. Our neighbors, the prospectors, were already up, and one of them had washed out three pans of dirt taken from a nearby hydraulic mine idle for want of water. He found a dozen "colors" which interested Florence considerably.

After breakfast she and I started to make our fortunes, not out of the other man's idle mine but by getting gravel up on the hillside where another hydraulic miner of the long ago had left a few handfuls of gravel in a crevice. We filled our pan with the overlooked wealth, and then put two more pans into a water pail to carry to the creek, panning the three with great care. Mrs. Clark had been kept out of it and at work about the camp by being promised the excess above $50,000, and seemed quite disappointed when informed that there was no excess. In fact there wasn't anything. Those old miners had not overlooked those three pans of gravel—they simply knew there was nothing in them that they wanted. The white man may have missed some occasionally, but after him came the Chinaman, and what he overlooked simply was not there.

One exception to that rule one of the prospectors told us the night before. A green young easterner had come onto Willow Creek in the western part of Trinity county, and began working once more a bit of creek bottom which was supposed to still have a little gold—a job of gleaning as it were. His cabin was some distance from the creek, and he did not take kindly to the old miner custom of carrying water from the creek regardless of distance, so he sank a well, the house being but a few feet above the creek level, thinking the water would seep through and be clearer and purer than the creek water, as well as handier. In that well he struck a little bit of an old gravel bar, from which he washed out $70,000!

It is tales like this, some true and others apocryphal, which keep men hunting through these mountains for the treasures overlooked in the previous years. And once in a while somebody finds the spot for which he is looking, and immediately there is another rush to the mountains. Other occupations usually pay better than mining, but there is a lure about placer gold, the ease with which it may be obtained if one is lucky, and the quick returns—no waiting to market anything and get your money in course of time—the physical possession of wealth, or rather the possession of the physical wealth, and not merely some figures on a piece of paper. Even oil does not have so much attraction for men, because it always represents some actual investment, small though it be while the gold may come from the labor of an hour otherwise idle.

"How many mountains to cross between here and Eureka?" we asked the prospector who was most at home in this part of the world before he left that morning. "Just one; all the way," was his reply. The *Blue Book* told us it would be a little over 100 miles yet, so we left camp the middle of the forenoon.

The statement that there was just one mountain and it continuing all the way was hardly fair. We crossed one sizable mountain soon after we started and then we followed for 40 or 50 miles along the Trinity river. Of the great gold producing rivers of California, this river will come at least third, and possibly even higher, and throughout its entire length its gravels have been washed over and over, much of it by a dredge the last time, which picked up, washed and laid down in serried rows all the millions of tons of gravel which had occupied the valley. So it is no longer possible to find field or meadow in that valley, nor even to make a road except it be surfaced. Squirrel, goat and man are about the only animals that can get over the piles of tailings, and not one of them can live in the valley. So when the time came to build a road it had to go onto the mountainside. Occasionally the canyon walls would end in precipices, and the road would climb high up, but ordinarily the road was from 100 to 200 feet above the river, and one could toss a pebble into the stream, or at least onto the piled up gravel with which it is lined. Today the water is almost clear, having that little color which tells of a quartz mill somewhere above or else in tributary fed by that greatest of all rock grinders, a glacier, but when the rains of winter fall and the placer miners get busy, the waters, swollen to many times their present stream, run to the sea red with the clay and sand of the hills and mountains.

But beside that long run alongside the Trinity, we climbed three separate and considerable mountains. The road along the river had been easy. Sometimes it was too narrow to pass, and so nearly was the river one that it was a dizzy operation, even the passengers not caring to look down, while the driver's eyes were fixed upon the inner edge of the road. But the mountain climbing added heavy grades and many short turns which did not add to the pleasure of the day. Some whom we met described the road as "terrible," "horrible," "awful" and in other ways expressing undesirability. But we voted it not so bad. A little trying to the nerves, but not particularly danger-ous to the careful driver—and somehow it seemed to take the reck-lessness out of all the drivers we met.

"There are some detours over in Humboldt county where they are building road that are very bad," Nelson Wilson had told us at Weed, and we found it correct. One detour around a bridge involved a long descent which was the steepest we had found on the entire trip, and was a test of the brakes. The other was caused by a torn out bridge and took us several miles from one highway across to another, over a pretty high mountain, where the road was rough—including some of that rarity now, once so common, corduroy road.

These three mountains of the day were from four to 12 miles on the ascending side, and about the same descending, being each a hard grind and preventing any fast time. So by the time we were down to the valley level along Humboldt Bay we were in humor for camp and supper, pulling into the camp among the redwoods at Arcata a little after 6 o'clock, the speedometer calling for 106 miles for the day, making the run from home 7,343.

That Sunday night, August 23, was one of the pleasantest spent on the entire trip, so far as accommodations were concerned. Our place in the camp was at the very edge of the redwoods, to the southwest being open ground with Humboldt Bay in sight not so far away but that we could hear the slosh of the breakers during the night when the tide was in. On the other side were the tall redwoods, not the giants such as abound in virgin forests, but second growth, beginning probably shortly after the discovery of gold brought settlement to California, they being now two or three feet in diameter and 150 to 200 feet high.

Many of them were sprouts from old stumps, and, with the strength of established roots backing them, made faster progress than seedlings would have done. The superintendent of the park, who had charge of the camping arrangements, was the most agreeable official of like kind that we had seen. At the very beginning he made us feel that he was honored by having a customer from West Virginia, and through all his talk he refrained from observing that we were "a long ways from home," which had been the invariable observation of all with whom we came in contact since crossing the Mississippi.

The height and size of the redwood trees undoubtedly dwarfed the Clarks' 1925 Chevrolet Superior roadster as they do these earlier-model motorcars. This view of the early Redwood Highway in Humboldt County, California, was made a few years before the Clarks' visit when they camped beneath the mighty giants. *Courtesy Save the Redwoods League.*

Then the arrangements were first class in every respect. Elsewhere we had found hot and cold shower baths; here they were to be had in privacy behind locked doors. The kitchen was so large that it also contained about eight tables, and we were privileged to eat indoors. Then there was a community house, clean, well lighted, comfortable chairs and a large number of magazines including files for a year or more of some of the best.

The one fault which might be found with it was the absence of any place where provisions might be bought. We were in need of none, but at times the tourist finds that a severe need. And the western grocery stores have a common practice of closing at 6 o'clock that is surprising to easterners and not at all popular with tourists.

Monday morning there seemed to be a number of petty things which united gave us a late start, and a stop was made at Eureka to have repairs made on the tire which had gone flat the day before, and a visit was made to the stump store during the wait. This popular place for the tourist has been in operation for 40 years, the owner then having begun making things of beauty and utility out of the redwood burls. Our visit there was enjoyed very much, for we not only saw a great many beautiful and curious things, but learned some things about the redwood trees we had not known before. These burls are peculiar to the redwood so far as I know, and are increasing rapidly. Some are of tremendous size. The finest, both in quality and size, that he has ever had was 60 inches in diameter and 80 feet long, as I remember the dimensions. He paid $1,000 for it and it cost about $400 more to get it to his shop. But he said he would have paid $3,000 had it been asked. From that they range down to small growing ones the size of a goose egg. These will sprout out fernlike limbs if fed plenty of water, and the limbs in turn may be broken off, planted in earth and will proceed to form a tree. I didn't ask what happens to the tree where they are sawed off. On the tree they produce no foliage.

With three flat tires in the afternoon, besides stopping at a small town barber shop for a shave, progress was slow, and camping time found us at the state park on the south fork of Eel river. The road had been good—gravel with a little concrete—but it was all uphill except in crossing points of hills, which would be both up and down and quite steep, and a large part of it had been too crooked to permit fast running. Much of the way had been through the redwoods, in one place passing where logging was in progress. Where they grew there was nothing else, and when we would come to a place where they met the fir trees, the line of cleavage would be almost as distinct as a line fence. As I write this in the park I am on one of those lines. To my right I can see no redwood, and to the left not a fir tree is visible. But oak, pine, laurel and a number of other varieties mingle freely with the fir; the redwood is as exclusive as a descendant of a Knickerbocker family.

Owing to the delays mentioned the day's run was only 101 miles, putting us 7,535 miles on our journey.

⁕

That camp in the redwoods where we began August 25 was not at all to our liking. Called a state camp, it really is a private affair, run by a lessee, and evidently his lease did not have much longer to run. The equipment consisted of sheet iron stoves and some of the regular camp style of seats and table combined. The ground was bare and generally uneven. The wood—take as much as you want—was good 16-inch redwood, but the stoves were chambered for 10-inch wood. A little grocery store supplied such things as the tourist must have to eat, but the prices were reminders of early days in Alaska. The charge was the same as we had paid for the desirable quarters at Arcata the night before.

When the touring by automobile began to be rather general, the western towns of any size with scarce an exception prepared camps for the tourists, and not only was their use free, but there was considerable rivalry between the different towns as to which could provide the most attractive camp. The tourist drove his car in, pitched his tent and spread out his belongings. When he decided to move on he did so and it was nobody's business.

After a time it came to the notice of local officials that workmen employed on the streets, in building houses, working on nearby farms, local garages and what not were all camping in the town's tourist camp, with wood, water and other necessities furnished without expense. Their children were enrolled in the local schools, and they were for the time residents of the town. But when tax collecting time came they had gone elsewhere.

This condition soon resulted in the establishment of stated charges for the use of tourist camps, and quite commonly a time limit to the stay there. Then private owners of suitable property began to establish similar camps, with such equipment as they chose. The result is that there are few free camps, and they where ground has little value, accommodations are few and the owner has things to sell the tourist, either to eat or for his car.

On the whole the tourist, the real sure enough vacationist and sightseer, is better satisfied. He feels that he pays his way instead of being under obligations to strangers, who are entertaining him from selfish motives in spite of all pretense to the contrary. He is not "looking a gift horse in the mouth," and feels free to demand that which is advertised as being furnished in connection with the camp.

But there is a wide variation in the accommodations and conveniences of the different camps even though the charge is uniformly 50 cents, and we felt that the state of California through its lessee gave as little for the money as any we are likely to find.

The next night in the camp where this is written, Santa Rosa, we found the dirtiest place yet encountered. The prettiest little city we have seen, its homes models of elegance, with grounds in perfect condition, its tourist camp was positively filthy. It is the dry time of year in California, and nothing green is to be expected where there is no water to make it grow, but the dirt here is human dirt, than which there is no dirtier.

We are told that the first of next month the municipal camp is to be abandoned and a private one opened, and that may be the reason this is so run down.

The roads for the day have not come up to the advertisements. In fact, none of the California roads have so far. Roads which a year ago were reported as finished—not by printed matter, but letters from local authorities—are found this year almost impassable and contracts under construction that will not be completed for two or three years yet. Of course repairs will always be in process but a lot of these "highways" have not yet had the surveyor's stakes set. But undoubtedly there are better roads ahead.

The redwoods disappeared early today, although much farther along the towns advertise as being in the redwood country, and there may be small bunches of them, or at least were such until they were cut out. But the big trees are gone, and in their place are new varieties, some unknown to us, but in the main, oak and laurel predominating.

The country was rough, the valuable timber all cut off, but little land cleared, and the settlement but sparse until we came to Russian river. Towns as shown on the road maps were far apart, and when we did come to them almost without exception they were merely points on the map. For 90 miles there was no railroad and then the first station we came to had only one little store.

Then we began to come to scores of new vineyards and orchards, mostly in their first year, although a few were in their second. Very rarely was an older one seen and they were small. Finally we came down to the Russian river valley and for the first time began to feel that we were in California. Settled by a Russian colony in the dim ages of the past, this climate did not prove satisfactory to them, and they finally deserted it to go up to Alaska where a man could really enjoy life. But for that, Russia might have held sway over the whole coast from San Francisco north. Such trifles are part of what makes us Presbyterians believe as we do in things theological.

Prunes, grapes, peaches, pears, oranges—all these grow in this valley, and there is no irrigation. Lawns in towns are plentifully watered to keep them green, but the fields, orchards and vineyards take the moisture nature furnishes and are content. The grapes are all wine grapes—no table varieties—and while prohibition makes it grape juice instead of wine, nobody but a prohibition enforcement officer could tell the difference.

Prunes are drying, a few in the orchards, but more in open places alongside where the sun can get at them. Hundreds and hundreds of shallow trays, about 3x5 feet. The fruit is shaken from the tree, gathered up by pickers into boxes holding about a bushel each, taken to the dipping sheds and dipped in a weak solution of lye, placed in trays and put in the sun to dry. No, I forgot one operation: they are run over a classifier which divides them into five sizes. Most of this information was gleaned from a man who was just here looking for more pickers. He said they paid $4 a ton to pickers, and a good picker would get about $5 a day. I tried to get Mrs. Clark and Florence to try it a day or two, but they are in a hurry to get home.

Early pears are all picked, the big work now being in the prune orchards. Once we saw a sign announcing the want of hop pickers, but the hop business seems to be on the decline. Many people find their summer employment following the berry and fruit crops from one end of the state to the other. It was because of them that free municipal camps were abandoned.

The run for the day shows as 170 miles, making 7,705 since the start.

❧

The morning of August 26 dawned with a decided change in temperature since the previous day. It seemed no surprise to the native when the sun failed to show itself that morning for they were sure that it was in evidence "over in the valley," and as for not showing there in Santa Rosa, they reasoned that such was the usual condition of the "coast towns." It is deemed a rare privilege to be a resident of that "betwixt and between" region which is neither baked by summer suns nor soaked by continuous fogs.[1]

The usual tire repair came early, one of them being flat when we awoke, although it was standing up all right when we went to bed. An examination found a slow leak in the tube, so trifling that it had stood up for hours the day before. Correction of the fault took some time.

There was another matter requiring attention: Santa Rosa is the home of one of the world's two greatest men, Luther Burbank, and his work called for attention.

There was no trouble in finding his "garden." I suppose the people of Santa Rosa have no more trouble in remembering or telling strangers that than the residents of Washington would in telling how to find the home of Calvin Coolidge, its great man for the moment, but not to be included in the same class as Luther Burbank.

It is situated on the direct route to San Francisco, and is one of the beauty spots of a town which has many of the prettiest places the mind of man can imagine. Gorgeous palms with bodies from one to two feet in diameter are a regular feature of Santa Rosa lawns. Flowers bloom there the year round with a profusion seldom seen in other latitudes. Trees of rare beauty which have been brought from regions far away and carefully trained in their growth, are on every hand. We could have spent a week there taking snapshots of beautiful homes and grounds and still have left plenty unpictured.

But the Burbank home was different. In one way it is disappointing. One who reads of great men and wonderful works will invariably imagine too much. We read how Burbank takes plants not usually considered related and by his artfulness produces from their crossing a new creation which has the virtues of both parents and the vices of neither. All this is true, but we read about it so much that we come to think of it as being mere child's play for him, and that he does it at almost a moment's notice and in profusion.

As a matter of fact he does such miracles, but only after they have been carefully thought out, and then at times only after long and repeated efforts. Indeed were Mr. Burbank to speak along that line, he would tell that he has failed multiplied times to where he has succeeded once.

Then again some of his greatest accomplishments have been given to the world, are now in common use, and he is no longer concerned in them. It is only the newer and the more promising that he exposes to public view on his block in Santa Rosa. There were flowers and vegetables in plenty—perhaps 30 or 40 different things—but many of them were not new, only improved strains of the old. One of the most striking of all was his new plant with red foliage. In a more northern garden I had seen samples of it grown from seed obtained from Mr. Burbank, and there seemed some doubt of its being all that he claimed. But in the climate of its birth, and in the hands of its author it is a thing of beauty and a blaze of glory. All nature produces nothing of a more brilliant red, shading on the lower leaves to a dark brown with only the appearance of being "red under the skin." Even a single plant would attract attention, and when grown in masses they form a striking picture in any landscape.

Perhaps of more practical value than any other plant now being grown on his grounds is his spineless cactus, for if it possesses the utility he claims for it, from its introduction will come value to millions of acres of our country otherwise worthless. The production of new gladioli, dahlias and other flowers lack the substance of utility, but in them may be found a lot of pleasure and happiness, and in any event it should be the privilege of an old man to do things solely for amusement sometimes, forgetful of mere utility.

An hour quickly passed in the examination of these wonders and beauties and again we were on the road, going but a few miles before leaving this beautiful valley, and taking to the hills of Marin county. But before we left it there came one surprise. We were running down that valley, as nearly perfect for human homes as could be imagined, as was abundantly proved by many of the homes by the road side. The question arose as to the sale value of the land in its natural condition. With my usual recklessness I risked the opinion that it could be bought at about the same sum today that northwestern Iowa farm land brought in the boom days immediately following the World war, $500 to $1,000 an acre. No sooner had I ventured that guess than we came to a large sign telling where to apply to buy that land in tracts of from three to twenty acres at $175 an acre! I was tempted to stop and buy up to the limit—I mean up to the limit of my resources.

Sausalito and mail came before noon, the first mail for several days, all very welcome. Then on the advice of the postmaster, who was naturally of an accommodating turn and in addition had for many years been a newspaper man, we drove out along the edge of the bay to look at the Golden Gate and incidentally see some of the preparations Uncle Sam has made to prevent any other nation from endeavoring to subdue the people in and about San Francisco.

Then Lena rolled aboard the San Francisco ferry and in 20 minutes we were in Yerba Buena. A call at headquarters of an automobile association sent us far out on Mission avenue to a tourist camp, and with the sun still behind the clouds we have been spending the closing hours of the day preparing for tomorrow, when we are to see as much as can be crowded into the short day. The women have been renovating some of the soiled clothes, and a few letters have been written.

The speedometer record is 85 miles for the day or 7,790 for the trip.

⁂

But before beginning the report of the leap made on the 28th day of August, mention should be made of things occurring prior thereto. San Francisco did itself proud in welcoming us to its midst. For three days it had been hot there, one of them so much so that the girl at the automobile association headquarters where I went for information told me that she went without her sweater in the office, for the first time this year. Such excessive heat annoyed her, and the average Friscoite naturally felt that it would be distasteful to visitors as well. So they ordered up another kind of weather for our delectation. The day we arrived a heavy fog rolled in from the Pacific Ocean—a controlling interest in which is owned by San Francisco. The mercury dropped to a degree which they aver there it never does reach, but that was because they did not test it in our immediate locality. With the fog was a delightsome breeze moving landward at a rate of 30 or 40 miles an hour, which made the cold all the more apparent—to visitors.

We could not contemplate sleeping in the tent for the next two nights, so rented a cottage at the tourist camp, and long before dark were indoors trying to warm the little house with a big coal oil stove, and failing miserably. Before dark the fog was wetting the ground wherever the wind struck, and soon the trees over the cabin began to drip. All night long there was a steady drip, drip, drip upon the roof. It was what in most lands would be called a drizzle, in Oregon would be an "Oregon mist," but in San Francisco was a "heavy fog."

Our time was limited and we had to see as much as possible while there, so in good season the next morning we started down town. The camera was forgotten, but it did not seem needed, so we kept on until when half way in we fell heir to a flat tire, so while the garage man fixed it we went back after the picture maker. I wore my overcoat for the first time on the trip, although we had traveled several days in and about Yellowstone with snow banks beside the road much of the time. And even the overcoat did not warm me. I really suffered from cold, and a similar experience in that city in August 1898, led me to believe that there was no place in the city where I could get warm. They claim to get used to it and like it, but I think they dress for it. It was the women of San Francisco wearing furs in the summer from necessity that put it into the heads of American women generally to wear them when lace would be more comfortable.

We drove out to the museum in Golden Gate Park and spent two or three hours in there, making a rapid survey of one wing of the mammoth building. This museum far surpasses any I have ever seen. The state of Colorado has one in the capitol at Denver which may surpass it in some ways, but when I saw it there was no real comparison between it and this one at San Francisco.

It was the gift of M. H. DeYoung, one of the newspaper owners who made his city famous (and sometimes infamous) with his paper, *The*

Chronicle. Others have contributed to it, some extensively, but the great mass of its contents came from Mr. DeYoung.[2]

We could have spent months in there without seeing all that it contained—without even seeing all that would have been of interest to us—but we could not devote the whole day to that one thing, no matter how attractive it might be, so we moved on. When we came out the fog was gone and the sun shining brightly. Still we stuck to our winter wraps until we reached the Cliff House and went into the Sutro Baths and Museum.

Tiring of that we drove down the ocean side and about the city, covering some of the most popular drives.

One of my cousins from Klamath Falls was in the city and by arrangement made before we left her home in Oregon, we dined with her at a down town restaurant and then went to see "No, No Nanette." When we reached camp some time after midnight the speedometer reported that we had run 66 miles during the day, or a total of 8,846.

The urge to get home again was growing stronger in some of the party so the next morning, Friday, August 28, we were up betimes, the packing requiring more time than usual because of Lena having been unloaded to the minutest detail for use in running about town, and the safety and protection the cabin afforded his contents.

First was a short visit to a cousin of mine living in the city whom I had not seen for more than 40 years, she being then the wife of an itinerant Methodist preacher. Her sons were away at their several duties and our visit was short.

Then the car was to be greased and the oil changed, and during that operation we were to visit Chinatown. This distinctive feature of San Francisco is said to be greatly changed since "the fire," and certainly the daylight visit now was very different from the night visit I made in the old days. Then all that we saw was what catered to the tourists, not always of the highest character, and perhaps in many cases not illustrative of Chinese domestic or commercial life. Here we found shops of all kinds and some stores that would be a credit to any city. Immense department stores and others which specialized in one particular line and carried stocks suited to every taste and purse. One show house announced that it was high class only, seats from 50 cents to $1.75, but no moving picture place did we see. It was time of day to eat and I proposed that we patronize a restaurant of the locality. The ladies promptly declined, thereby relieving me from backing out on my own proposition. Many markets displayed a vast amount of edibles, or things presumably edible, and the appearance of some of them may have influenced the decision.

We purchased such souvenirs of the occasion as suited the individual fancies of the party, ate lunch at a nearby eating house, redeemed Lena and headed for the ferry. In Oakland there was to be a call on Mrs. Pearl Wood Brandt, but the telephone indicated that she was not at home, we getting no response. Then there was an old friend in Alameda on the list, but she had moved to Southern California a month or two ago, so we were off on the way to Yosemite.

The day was warmer after we crossed the bay, but Mrs. Clark continued to wear her heavy coat as long as we were driving, our day ending at a pretty little three-year-old town in the San Joaquin valley, surrounded by a rich farming and fruit growing country. It was in the midst of an irrigated region with surprisingly rich soil, considering its sandy nature. Good roads were numerous, we having that kind all the way and seeing many others branching off in all directions.

Between the bay cities and the San Joaquin there were two distant ranges of hills, each presenting a considerable climb and apparently of little worth, being sparsely settled. Between these ranges was a valley a few miles wide, and then came the San Joaquin valley, so wide we could not see its farther side through the smoky atmosphere, and perfectly level. Usually "level" valleys have the swells of old sand dunes when examined closely, but this seemed ready for the irrigator as soon as he would plow up ridges on which to make his water courses. They need ridges rather than ditches. The speedometer reported 95 miles run during the day, increasing the total to 7,941.

Of the national parks so far visited, Yosemite is the hardest to reach, at least if one comes the way we did. I hold the long distance championship record as a taker of wrong roads, usually when there is logic and common sense on my side. Thus in coming from Manteca the road led due east for about 26 miles, as ascertained by inquiry at Manteca garages and demonstrated by speedometer. There, according to the *Blue Book*, was to be found a highway leading from Stockton to Yosemite. It was reported as coming in from the north, crossing the railroad, turning east immediately and "follow the concrete." We did that, and had the further assurance of state highway markings announcing Yosemite as one of the points to be reached on ahead. We continued to follow those highway markings through Waterford, LaGrange, Hayward, Coulterville and on into the mountains, going over range after range, but each time going up more than we went down. We came onto the Tuolumne river, its water dirtied from placer mining just as in the days of Bret Harte and Mark Twain; we came to a huge dredge slowly scooping the gravel from its old channel, just as Bret Harte and Clemens never saw it done; we saw acre after acre piled high with cleanly washed gravel which that same dredge or some other had piled up there, taking out every particle of gold, along the stream where those old writers saw the hydraulic miners wash other gravel into the stream to be carried down and clog the river to the ruin of the farmers.

We saw old mines abandoned years ago as worked out; we saw others recently discovered whose owners hoped to take millions from, as the owners of the others had done. All such reminders of California's past and hopes of her future we saw, but we did not see any of her present. In other words, we saw no automobiles going to or coming from Yosemite when there should have been scores of them.

Finally, having led us deep into the mountains, the highway marks disappeared. Freshly cut trees told of the operations of the woodmen; newly laid rails showed a standard gauge railroad evidently built to remove the timber. At intervals the road divided, each way about equally traveled and with no mark to indicate which way we should go. But we tried each time to take the oldest road, and finally were so fortunate as to come out at a ranger's cabin. He wanted to know how we came to get in on that road and I told him it was following highway signs and making good guesses. Then he expressed an opinion of the state road commission that put up those signs which was in thorough accord with my own. He did it more neatly and tersely than I could have done it, but he probably was more experienced than I, for we were the fourth car in a week that had traversed the same route, each to the sorrow of the driver.

The trouble started at Oakdale, where another road had been concreted since the *Blue Book* was issued, and we had taken the wrong one. Then the highway commission evidently intended to make a road to Yosemite that way, but the ranger said it was several miles farther and at the present time very much worse road.

We checked into the park and had 35 minutes to run eight miles, three of it up hill so steep as to require second and sometimes low, or failing in that we must wait until 7 o'clock before we could go down the grade onto the valley floor, the road being a one-way affair and traffic going up and down on alternate hours.

Now the matter of speed is more than a matter of temperament among our drivers. When we started out Mrs. Clark announced her objection to fast driving, setting 30 miles an hour as a rate fast enough for any occasion. So when I drive I hold myself to that rate, barring occasional spurts on very good roads when her attention is directed elsewhere. But Florence knows no boss, so when time is to be made she takes the wheel and forgets all about speed laws. In fact that morning of August 29 while coming from Manteca to Oakdale over a new perfect road, Mrs. Clark herself occasionally forgot about her rules and steered Lena gaily along at 35 miles an hour or better.

Now when we were trying to get down that mountain there was no protest when Florence went at a rate equivalent to 100 miles an hour, condition of the road considered. In the midst of her effort came a flat tire. We made the change as quickly as possible, but arrived at the control station three minutes too late!

The ranger was a young man, Florence smiled at him, and he told us to go ahead, but be sure to reach the checking station at the foot of the mountain before 6 o'clock. That is the way Uncle Sam does business. He makes rules and provides penalties for their infraction; then he insists that you willfully and deliberately violate them. The rule set a speed rate down the mountain which made it impossible for us to get down by a certain time and then the officer enforcing the rule stipulated that we must go faster than that. We got down before 6 o'clock, the official in Washington who made the rule did not know it had been violated, no harm was done, and we all had another proof that the best law of all is common sense.

At the bottom we checked in, ran up to the superintendent's office, registered and were assigned to Camp 7 during our stay in the park. It proved the best of all the 20 camps to our notion, for there was an abundance of high grass on which to make our beds, and we saw none in any of the others. The speedometer reported 139 miles for the day, making 8,080 from home—two-thirds of the way according to the estimate.

⁂

[Leap LVI,] which also includes the loitering about Yosemite on August 30 and 31.

This was not so enjoyable a time as might be supposed, for there was a dark cloud hanging over our camp. The morning we left San Francisco Mrs. Clark woke with a sore mouth. At first I attributed it to eating fresh figs, even though she had eaten but one and I never knew one fig to cause a sore mouth. But during the day it grew worse and by night there were a number of festered places all over the inside. A suggestion that we consult a doctor met with disapproval, and the assurance that it was better the next morning, followed by her taking the steering wheel and driving with more readiness than usual, gave us some confidence. But later in the day when we struck the worst of the road already told about, she was evidently worse, and there was more wrong with her than a sore mouth.

Sunday morning she was better so far as the mouth was concerned, but was ill otherwise and had no appetite. Still she turned a deaf ear to suggestions of medical advice. The forenoon was spent in a lot of cards for mailing, and in the afternoon we drove about the park, she seeming to feel better. Especially did she show improvement when we encountered bears down near El Capitan.

Two cars were stopped in the road and a big brown bear was in the woods a few yards away, the people and bruin evidently entertaining each other. Remembering our Yellowstone lessons, we rang the dinner bell for the bear. The regular bell is to rattle a paper sack, but in the absence of any I shook a large map which made a good noise and the bear promptly came over to the car to see what we had to eat. Mrs. Clark was much interested in the new boarder, and began feeding him some of the buns planned for our supper, keeping it up until the bear got his front feet up onto the-running board in order to get closer to the sources of supply. Invitations and commands that he get down having no effect, Florence started the car and ran away from him.

On the return trip near the same place there was a black bear beyond a wire fence and Florence wanted to coax it up to the fence and feed it. She rattled a paper industriously, and it came back quite a ways, halting and turning away again from time to time, but evidently was not hungry and had no desire to waste time conversing with a young lady.

Monday morning the sick woman was better, and the post office being open, a goodly lot of mail helped wonderfully; so was started lap to Vernal and Nevada fall, the only ones in the park at that time which had enough water to really reach the ground in a stream. It involved a six miles walk and a lot of hard climbing, so the women stopped at the foot of Vernal Falls while I continued on up to the higher, finer fall which had been named for my wife.

In the other parks we had visited—Yellowstone, Rainier and Crater Lake—California cars had been more in evidence than any other state, except the home cars from the nearby cities at Rainier, but here they were all Californians. We were in Camp 7, and with 50 to 75 cars there, changing daily, I saw only three or four that did not bear the California tag. When we checked into the park, the ranger said Lena was the first West Virginia car he had seen this year, but the superintendent said there had been two or three others.

We had seen but one Florida car in many days, accounted for perhaps by the intense jealousy existing between the two orange growing states. Any Californian can tell you how Florida has nothing but boom and the Floridan, Floridian, or whatever he is, can see nothing in California to attract people. I suppose that in Florida the California car is not much in evidence, but elsewhere it occupies much of the space on the road.

After two days spent on the floor of the valley the desire for home overcame that for rest and recreation and we started on. A new schedule had been prepared in order to let our friends reach us through the mail, and to meet it we must make Fresno that night, so we were off early. The road out of the canyon met all our expectations, being almost an exact counterpart of the one we had come down in entering. Until this year the lower two or three miles of it had been one way road, with up and down traffic using it on alternate hours, and while the control was taken off this year and the road made two-way, the public generally did not know it, the latest government publications not noting the change, so we thought by getting off early we would meet few cars there. Indeed we met only one.

Thirteen miles from the start we came to a side road which would take us back to the top of the mountain directly above where we had camped, so we went back to take a look at Yosemite in the altogether. It was a very bad road, but we did not regret the extra 26 miles the trip required. It ended at the crest of Glacier Point, the spot from which the fire falls nightly.

The fire fall is one of the events in Yosemite. On the summit of Glacier Point a big pile of dry wood is prepared daily during the tourist season, and at 8 o'clock it is fired. Like a very bright star appears the fire to the visitor 3,250 feet below, or more than a half a mile. By 9 o'clock the wood is burned to coals or small embers, and there comes a cry of "Ahoy, Camp Currey," and a voice at Camp Currey replies, "Let it come." Then with long handled rakes, men begin showering those coals over the cliff. It falls about 1,000 feet in one sheer drop and then strikes a sloping ledge which swerves the larger pieces to the eastward, the smaller lodging or being already burned out. Some of the more solid portions continue their way perhaps 1,000 feet farther before coming to rest on some tiny ledge.

The effect to the observer below is as though a stream 40 or 50 feet wide plunged over that cliff, but the stream, instead of being water, was red hot molten metal. It lasts from five to eight minutes, and after the last is sent down, there is a gradual disappearance, the red beginning to fade first at the top, and one cannot say certainly just when the last glow ceases.

From that lofty elevation one can see not only all of Yosemite, but thousands of square miles of Sierra Nevada mountains beside. Some of it is disappointing, or rather is disillusioning. Those lofty domes which from below seem almost to graze the moon are here found to be overtopped by other, greater heights beyond, although not to an extent to make them seem insignificant. North Dome, which from the valley reminded me of the dome of the National Capitol, is rather a puny affair seen from Glacier Point, but the Half Dome on the other wall is magnificent, and nothing earthly can make El Capitan appear puny!

Turning our backs on Yosemite with regret we began the back trailing to the Fresno road. Much of the way over the driver had complained of carbon which kept the car from pulling. There was no power in the engine. When we made the return trip we found that those gentle slopes up which we could not go even in second were so steep that we could not go down them except by low gear, cutting off the ignition and then using the brakes copiously.

On the way over we saw a four-point buck grazing beside a ranger cabin, looking unconcernedly at us 50 yards away; a little farther on a doe with her fawn stood in the trees beside the road and remained there while we stopped, backed up alongside and started to take a picture at a distance of two rods, but started before we could focus the camera; coming back we saw another doe near the same place, trotting across the road just ahead of us. We were in a game preserve, and the animals were unafraid. Over the rest of California, deer were fleeing for their lives at the least scent of suspicion of man, for the open season for deer began that day, September 1.

Back on the Fresno road once more, we stopped for lunch and discovered one of the tires had a slow leak so we had to change it. A dozen miles more and there came the road leading to the Mariposa grove of big trees, a thing not to be missed, especially since through following that state routing into Yosemite we had missed the Tuolumne grove. It was only five miles off the road, and we made two of that before the flat tire came. This time we had no spare, but must pump by hand.

We did.

Then we went on and saw the big trees. They were a wonderful sight but the rough roads and troubles of the day took from us much of the pleasure and satisfaction of seeing them.

Once more back to the Fresno road, it was almost camping time, and no supplies in the larder. We did not know how far ahead was a store but there proved to be one at Fish Camp, only three miles farther, and there we camped for the night. The speedometer showed only 79 miles for a hard day's run, which took us only 33 miles on our direct route, making 8,192 since leaving home.[3]

CHAPTER EIGHT

Southern California and a Quick Visit into Mexico

Our camp the night of September 1 was at a resort place, where there seemed to be a close community interest between the hotel, garage, store and camp ground. For the first time we got the prices which are supposed to prevail at resort places. Milk was 25 cents a quart in a region which should be a good milk country, although it would be hard to market except as cheese or butter. When Florence asked about cream, the salesman hesitated, then replied, "Yes, we sell the cream in the milk!" Round steak was 35 cents a pound in one of the best beef sections of California. Most of the stuff on sale we did not dare ask the price of.

We got away in good season and had gone nearly a mile before a tire went flat. The first flat tire no longer bothers us; it is the others that go wrong before the first is repaired and filled with air. Our road lay through the lower parts of the Sierra Nevada mountains, and besides being extremely rough, was too crooked to permit of making any time, even had it been smooth.

A saw mill was working on the pine and cedar timber, being supplied by a railroad which not only ran up the canyons and brought down the logs, but also hauled the lumber out to connection with other roads. It apparently had been there for many years, for the evening before we saw several miles of old bed where the rails had been torn up. The timber was of indifferent quality and only a sparse growth was found generally.

There were a few stations of one or two houses inhabited by people who live off the traveling public, but it was a mile before we saw an honest to goodness settler. There was nothing in the country to induce settlement. The small tracts of timber land were doubtless gobbled up by mill men long ago, and there was no place where any of the standard crops could be raised. Occasionally there might have been small orchards unless the lack of water would have killed the trees, but the few creek bottoms were nothing but rock, and the hills all rock or sand.

Finally we came to one house, with a sign out announcing milk, melons and peaches for sale, and we stopped to get some. Melons were two cents a pound, which they said was the price down in the San Joaquin valley, but as we had bought them there a few days before at a half cent a pound and hoped to get back there in a few hours we only took some peaches—small but very good flavor. A fig tree and some sort of nut were growing in the yard, and in the orchard were a few pear trees. The owner told me he had about 100 pear trees killed by grasshoppers last year.

A few miles out of Fresno, Florence announced that the tire under her was getting flat, and after we stopped the air continued to whistle out of it for some time. Before we got it changed the front tire on the same side was found to be in a similar condition, but we pumped it up and got it to hold until we ran into Selma, where we had the three put in shape for use—the only tire incidents of the day up to the hour of writing this letter.

North of Fresno there seemed but little settlement in the San Joaquin valley, and that little recent, but from there south it is a garden land. Grapes are the principal crop, raisins being the one big industry here. Most of the vineyards have been picked, and between each alternate row of vines are rows of trays about three feet square filled with grapes which the sun is turning into raisins. At a wayside stand where grapes were on sale we stopped and bought some. They were of two varieties. The larger, a greenish white, make the standard raisin; the others a milky white, growing in intensely thick clusters, and from them are made the small seedless raisins. They were sold to us at eight pounds for 25 cents, the cheapest grapes we ever bought, and quite good eating although not equal to some of the regular table grapes. The price at which the boy retailed them is probably two or three times what the grower will realize for them turned into raisins.

Fresno is the heart of the raisin industry and turns out about $12,000,000 worth annually.

The soil on which these grapes grow is sand pure and simple. The beaches along the seashore do not show a purer quality of sand than is found in many of the vineyards and orchards in the San Joaquin valley. Except by irrigation nothing can be grown, and that is accomplished by flooding the ground until it is a regular lake. Instead of little ditches to lead the water over the ground where the vegetation is growing, there are embankments thrown up, cutting the ground into tracts in size from one to two town lots, and those enclosures are filled with water several inches deep.

The weather of course is warm all through the growing season, today is the first warm one we have had for a long time, but in camp here at Tulare this evening it is quite comfortable. Cool they call it, for in this town the thermometer sometimes goes up to 118 in the shade, as the people freely admit. This morning we woke to the sound of thunder, and appearances were quite threatening for a time, while several light sprinkles interfered somewhat with breakfast. Marks of the shower showed in the road most of the day, and here they had a few drops but the rain storm passed. With a single exception, this is the first day rain has fallen on us since we left Yellowstone two months ago. One of the big advantages the Pacific Coast has to offer the summer vacationist is the assurance that it will not rain on him. He may also be reasonably certain that forest fires will make it so smoky that he cannot see very far in the mountains, and the lack of rain, except as to few streams fed by glaciers, will make water so scarce that late in the season waterfalls will not amount to much as spectacles.

Speedometer record for the day, 126 miles, mostly made in the afternoon; total since leaving home, 8,318.

❦

[Leap LVIII,] in which we arrive at the City of Angels on the 3rd day of September.

The report of the last leap was written under different circumstances than anything I had ever written before. I was seated in a summer bower, somewhat perhaps like that in which Jonah sat, and the shade over me, the thatch of the bower, was made of the fronds of the huge palms of that region. It made me feel somewhat like Robert Louis Stevenson writing from his South Sea Island home.

The palm had been a prominent feature of the landscape for several days, as had also the eucalyptus, but if either of them has any use except for ornament I did not learn it. Some varieties of palms are beautiful, but there is one very common one that I would want to charge high rent to occupy space on a place of mine. The beginning of it is beautiful and the top forms a pretty tuft, but in between there will be from five to twenty-five feet covered with the long leaves dead and hanging down like the skirts which the hula-hula girls used to wear, according to the pictures I remember seeing in the days when they were on exhibition in this country. One can't help but want to get up there and strip that dead stuff off. I don't know whether it is ready to come off or not, but if it isn't that is all the more reason for not wanting the things around.

I wanted a section of one of those stalks for my curio cabinet, and found that getting one was no simple matter. I pulled one of them out of the thatch and found that the stem was some three inches wide, armed with teeth on either edge like a sword fish. I tried to cut it with a pocket knife and failed, having to resort to an ax. I think a saw would be the proper implement to remove them from a tree, and as one would have to get up under some eight feet of drooping leaves and stalks, it is evident that it is easier to let Nature take her course.

We were away betimes that morning, our first objective being Bakersfield, the county seat of Kern county, a few years ago only a spot in the desert, now the producer of one-fourth of the world's oil supply.

There we left the San Joaquin valley and for 50 miles or more ran through mountains as desolate as those which border the Dead Sea. Only sage brush, greasewood, chaparral and yucca palms deign to grow there, and none of them are of a size or color to decorate a landscape. The rocks and sand blend with the sage brush so that it beats the monotonous gray of the desert, so dear to Zane Gray.

That 50 miles of mountain highway is known as the Ridge road, and it is a wonderful road. Note that I did not say beautiful, but wonderful. Beautiful it could not be, for there is nothing in the whole scene to make beauty. That whole range of mountains has but two purposes so far as I can conceive—to give the highway engineer an opportunity to show his skill, and to afford an entrance way to Los Angeles. I doubt if there is a single stretch of one-quarter mile of straight road in the whole 50, and feel equally certain that it will average a curve for each hundred yards of length. Many of them are very short, too, and driving over it not only requires constant vigilance but no little exercise of muscle besides. Even the worst of politicians is straight compared with that road.

We finally came down into the San Fernando valley, with some irrigated places, which soon widened out into a considerable valley and we were into Los Angeles. In fact we passed through the last hill in a tunnel and, at its outlet met the sign informing us that we were within the city limits of Los Angeles. We were still some 30 miles from the business center, and between us and there were several incorporated towns of no mean size. No wonder San Francisco is jealous of the metropolis of Southern California. It is likely to wake up some day and find that it is merely certain wards of the City of the Angels.

A brief inspection of the old mission at San Fernando, after picking up an old friend to guide us through the city; then around through some of the residential corners; through Universal City, where the scenes are shot, many of those far off desolate pictures we had seen on the screen being before our eyes in reality; then through Hollywood, where the actors whose likenesses appear on the screens of the whole world; then into Los Angeles proper, to spend a day or two visiting and sightseeing, the women with a preference for Hollywood and I for the old city and the people who go to make it, but hoping that if they make a contract at Hollywood they will make a good one.

The speedometer says we ran 213 miles getting here from Tulare and 8,531 coming from Ravenswood.

⁂

[Leap LIX,] in which the jinx pursues us through Saturday, the 5th day of September.

There was one exception to the monotony of that Ridge road which I failed to mention. Once on topping a summit we appeared to be far above anything on the southern side, the first impression that we were looking at the sea. Those who have seen the sea or a great lake will recall how the water in the distance seems to stand up like a far off mountain. There we had the same impression, although we were looking at the sky and it really was above us although we had the sense of looking down onto it. Also I did not tell how the kinks are being taken out of the road. Many men are now working there, and much of the excavating and filing is done, although it still is to be surfaced. Nearly every curve will be lessened some, and many of them nearly eradicated. Its completion will make the road no less wonderful, although the wonderment will be from a different cause.

These omissions came to me while the women were on their Hollywood expedition, and I was seeing the city in my own way. They were late getting back to the agreed meeting point, but we had our evening meal before the company began to arrive. The latter consisted of my cousin with his wife and four of his children, and seven of our old South Missouri friends, representing three different families, one of them having acquired a wife since those days. It was midnight when the last goodbye was said and the guests had departed.

Saturday morning we made an early getaway, being due to lose some time visiting along the road that day. We were not out of Los Angeles until the flat tire came, and its repair at Anaheim cost considerable time. Then we ran out to the Deming home, finding them just returned from their eastern trip, but with the sorrowful intelligence that morning that the mother from whom he had so recently parted at Oil City, Pa., had passed on, and he had started back on the morning train.

A short chat with Mrs. Deming and the girls, a hurried view of the oranges, lemons, figs and walnuts growing in their groves and we were once more on our way, our hope of reaching San Diego that night all gone. Forty miles out of Anaheim, a road hog gave me the choice of going off the road into freshly piled dirt or being knocked off, and my choice cost us a blow out, ruining the tire we had bought in Portland, and which was beginning to seem like an old friend.

In and about Anaheim had been the most prosperous appearing agricultural country we had seen. There really seemed a little soil mixed with the sand in many places, and the crops looked well. Oranges took the lead, there being some large groves, and in some there was a large part of the crop still unpicked. Oranges which ripened in June were still hanging on the trees. Walnuts were just beginning to ripen, and there were a great many of them. The land was apparently level, and the irrigation water is carried in pipes, so that there can be sufficient pressure to make it run.

We finally camped beside the ocean a few miles below Escondido, with a constant stream of autos passing and repassing, but the majority bound south. Monday will be Labor Day, so the week end will cover two days, and Tia Juana, Mexico, saloons will reap a harvest during the time. There is plenty of talk here about everything being wide open in all the towns, and a man can get anything he wants without any trouble, but just the same, when time permits, there is a great hegira to Tia Juana, which is to Southern California what some years ago Pomeroy was to our part of West Virginia.

Tonight we get camping ground for 25 cents instead of the regular 50, but have to buy wood. The speedometer shows a run for the day of only 129 miles, much of it over the El Camino Real, California's crack road, making 8,660 since leaving home.

⁂

The situation at that camping place of September 5 brings to the front a condition which is not pleasant to contemplate. In one of my previous letters, reference was made to the jealous feeling between California and Florida, and the claim of the westerner that the southeast state had nothing to persuade people to buy land except boom conditions. Now the fact is, and a number of Californians stated it to me in conversation, that aside from its fruit the southern half of the big Pacific state is living on the money easterners bring there to invest. Nothing is grown without irrigation, and it looks like about all the available water is already utilized. New projects may be established to impound water and furnish a supply for additional acres, but it will be expensive water. In several instances it has already been found that projects have been created where the cost was so much that it could not be profitably used, and common sense will tell us that the cheaper projects were established first, and those yet to come will be at a steadily increasing cost.

Now these town lots and small acreage tracts that the easterners are buying are not worth a dollar a square mile unless water can be brought onto them. That the end of the water is in sight can be deduced from the fact that Los Angeles is seriously contemplating getting water from the Colorado river, having not only to bring it 300 miles through canals and aqueducts, but also to pump it up a vertical distance of 1,600 feet. True, some of the cost of that pumping would be repaid by power developed when the water came down on the other side of the mountain. But water cannot be moved such distances, under those conditions, for the use of growers of any standard crops, especially when they require such quantities as the grower of Southern California.

So the end of the water is in sight, and there can be no material increase in the productive population of that region who depend upon the soil for their production. Yet every additional citizen of the region at the present time means an additional demand for water if he is to do anything. The 60,000 people of Wheeling produce far more of things not dependent upon the soil than do the 1,250,000 people of Los Angeles. In all the southern part of the state there is not a single factory that would rank as a third class one in any eastern city of 100,000 people. Every block in Los Angeles has a real estate agent, but from the top of its highest mountain you cannot see the smoke of a factory which employs 2,000 men. Even an assembling plant of a fifth rate automobile—rated in quantity of production—is hailed as an important addition to the city's institutions which will furnish employment to some of its citizens.

As already stated, they are living off the money of the easterner, either by selling him real estate or building houses on the lots he buys. Apparently most of the others are selling him gasoline for his car. As soon as he buys a lot and builds a house he becomes a detriment instead of a benefit to his country, for he demands some of that diminishing supply of water, and also employment at something by which he can live. Unless he is a carpenter the only thing he can do is to open a new real estate office or filling station, and there is no room for either unless there are more towns.

That brings me back to the starting point.

Along that coast for miles and miles are the nicely painted stakes with beautiful figures on them which mark the boundaries of lots in news towns or additions to old ones which already have more people than they can provide employment for.

The only hope for Southern California to continue to grow is for it to open up factories which will employ its people and produce goods which can be sold at a profit where we camped was a new town. Several streets were graded, there was a grocery store—selling supplies to tourists—water mains were laid, and three houses were under construction. The lots were piles of sand. They stood up 50 feet above the ocean, commanding a beautiful view, but there was no possible way for the owners of those lots to make a living except to open a real estate office and resell the lots of dissatisfied purchasers or put in a filling station and sell gasoline to the tourists. Unfortunately the road ran so that the same lot did not both front on it and overlook the ocean!

We did not rush the morning of the 6th, but broke camp leisurely. Once in the road, however, we had to run fast or we might have been run over. All night the streams of cars had been passing, some of them to the north but a much larger part toward Tia Juana, where on Mexican soil with open saloons a big time was in prospect for Sunday and the holiday of the Gringoes which was to follow. During the evening hours the stream had been constant, but we expected it to wear itself out sometime in the night. A dozen times I was awake, and every moment there was to be heard the roar of the automobile, and with the coming of the morning the number seemed to increase.

So we dropped into the maelstrom, and in due time came to the city of San Diego, that point on the Pacific which had been discovered and preparations made for the city there which should civilize the Indians, three-quarters of a century before the Pilgrims brought Plymouth Rock into notoriety.

In due time we arrived at the home of S. G. Wilson, once the maker of bread for Ravenswood and the pumper of water for the B. & O [Baltimore and Ohio Railroad]. With Mr. and Mrs. Wilson and their daughters we spent a pleasant afternoon, aided by some newlywed neighbors, the whole party in two cars paying visits to Balboa Park, San Diego's greatest beauty spot; Point Loma, where Uncle Sam has arranged to prevent any other power from interfering with his most southwestern city; and some of the beaches, where San Diego's people dip into the surf every day in the year, although this September day was so cool that a very few people cared to get wet.

It is a beautiful city, pleasantly situated, and has a fine harbor which Uncle Sam has recognized the worth or much more than his commercially inclined sons. The western sky was heavily overcast, and in any other country rain would have been almost certain, but in San Diego they know it will not rain in September. As the Englishman says: "It isn't done you know."

So long prolonged were the pleasures of the afternoon that it was dark when we got to camp, and we had to put up the tent by the light of the car lamps. The speedometer reported 104 miles for the day, making 8,964 thus far.

⁘

[Leap LXI,] being that made on September 7 when the jinx followed us up onto the mountain.

We made a short back track the first thing Monday morning, running back to La Jolla to see two people and were doubly disappointed. Before leaving West Virginia I had an invitation from Walt Mason, who has made La Jolla his home for two or three years, to call and see him when I came through. I had scarcely wanted to make the call on Sunday, so passed by on the way down the coast. Then a dear friend of the early days of Eastern Washington whom we had not seen for about 20 years moved there in June. We had expected to find her at Alameda, but at her old address only learned that she had moved. At the post office we could get no trace of her, and the Methodist pastor who could have told me where she lived was nonexistent, there being no Methodist Church there.[1]

At Walt Mason's home I was again disappointed. Walt had not joined the rest of California and gone down to Tia Juana, but he had "gone down town" a short time before, and like so many other women left at home that was the extent of Mrs. Mason's knowledge regarding him. It was Labor Day, and therefore he would do no labor, not even spending the few minutes at the typewriter to copy off the little poem which in its allotted time would be read by some millions of Americans. He had just "gone down town." Where he went when he "went down town" of course she did not know, no good wife ever does, for it is not intended that she should, and on this day when even his usual cronies were out of town it would be more doubtful than ever.

We had picked a bad day, and realizing that we had made what we used to call a "water haul" when hunting moonshiners, we turned the head of Lena back and were soon again at San Diego. Turning east we entered the city we felt for the first time that we were homeward bound, with the Ohio river ferry only about 4,000 miles away.

There were heavy clouds that morning, but a query as to the possibility of rain brought the assurance: "There isn't a ghost of a show."

But there is no spot on earth known to man where rain does not fall sometimes, and Labor Day, 1925, was a freak in Southern California. Twice that morning enough drops fell to spatter up Lena's windshield. It may have been a real shower in places.

Out of the city, the country began to go to the bad rapidly. Even at the start there was much waste land, and in a few miles there was very little ground tilled. The guide book or highway sign would announce a town ahead, but when we came to it there might not be a dozen houses, counting all sorts. Here and there would be a little valley which had all been covered with the life bringing water, but in the main it was dry, and a large portion was rock.

We were gradually climbing, running up and down, and by noon were up onto the mountain, some 4,000 feet above sea level. The character of the country grew steadily worse until we topped the summit and began a long run through the mountain. For 50 or 60 miles the road is up on the mountain, ranging from 3,000 to over 4,000 feet above sea level, and for a considerable part of that distance there are occasional trees. Mostly some inferior sort of oak, and in a few places some small pines. But it is all covered with mountain laurel, greasewood and other shrubs, so that there is a decidedly green cast to the landscape, a relief to the eye after resting for hours on the dried up dead hills of the last few days.

Then came the jinx. In four hours four tires went flat, one of them blown to kingdom come. One was the fault of the garage man who fixed the tire, in failing to find the break in the boot which had caused the trouble, so it promptly pinched another. It was one more than we had had any previous day and caused considerable loss of time.

We had a concrete road from San Diego up to the summit, and a good gravel road beyond that, changing to concrete again when well along on the mountain top, with gravel again for the descent. This latter was a very marked escarpment, there being a continuous down grade—much of it quite steep—down into Imperial Valley. This descent was something different from any country I had ever seen. It was not simply waste land, but it had a lot of frills different from other waste tracts that made one feel that it was more utterly waste than any other kind of land. I have always heard that the shores of the Dead Sea are more utterly barren than any other region on earth, but I doubt if one could tell the difference between the two were he taken there without knowing where he was. The hills—they did not seem to rise to the dignity of mountains—were nothing but rock. All were rounded as though by the action of water, ranging from tiny things up to rocks as large as a car or Southern California bungalow. Universally they were granite—which seems to make the most worthless sand when it is crushed—and a peculiar thing about them was that they all appeared to be freshly washed. All were clean, and down between there was no sign of earth. At first we thought the wind had blown all the dirt away, but after we came around onto the other side of the hill where it should have lodged and found just the same conditions we knew that there never had been any dirt there!

After seven or eight miles of coming down the mountain we came to its foot, and there the country sloped away into the desert. Pushing in the clutch and throwing off the ignition we coasted for two or three miles, simply touching the brake occasionally to hold Lena down to 40 miles an hour. Alongside the concrete was sand—thousands of acres of sand—and in that sand grew cactus. Different from any we had ever seen, they looked like clumps of willows eight or ten feet high which had lost their leaves and by rough handling the smaller branches had been broken off. Mile after mile we flew, the only variety in the landscape being the difference in the variety of the cacti. Another kind were short and rather thick, growing in single stalks, and at a glance reminding us of the picket pin gophers which had adorned the landscape so much of the way this summer, only the cactus would be the old grandfather of the gophers.

The same dull gray of the granite mountains continued down here in the valley for this sand is granite too. We came to the railroad and then to a station, where there was a grocery store and supplies could be had. We bought some but voted down a suggestion to spend the night there. It was getting late; the clouds of the morning, which we had been assured would disappear when we got over into the valley, still covered the sky and darkness would come early. So we kept on and in time reached a tourist camp at the edge of El Centro, the capital city of the Imperial Valley, and seat of Justice of Imperial county. Some miles back we had crossed the dead line, the first irrigation ditch, and from a desert the country instantly became a paradise. It was the first irrigation project we had seen where the country had all been redeemed from the wilderness. In the others there had been high places where the water did not reach, but here all were on the same level. It is not my intention to tell of the Imperial Valley here, for it deserves more than such brief mention. It is not part of California that is being boomed, for there are some objections to its climate, but it is making good every promise made, which I fear some other parts of the state will fail to do.

The camp man furnished us big chunks of ice, otherwise we would have found the water poor drinking, we later finding that same water delightful for shower baths, just as it ran from the hydrants. The clouds still hung heavy, and the camp man acted as though possibly it might rain, although he did not answer my question as to whether he ever saw it rain here, and we went to bed with the wind blowing so we had to make extra stakes to hold the tent down, the speedometer reporting 160 miles for the day, or 8,924 from home.

◦❀◦

The same [Leap LXII] being made on September 8 principally beneath the depths of the sea somewhat in foreign lands.

We were down in the hot country now. For days our friends had commiserated with us over our distress while going through the hot interior and the desert. When the Californian is away from home he loudly avers that his state is not only the greatest of all but perfect in every detail; when he is at home, the particular spot he honors by making his abode is the one perfect place and all other parts of the state have imperfections, some of them quite pronounced. And one of the worst conditions was the heat of the interior valleys and the desert. We had slept comfortably, rather too warm at times in the night, but were prepared in our minds for a blisteringly hot day.

When I rose early to write the happenings of the day before the sun was announcing its imminent appearance in the east with a rose tint on the clouds which I had never seen equaled before. I have seen "glowing sunsets" many times but never one with the depth of color or width of display of this sunrise. Such a display in most lands would have betokened the coming of a heavy rain and in West Virginia we would have known the ground would not be dry more than an hour or two longer. Here there was no thought of rain, because it does not rain in September. But it did presage a cloudy day, as we found to our satisfaction. The clouds continued all day, with only broken places through which the sun shone at times. Later when it was streaming through and Florence asked a filling station man as to the heat, he said it at times reached 126 there, but today was cool, the mercury not having gone above 100.

We were below sea level when we awoke that morning, the official figures for El Centro being 52 feet below sea level, and I doubt if there is a variation of two feet in the elevation of any two spots in the town. We patched some tubes in readiness for the remands of the day, and set out for dual city on the international line, Calexico on our side and Mexicali beyond the Mexican border.

I have read that the valley of the lower Nile is practically flat, the river having a fall of only six inches in 1,000 miles. I doubt the truth of the statement, but one could easily believe that this road was absolutely level. Really it does rise toward the border, for water in the irrigation ditches flows to the north. In fact one rises almost to sea level in that 12 mile drive, but the grade is uniform. You cannot look ahead and see the dips and rises in the road as in other roads. Never on ahead can you see where a change in grade makes the road come on a level with the eye so it looks like water. It is just a regular "climb" of so many inches in a mile. The only rises in the road are where it crosses an irrigation ditch, for the ditches are not sunk into the ground but built up on it. The silt which the water deposits keeps filling them up, and at times they have to be cleaned out, so the ridge on which they run keeps growing. At the boundary line the customs officer told me we could walk across the line and back without question, but an automobile with baggage would be subject to a lot of inconvenience; also that I would not be allowed to take my camera. So we left the car parked on the American side and went abroad on foot.

The two towns join for a half mile or more, but in only one place do the streets connect. Each nation has its custom house, about two rods apart, and the cars going and coming are lined up for examination. Pedestrians pass and repass along the sidewalk, but the eyes of the customs officers are on them, and any real attempt at smuggling would soon be detected. Of course the real smuggling along the border is in the country and it is there that the line is really watched on both sides. But the traffic by car was in marked contrast with that along our northern border, where sometimes the customs houses are miles apart.

We wandered about the streets of the foreign town, visited the newspaper, whose linotype operator was a member of the Typographical Union of New York. His machine was thoroughly familiar, but his copy would have defied any one of the visitors to make time setting, typewritten though it was. But we did make something out of the paper we got, much having an Englishy appearance through its Latin origin, and in days of yore I possessed a smattering of Spanish, both oral and written.

At a bank we got a few Mexican coins, and learned that the coinage of Mexico has been remodeled and put on a gold basis. The old Mexican dollar is gone. In its place is a silver coin of the same name—peso—but only 50 cents in size and value. The only difference the banks make in the two coinages is a nominal charge for exchange. The old "bit," or eighth of a dollar, is gone and in its place is a tenth—rather a fifth of a peso—or dime, and a silver piece of half that value but only a shade smaller. The pesos and 50 centavo pieces, or halves and quarters, have the Mexican motto stamped into the edges in lieu of milling, but the smaller pieces are milled, although with a different mark from ours.

Having "done" Mexico with our eyes, our stomachs must also be treated and having sifted out two or three alleged eating places which were really only saloons, Florence selected one where we each had a piece of pie and coffee. (It really was a Chinese restaurant, but that was all right for a very considerable part of the population of Mexico is Chinese. The bank had one Chinese teller expressly to handle the accounts of his people.)

We walked back to our car showing the customs officer the souvenir handkerchief Florence had bought, and were dismissed with a wave of his hand and a smile. Then back to El Centro and on north toward the real beginning of the eastern journey where we would enter the Mojave desert. The beautiful farms of El Centro were repeated again and again. Alfalfa, fruit, cotton, garden, these were oft repeated, and luxurious growth was everywhere. We passed Imperial and several smaller towns until we came to Westmoreland and shortly thereafter the edge of the irrigated tract and consequently the edge of the desert. Here and there was a house and of course a little water and a filling station, until we came to one which announced that it was the last water for 30 miles.

Off to the right, in sight, and at its nearest point not more than a mile away, was the deep blue water of the Salton Sea, but that water is salty from absorbing the deposits of the sea which long ago flowed unrestrictedly in here and made the beach mark which shows so plainly on the mountainside on both sides of the present "sea."

The rich soil of the Imperial Valley was gone. It was no longer the silt of the Colorado but the gravel sands and pebbles of the mountains to the west through which we came the day before.

Finally came Oasis, where dates seemed the principal business, and for a few miles we were in fairy land again so far as vegetable growth is concerned.

Then all at once the genuine desert, for the land was all covered with cacti, profusely as to both quantity and variety. There were even some which we had not seen where we came down from the mountain.

On and on up the mountain we went, climbing slowly it seemed to us, but not so according to the long freight train we passed, with one big engine at the head and another two-thirds of the way back, both of them struggling mightily.

Signs galore had told us Banning had an auto camp, and we found it a very nice one, reaching it just at camping time with the speedometer reporting 170 miles for the day or 9,094 for the trip.

※

[Leap LXIII,] made on September 9, beginning on the edge of one desert and ending at the edge of another.

That town of Banning seemed to be mostly a Mexican town, nearly all the people we saw being of that race, but maybe there were others whom we did not see. The region was mainly given up to prunes and almonds, and it may have been a case of the owners living in the country and the laborers congregating in the town.

We passed out of the desert proper only a few miles below the town, the cactus and sage brush reaching almost up to that place. I did not learn the source of the water supply, but in the camp ground there had been an orchard, and at each tree still living there was a spigot, from the waste water of each, the tree getting some of the life giving fluid. There had been a number of other trees, some of them quite well grown, but they were either dead or had been cut down.

The almond crop was just being harvested, and seemed to be very large, the trees being loaded heavily. The pomegranates, figs, dates, olives, oranges, lemons and other warm country fruits which had been so common for days were gone, although the change in temperature was but small. I did not learn the elevation there, but at the next station, six miles farther on, came the top of the mountain at 2,600 feet above sea level. Banning must have at least 2,000.

Down the mountain by any easy grade brought us to the San Jacinto valley, a beautiful valley if it only had water, but the only sign we saw of any, except at an occasional well pumped by a windmill, was the sprinkling cart which kept down the dust on the detour where they were building a new road. The valley was wide, level and attractive to the eye, except for the lack of anything green.

Riverside, near one of the first big irrigation projects in Southern California, appeared in a few miles. It claims a population of near 30,000, and embraces an area of about 40 square miles, the original Riverside being an irrigation project where the people would each own a small orchard tract rather than a town in the usual understanding of the word. Its 28,000 acres are planted almost entirely to citrus fruits, and few of the boomed places have been so well handled as Riverside. I distinctly remember when the project was started years ago and it was with difficulty I might add that the land was sold at about what it was actually worth instead of the fancy figures at which many other projects have gone on the market.

Before reaching Riverside we had passed one region given over to the hen almost exclusively, and in two or three miles we saw a considerable source of California's egg supply. Probably, more hens are grown and eggs laid than in Petaluma, although the latter hatches the chicks and sells them as day olds. Speaking of hens and eggs brings to mind a bit of experience at San Diego. We were to buy some eggs at the camp store and the lady said she had them at 43 and at 52 cents a dozen, each equally fresh. Then she explained that under the law of California all eggs sold as real sure enough eggs had to weigh a certain amount per dozen and eggs weighing less had to be sold as light weights, with the customer's attention called to the fact that they were not standard size.

Ten miles beyond Riverside came San Bernardino, and then over a cement road we went 40 miles farther, the country bordering more and more onto the desert. At Victorville the concrete came to an end, and the maps informed us that it was on the edge of the desert where the Santa Fe Trail crosses the Mojave river. Mammoth cement plants are located there, and it seemed a live town, although the surroundings were not attractive to the eye. Before that we had seen the Yucca palm, the truest sign of the desert, the trunks growing a foot or more in diameter with branches like an oak tree. In places there were regular forests of it. But on the other hand for miles after the concrete road had vanished there was a stream running beside the railroads, with green bushes all the way and green fields and orchards generally, entirely unlike the desert. Finally came Barstow, usually recognized as the door to the point where no man can exist without outside aid, and there we camped for the night. The story is that there are washouts ahead which may make it impossible to get through to the Grand Canyon. We hope to learn more of the situation from travelers from that direction. We are back on the Old National Road today, and are meeting cars from everywhere, instead of only Californians as has been the case ever since the day we entered the state.

The speedometer credits us with 135 more miles, bringing the total up to 9,229.

⁂

[Leap LXIV,] in which the major part of the Mojave desert is crossed in a daylight run.

The guild book advises that because of the intense heat the tourists frequently run across the Mojave desert at night, and it had been our original plan to leave Barstow in mid-afternoon and keep going until

The early National Old Trails Road through the Mojave Desert in California was more of a trail than an established road through the snow-white alkali. *Courtesy Federal Highway Administration.*

we were across the desert, which we hoped would be before the heat of the next day. But our own experience in the Imperial Valley, added to that of fellow tourists who were crossing the desert daily, caused us to change our plans and undertake it in daylight. From what we gathered in various ways we decided that one objection to making it as a night run was that we would not know when we got across. We had been in a desert-like land for more than 50 miles before we got to Barstow, and would be for 800 beyond, although the map shows desert for only 270 miles. Even after running through it I find it impossible to tell why there should have been such boundaries set as were. There is a vast region, reaching from the ocean eastward well into Texas where nothing will grow unless water be added to the natural supply, and only at rare intervals in that region is there water. That makes it all desert, and yet an irrigation ditch anywhere almost would make the ground it covered anything except desert.[2]

The camp at Barstow was one of the nicest we have encountered. In view of the conditions, it might be called the finest. Clean, with excellent accommodations, friendly spirit and capable management.

We were off before 7 o'clock, and ran as fast as the condition of the road would permit. Running alongside the Santa Fe railroad, usually at a quarter to half mile from it, the road in general was surprisingly good. We had heard many stories of the road, mostly to its discredit and had expected it to run from bad to worse. On the contrary in the main it was good. Of possibly 20 miles of the day's run we had to hold down and go very slow. Once in meeting a car I gave the other fellow too much room, and hung up in deep sand. The little shovel brought for such emergencies had its first job, and finally helped us to get out, but it took a good deal of effort, and part of that was contributed by two friendly travelers who came to our aid.

Then there were 20 or 30 miles where the sand was so deep and coarse that it was dangerous to run fast, as the wheels would not track with any certainty, and did not steer well. The rest good for 25 to 35 miles right along.

In one place we came to the sign of city limits, with the usual speed limits, and the city by actual count contained three tourist camps, each with a small grocery store connected, and two garages. That was all. Not even a chicken coop in addition.

CHAPTER NINE

Arizona and New Mexico

LATE IN THE AFTERNOON WE CROSSED THE COLORADO RIVER, BIDDING CALIfornia adieu and being welcomed by Arizona. We had seen the river water in irrigation ditches in Imperial Valley—indeed it is known that the Colorado carries more silt to the gallon than any other river in the United States—so we were ready for its appearance. The old saying of the Missouri that it was too thin to walk on and too thick to swim in describes the Colorado pretty well. Possibly it was a little worse than usual, for there had been rains in this country. To look at the land we crossed that day it is hard to believe that it ever rains, but there was ample evidence that it had done so within the past few days, and when it rains there something happens. A week before we knew El Paso had suffered from floods, but did not know it was so wide-spread until we heard from tourists of damage to the very roads we were to traverse, and some of that damage had been in the very desert we were crossing.

At Oatman, surrounded by mines now idle for lack of water, we camped for the night, the speedometer reporting 216 miles for the day, making a total of 9,645.

[Leap LXV,] made on the 11th day of September, taking us out of the desert and to the edge of the "Biggest Ditch in the World."

That town of Oatman was a typical mining camp—a thing with which we were all familiar years ago, and which none of us ever admired as a place of residence. In addition to the drawbacks which afflicted all mining camps this one had the additional defect of being practically without water. I do not know what was the source of the supply we had, but it tasted like it might have come out of a mine; hard, sulfurous, vile smelling and worse tasting, it was bad to use even a single night. Fortunately we had our two-gallon jug filled with good water obtained at Barstow.[1]

The ground on which we camped evidently was filled in with the waste from a mine, and was so hard that we could drive the tent pins in only two or three inches. Across the street was a moving picture theater, the barker of which evidently had seen service at some traveling side show, and did his best to draw a crowd from empty sidewalks. The dog crop was the only prosperous thing in town, and most of them came to the show. There were a number of free for alls among them while the people they accompanied were watching the "Ten Commandments." When the show was out the soft drink man loudly proclaimed the virtues of his wares, and then an engine started somewhere near and continued throughout the night, its chug, chug interspersed with what sounded like car loads of ore dumped on a wooden floor. Taken all in all it was the worst camping place we had anywhere on the trip.

Out of Oatman we climbed steadily for five miles, bringing us to the top of a picturesque range of mountains. All the way up there had been prospect holes and some sure enough mines equipped with concentrating plants, some of them with many houses nearby and apparently at one time affairs of consequence. All were closed down and empty now.

Kingman was the next town of consequence, being really an important place, although still in a sterile region. Out of there a few miles, we saw a few blades of grass, the first for two days, and in a few miles more it became quite common. Indeed before reaching Kingman, just over the mountain from Oatman, we saw one cow by the side of the road, and she seemed to be eating something, although it was not grass and she could not have eaten cactus.

But if that cow had been a cactus eater she could have taken on a widely assorted meal and yet not gone out of that popular desert

This circa 1925 photograph shows a touring auto on the National Old Trails Road near Kingman, Arizona. *Courtesy Federal Highway Administration.*

family. Never before had we seem so many varieties of the cacti family since entering the desert. There were the Yuccas—at least we called them so—which grew into respectable trees a foot or more in diameter and 25 feet high; there was one we called the elk horn because of its resemblance to the elk's antlered head; there is the common old thick-leaved kind where one leaf grows out of another at all sorts of angles, and the tall, slim fellows which look like a bunch of hazel bushes, except that are as big at the top as where they come out of the ground. These only name a few of the more common sorts. Sometimes there will be only one kind for miles and that possibly quite scarce, and again there will be mixtures of a dozen varieties and the ground may be well covered.

Even with the coming of the grass the cactus did not disappear, although miles farther on when we came suddenly to pine timber it seemed to spell the end of cactus. But that was much farther on. Before then we had stopped at Seligman for lunch, set our watches an hour ahead because we had reached the beginning of Mountain time. Also we found that the Oatman price of 25 cents a quart for milk still prevailed, and tomatoes had gone up to two pounds for a quarter. But I would not undertake to produce either of them there at these prices.

Before night we had seen a good many cattle, but all were the white-faced Herefords, and everybody knows they have no place in a milk factory. For the accommodation of the cattlemen the country is cut up by wire fences into immense pastures. I have no idea that they own the ground, but except on the forest reserves they probably put up the fences. Where the road goes through a fence there is a cattle guard somewhat like railroads have. The first one we came to had two ties put in lengthwise the right width apart for auto wheels, and if one ran off he would land on poles crosswise and spaced well apart. I took pains to keep on the ties. For horse drawn vehicles or moving cattle through, there is a gate at each crossing. I suppose the law recognizes the cattle-man to the extent of making such roads lawful. In any event there are few horse drawn vehicles on the road any more. We saw just one span of horses in Los Angeles, and holding up for it caused us to get run into.

Even before we came to that pine timber we began to see signs telling how far ahead it was to Pine Springs tourist camp, and we antici-pated a good drink at last. For two days we had had to drink out of the canteen and the water was very warm. Finally we came to the Pine Springs camp, and driving in asked where the spring was. We were told that water in the can there was for radiators and the drink-ing water was in a truck behind the house! We drove on, but four miles farther came to a camp where the water in the spigots was said to be spring water, and evidently was.[2]

Right at a garage in Williams the engine died, and examination showed a clamp on the battery corroded in two, and while the new one was being made we took a look at the town and mailed some letters. A professional sign in a window bore a name once familiar to me. I never knew another man of the same surname, the initials were the same, one of them being X, I felt pretty certain. Stepping into the office I found I had not been mistaken. Nearly 50 years ago the man had graduated

Two men pushing a touring auto with two women walking behind on an Arizona highway circa 1925. Auto breakdowns were common at the time, and vehicles often had to be pushed by hand to get them to start. *Courtesy Arizona Historical Society, Tucson.*

from a university, located in a growing city and by his friends was considered to have as bright a future as any man in his state. In a few years he disappeared, and I think all of his old friends lost all track of him. We chatted a few minutes and he told me briefly of his life. He went abroad, became counselor for a big church dignitary; was rich three times; went broke the same number. Came home and was offered a lucrative practice by old friends, but disdaining them went where he was not known to start again. He said at the time he could not have bought a 10-cent book. Once more he is up in the world; not rich, but where he does not have to work unless he chooses.[3]

It was an interesting talk, and yet I felt all the time that between the lines there was another story. That what he did not tell was of more interest than what he did, and that it would all have centered around one thing. A true history of his life probably would be of more value than though he had achieved the fame which his friends long ago predicted would be his.

With Lena's fires once more restored we began a race against time for the Grand Canyon. It was about 4 o'clock, a distance of 64 miles, the road said to be rather bad in places, and there was no camping place between. We made half the way in half the time we had allowed; then a tire went flat and we lost a few minutes, the road became rougher, and by the time we were through it was too dark to see anything. After considerable hunting we located a camp, drove up among the junipers and camped, our neighbors on either side having arrived a few minutes before so we could get no information from them. The speedometer showed a run of 239 miles, making 9,684 all told.

✦

[Leap LXVI,] preceded by a day spent at the Grand Canyon of Colorado.[4]

The selection of a camping place in the grounds at the "Big Ditch" was not a matter of choice but of chance, as we arrived when it was too dark to make any selection. The camp is in an immense grove of about equal numbers of Piñon pine and juniper. Neither grows taller than well pruned fruit trees and about the proper distance apart for orchard trees. The branches were high enough that the wood was very open, and a car could be driven almost anywhere. The ground had a little too much slope to make it ideal to sleep on, but we managed very well. There was an abundance of wood, and, very much to our surprise, a spigot furnishing very good water.

The Grand Canyon is the only one of the national parks we have visited where admission for a car is free, the others running from $2.50 to $7.50. But heretofore there had been a charge of 25 cents a day here for water. It is hauled from Seligman, 150 miles away. But this season water is being furnished free to the tourist, at whose expense I know not.

We woke early Saturday morning and were greeted by some new sights. The country, which had been birdless for so many days, was plentifully supplied with three varieties, blue jays, robins and a small bird which was strange to us. Also we had a new animal—the prettiest squirrel any of us ever saw. Those acquainted said it was a pine squirrel, but it was no relation to any pine squirrel I ever saw before. A bright clear gray, long body and well rounded, with a brush as beautiful as that of a fox and fully as long as the body, the whole animal more than 18 inches long. It was very friendly, and of course the blue jays ordered us aside whenever we came in the way, which is the way of the blue jay, and the other birds were very tame.

The morning was cloudy, there was only one letter at the post office for us—the first mail point at which we had failed to have a good supply—and everything started off wrong. By the middle of the forenoon it began to rain, and although it was only a little thunder shower, it proved to be one of a large family, and during the remainder of the day rain fell fully one-half the time, and we had to ditch around the tent to keep the beds dry. In the afternoon we drove westward along the rim to the end of the road, and saw many beautiful sights. One in particular would appeal to any Mason. At the point dedicated to Major J. W. Powell, who first went down the canyon, the rim runs out for more than a hundred yards, the neck connecting it with the land being just wide enough that for fear someone would try to run a car out there, a post has been set in the middle, thoroughly blocking any such effort. At the outmost part the top is circular and large enough to turn a short car around in, and on that the Powell Memorial has been built.

That is the setting as well as I can easily describe it, and out on that peninsula a Masonic meeting was held and the third degree conferred. I wished I had been there. I would have liked to have been the tyler, and as I guarded the narrow neck I would have been sure that no cowans or eavesdroppers were interfering at any other point, for on all sides the wall dropped off sheer for hundreds of feet, and a stone rolled over there would not have stopped until it had gone down a mile with more than half the distance vertical.

At 8 o'clock there was a lecture and moving picture show of the park shown at the hotel, which I attended, but it was so wet and nasty underfoot that the women preferred to stay in camp.

Before morning the clouds disappeared, and early we were off to see more of the canyon. When I left home I had intended to go down into the canyon, but later changed my mind. It has been almost 25 years since I was astride an animal, and almost none at all for many years before that, during which time I have added a good many pounds of my weight. Then, too, I learned that the one-day trip is not only a hard one but very unsatisfactory, and time forbade taking the two- or three-day trips. In addition to all this I had got an insight into the kind of people who take the riding trips in the parks. I don't know what pay the guides get, but they certainly have a lot of fun. Even the mules must see the fun at times. When some he or she dude from the east—and they do a good deal of the riding—comes to take a trail trip, there is a display of apparel which would drive any animal wild except a mule, and the training in a riding school, which has often been taken as a preparation for the trip, would get even a mule's goat. The questions put to the guide would form the base for the funniest book ever written, except that there is scarce variety enough.

So considering it all I abandoned the trip down into the bowels of the earth. The running around in the park aggregated 29 miles, putting us 9,713 from home.

Before noon we were on our way homeward again, running first to Maine, where we connected with the Old National Trails road, the distance being about the same we had run from Williams in, and the road perhaps a little worse, the rain of the day before having hurt it a little, although there had been no rain at Maine.[5]

Shortly before we reached Maine we came to a number of settlers' cabins, some of them farming considerably. We had run 340 miles in Arizona, and up to that time had not even seen a garden, and the fields of oats, wheat and corn looked good, even if the latter had recently been badly bitten by frost. We were up nearly 7,000 feet above sea level, and the seasons must be short. Oats, which were being cut in Montana two months ago, here were still much too green to cut even for hay, and wheat was showing no color of harvest. For

The Clarks saw several trading posts on their journey across the southwest. They probably saw Rimmy Jim's Trading Post between Flagstaff and Winslow, Arizona. It was typical of most such establishments selling curios, including Indian blankets. *Courtesy Special Collections and Archives, Cline Library, Northern Arizona University, Flagstaff.*

several miles the land was largely farmed, and then we came again to a rocky, barren region, the junipers suddenly disappearing and only a broad mesa spreading out before us with mountains here and there in the background. At 5 o'clock we came to a camp ground and turned in, the speedometer showing 128 miles for the day, bringing our total up to 9,341 miles.

꧁꧂

[Leap LXVII,] in which we saw the Petrified Forests and Painted Desert of Arizona and quit that state, entering New Mexico.

The ground of our camping place at Canyon Diablo appeared so hard, and the certainty of rock just beneath the surface so certain, that we did not put up our tent that night but slept in the open for the second time on the trip. There was but one other car there at bedtime but three others arrived after I had gone to bed. Some travelers stay late on the road and at almost every camp they are arriving until well into the night. Others are up and off at daylight or before, so the hours of undisturbed repost are few.

The road improved shortly after we started, and we made good time, except through Holbrook, which had streets which reminded me of the kind so popular in Ohio towns up to a few years ago. The good road continued on to the petrified forests. We took the Springerville road down to there and then ran through the forests to the Gallup road. Apparently realizing that his nephews would steal all his hardened wood if he tried to keep them from having any, Uncle Sam left one fine orchard out of the preserve and invited the people to help themselves there. I had been told the samples out there were not so nice, but did not notice any particular difference.

Aside from sending many things back home by mail and express, we had accumulated so many specimens and souvenirs that Lena was loaded about to the limit and we had to hold down to a few pieces of the petrified wood. The really nice ones—the kind one would really like to have on his lawn—weigh from 500 pounds to two or three tons, so we had to leave all such for others, although there were thousands of them.

The road across to the Gallup highway was much longer than we had anticipated, and was rather rough. Midway of the distance we had a startling illustration of the dangers which civilization has not been able to remove from the west. We had crossed the channel of a stream, the flat sandy bottom of which showed that the last water had been about 100 yards wide, and in extreme flood it was about twice that. The sand was still wet from the rain of a few days before, although no water flowed. The sand was deep, and we all watched Lena's performance with interest. Another car just ahead had hesitated over some of it, and with Florence at the wheel I had warned her to wait until the other car was across, as she not want to take chances on being stopped in there. Safely across, the other man stopped and waited to see us through. They drove on and we stopped for lunch. As we were starting away a new arrival asked if we saw the wreck and took us back to the stream and showed us a Dodge car in the sand. Four days before, while driving

This touring auto is crossing a bridge made of heavy fencing wire on a road somewhere in northeastern New Mexico. Road maintenance was a local responsibility, so in many areas makeshift solutions were used to keep the roads open. *Courtesy Federal Highway Administration.*

across in about a foot of water, the owner stalled his engine. Before he could start again, a wall of water came down which began moving the car. He got out safely but saw the water roll the car over a few times, when it began to slowly settle and finally disappeared in the sand. He located the spot as well as he could and offered another man the car if he could reclaim it.

It took a long search with iron rods to locate it when the water subsided, but they finally found it about three feet below the surface. They had been working two days, had dug a hole about the size of our tent, clearing the car and prying it up until they hoped to get it out that afternoon, raising it with block and tackle. Quicksand has always been one of the terrors of the western prairie streams.

When we left Los Angeles, gasoline was the cheapest we had found it. A war was on and a fair grade was selling at six gallons for 90 cents with a quart of oil thrown in. It had gradually gone up as we went east until this day we reached the high point at Sanders—three gallons for a dollar. We have the assurance of travelers that from here on east there will be a gradual reduction. Off the main roads of course it is higher. We paid 35 cents in Yellowstone, 33 at Grand Canyon, and far out in Trinity county, California, we bought a few gallons at 40 cents.

The latter part of today was spent on the Navajo reservation, and it is a wonder how they live. Their only stock seemed to be a few—very few—sheep and goats, the latter the more numerous. We did not see a band of more than 200 if that many, and the flocks were few. Small patches here and there had been planted to corn, about a dozen grains in a hill, and it had neither been thinned nor cultivated. The rock formations made some of the scenery fine but nobody but a Californian can live on scenery.

The last few miles of the day we ran through adobe flats which had been traveled while wet a few days before, and we did not enjoy them, although glad they had dried before we came along.

About 5 o'clock we crossed the line between Arizona and New Mexico, still on the reservation and an hour later rolled into Gallup, a town in the heart of a stock country, which gets its milk from Albuquerque, 170 miles away, where the nearest dairy is kept!

Late in the afternoon we all watched the speedometer roll up the 10,000th mile of the trip, the total tonight being 10,030, the run for the day, 189 miles.

⁕

[Leap LXVIII,] during which we return to a country appearing a little more normal, although with many peculiarities.

"The road from here to Albuquerque is good." "The road to Albuquerque is good for a few miles out and a little at the other end." "Some places are almost impassible; I ran into one hole filled with water that almost killed my engine." "There are one or two bad places on the road, but if you take them easy you can make it all right—don't try to run fast, but keep going."

Such were the road reports described by men who had gone over them that very day. When a man tells you of road conditions you know little until you know what kind of a car he drives and what kind of roads he is accustomed to driving on. Our neighbors in camp at Gallup were from Chicago, have been out a good while, have been over all the good roads we have traversed and some others, but missed most of our bad ones, and yet his memory goes back to the boulevards of Chicago and he is afraid of these roads which he asserts are awful. He is dead sure he is going to break a spring, just as he met another man who had when he was 40 miles from where he could get a new one.

Our opinion since arriving in Albuquerque is that the road was fair, although we did not make a very long run. We drove late last night and my record was not written until this morning, so we were rather late in getting off. Somewhere yesterday or today we crossed the continental divide, but I don't know when or where. There was nothing to indicate it. We crossed a few low divides, but nothing which had any appearance of a real summit. Neither has there been any marked change in natural conditions. The country continues dry and barren, even when there are mud holes in the road and washouts occur every little way. Only once was there any doubt as to getting over the road, and that was when some trucks stalled in a mud hole and made us wait. Lena was choking the bit to get at it and go through, but had to wait nearly half an hour for the trucks to get out of the way.[6]

The mystery to me is not why these roads are not better, but how did they ever get the money to make any kind of a road, much less as good a one as we have had since entering Arizona. We have crossed that state from west to east without seeing a garden or a dairy herd and only one small orchard. One saw mill and two or three rock crushing plants have been the manufacturing enterprises. We are nearly across New Mexico and late today saw the first dairy, have seen no mill, and until within about 25 miles of its chief city had not seen an orchard or a field of grain; no country that would bear a crop without irrigation, and up to where those fields appeared had seen only one irrigation ditch, the one which made the bad mud hole because its water ran to waste instead of being used. Of course there are better spots, but the counties through which these roads run do not have them.

While we waited for the truck to clear the way a local car stopped and the wife told us something of conditions. Four-fifths of the population of that county is Mexican, which reminds me that so great is the Spanish speaking population of the state that all acts of the Legislature have to be printed in both English and Spanish, and there has to be an interpreter in constant attendance at the meetings of that body. And yet they have built roads which compare favorably with those of better known states in localities where the population is much denser and better off financially.

Our road practically all day followed what was once a stream's course—may be one yet in the proper season. On one side all the time, and occasionally on the other, were bluffs of parti-colored rock, often hundreds of feet high and not infrequently perpendicular as high as big modern buildings. Water and wind worn, there were some majestic spectacles. I think the domes of all the state capitols as well as that at Washington can be duplicated; many of Uncle Sam's departmental buildings look like the rocks here, and the pagoda style of architecture seemed all the rage when these fantastic carvings were made. Occasionally vast figures seem so life-like that one can scarce help thinking the cliff dwellers had left evidences of their artistic skill.

For a time this morning we continued across the Navajo reservation with all the squalor of the Indians as evident as the day before. There were still the occasional small herds of sheep and goats, and the little patches of corn producing nothing for lack of care. The houses were newer than many we saw the day before. These are made circular in form, all about the same size, 12 to 15 feet across, built up of sticks and their dome-like roof and sloping sides covered with earth. There may have been a hole in the center of the roof for smoke to escape, but if so it was small and we did not see one. The only opening we saw was a hole in the side about three feet high, the same width and rounded at the top. I know those today were newer than the ones we saw yes[ter] day because these used old discarded ties of the Santa Fe railroad instead of sticks cut from the hill sides.

Timber in this part of the world is scarce. Within reach of the road there was nothing except juniper and occasionally a Pinon pine, but to the south the mountain evidently had some good pine timber as there were a number of branch railroads running in that direction and at junction points, cars stood loaded with logs.

After we left the reservation there came a change in architecture and we began to see the houses so well known as distinctively New Mexican—the flat topped house of adobe brick. Some of these were quite old and the brick seemed badly washed by storms. Some were finished by plastering over with some of the clay, but the larger part proudly showed their composition. The brick seemed oversized and somewhat irregular in size, as though molded by hand.

Ere long we began to come to occasional pueblos, some of them of considerable size. One a short distance out of Albuquerque had hundreds of houses. As soon as we were fairly into the valley of the Rio Grande a new kind of decoration appeared—festoons of red peppers. Some houses had a whole side covered with them drying in the sun. It was a good while before we found where they were grown, but finally we saw the fields containing several acres each. The combination of adobe houses and yards and yards of red peppers made a picture which had long been familiar through reading but never seemed actually real.

The Rio Grande valley for over 20 miles in length and possibly a mile in width was nearly all farmed by the aid of irrigation ditches, but all the people we saw were Mexican. Not a single white face appeared in that entire distance. And as for the houses, adobe buildings were as common there as bungalows in Los Angeles.

It seemed too late to make the next town where good accommodations could be secured, and a good camping place appearing, we tied Lena up for the night, the speedometer showing 181 miles for the day with a total to date of 10,211.

❧

[Leap LXIX,] wherein we visit the ancient city of Santa Fe and see the oldest house in America.

This was to be a day of sightseeing and little labor or travel in it, so we made no effort to be off particularly early. The run to Santa Fe, a little under 70 miles, started up the Rio Grande, but the country was quite different from the evening before. No longer were there adobe houses covered with red peppers drying in the sun. The gardens were replaced with meadows, and alfalfa seemed to be the principal crop. I had intended to buy a string of peppers for a souvenir. Not one of the full grown strings larger than one of Lena's tires, but a modest little string. But when we suddenly ran out of the pepper district it was out of the question. I could not go to a man whose entire pepper crop would have gone into a gunny sack and ask him to part with some of them to a stranger for a little filthy lucre; as well have asked him to part with one of his dogs!

In the little village of Bernalillo the children were going to school, some to the village public school and others to the Catholic school at the edge of the village. It was noticeable that those who went to the latter averaged much darker in complexion than the public school pupils. The Catholic Church is the dominant factor in the life of New Mexico—or at least a very great one—but it is only through the voters of Mexican blood, and because of their low grade or the weak hold of the church, it has never made itself as prominent in public life as the Mormon Church in Utah.

Half way to Santa Fe we left the Rio Grande, never to see it more, and I learned a bit of geography, for it was my recollection that New Mexico's capital city was located on that river. Instead it is far above it on an immense mesa.

The penitentiary, deaf school, and of course the capitol building are there, along with many ancient structures, largely owned by the Catholic Church, including what is said to be the oldest house in the United States. All those old buildings are made of brick, and have been repaired as often as the roof of a wooden building would have been relaid. The outer walls usually have a plastered coat of the same dirt that was used in making the brick, and it is replaced from time

La Bajada Hill, south of Santa Fe, New Mexico, some years before the Clarks traveled over the terrain. *Courtesy Federal Highway Administration.*

to time or else the brick appears badly washed and about to melt down. Indeed, many old walls are melting down.

The streets are narrow and crooked—almost as much so as those of Boston, and without a map of the city one is uncertain where he will land when he starts down one of them.

Roads radiate out in every direction. The one we came in on is one of the most important in the state, and is paved with concrete nearly a third of the way from Albuquerque. The rest of the way it is a good gravel road, somewhat hilly, but in only one place is the hill bad. That is one of the noted places in the state's highway system, Bajada Hill, rising almost perpendicularly—quite so much of the way—for 500 feet, and the road requires several hairpin turns to get up it, accomplishing the feat in what seemed little more than a mile. At several places on the hill, this sign may be seen: "This road is not fool-proof, but it is safe for careful drivers. Watch your step."

Just before starting up the hill, a bright, glistening snake, about four feet long, and shining like a new copper cent, skimmed across the road

A touring car on an unidentified street in Santa Fe, New Mexico, a few years before the Clarks made their visit. *Courtesy Federal Highway Administration.*

just in front of us. A quick step on the gas and we raced to catch his tail, but missed it by a hair's breadth, his speed having increased until he almost scorched the grass at the side of the road in his getaway.

After reading the mail received at Santa Fe, we spent some time in the museums. The Palace of the Governors, one of the oldest buildings and one of the most interesting, stands fronting the plaza, and is occupied jointly by the Museum of New Mexico and the State Historical Society, while across the street is the state Museum, a separate institution. We saw all these, the collections being interesting but not large, the state still being young, and the collections being confined almost entirely to things connected with the state. At one of the stores a Mexican was weaving a Navajo blanket. His loom was one of the aboriginal kind and the plan of weaving is likely that of the Navajo. This disturbed one of my theories, which was that all Navajo blankets now came from Connecticut, just as their pottery does from the Ohio valley. For two days a common sight beside the road was the body of a wrecked auto or some other form of shade, and as we approached, from behind the shelter would rise a squaw with a piece of pottery in each hand, and the oven in which it was supposed to have been burned is a common sight in the back yards.

And Navajo blankets!

In the store of Arizona today there are more Navajo blankets on sale—all of them new—than the whole Navajo tribe has made in the last 100 years. The eastern highways are lined with curio shops, but the west has fully as many—difference in population considered—and the Navajo blanket is one of the choicest. I thought we had seen them all while passing through Arizona, but here they are even more plentiful in New Mexico, and a factory actually turning them out before our eyes—at the rate of about one a week. But it was a good bit of advertising, and I doubt not that every week that place sells the entire life product of the old Mexican.

We first planned to spend the day and night in Santa Fe, but tiring of adobe buildings we bought some supplies and hit the trail again. Our road was a new one, well graveled, leading pretty directly southeast, over a mesa. It was a gravelly country, sometimes rocky, but not often so until approaching the enclosing mountains. Much of it was devoid of timber and what there was consisted exclusively of juniper and Pinon pine. The latter was but little higher than my head, but loaded with burs which were just opening and dropping the ripened nuts. In early days these nuts formed a large part of the provender of the Indians, and are now an article of commerce in a small way. We stopped and gathered a pint or more in a few minutes.

In the midst of these thousands of acres of nuts I wondered where the squirrels were. We had not seen a one since leaving Grand Canyon. The prairie dog had not been in evidence since getting into Arizona and we saw only a few of them today. The mystery of New Mexico's roads grew with the day. We were on a beautiful highway with barren ground on either side. Once we ran 23 miles without passing a habitation, and in 70 miles we saw only four that were occupied, while three teams and three other autos made up the traffic. One lone sheep herder was the rest of the animated landscape.

The merchant in whose adobe house we are spending tonight tells me that this is a fine country. He has been here 14 years and thinks it the best ever. It was a great sheep country, but for four years there has been very little rain and much of the country has been deserted. Rain has been plentiful during the last few weeks, the grass is green, and hope is reviving.

The speedometer showed a run of 156 miles, making a total of 10,367, while the flat tire record was increased by one, and another blow out ended the life of the last of the original tires of Lena's, one which had been kept exclusively as a spare "to run in on."

* * *

[Leap LXX,] being the run through the eastern half of New Mexico on September 17.

The cactus had been with us most of the time since we got over the mountain from San Diego, but the varieties had varied with the different localities. Through this eastern half of New Mexico a new one appeared, but also there would be considerable distances where none were in evidence. The sage brush appeared occasionally, and the jack rabbit was back on duty. We saw no live ones, but dead ones in the road which had been killed by passing cars were common. We would probably have seen them had we been running nights, but they are out less in day time than just after dusk, and in the dark the lights of a car seem to blind them and make them easy to run over. Practically all the animals common to the country were found dead in the road except the prairie dog. He has been seen frequently ever since approaching Williams, Wyo., and while the most clumsy of all the squirrel or gopher family, and not at all wild, he seems to dodge the autos successfully.

We saw several coyotes dead and hanging on fence corners, though we have seen none alive. Florence heard some in the night, and described the sound as so terrifying that "it froze her blood in her veins."

Our road today was the worst we have found for a long time. Much of it was never much more than the kind of roads country neighborhoods allow to make themselves, and recent rains had done much damage. Except where there was a gravel surface they were so rough no time could be made. The route lay nearly due east across the prairie, with abundant grass most of the time and but little live stock—mostly cattle.

A new industry appeared about noon. For several days there had been some bear grass along the road but not until today did it become common. It grows in bunches, blades a half inch wide and one to two feet long. There will be from one to two hundred blades in a bunch, coming from a common root, and at one station we saw where it was being cut, hauled to town and baled. We asked some Mexican teamsters what it was for and they explained that it was for weaving mats, hats, etc. I don't know what they get for it, but the crop is unlimited.

In mid afternoon we came down into the valley of the Pecos river, crossing it soon after. It is larger here than the Rio Grande where we crossed it below Albuquerque, and carries the same full charge of red mud that the Colorado and Rio Grande do. The valley was generally under cultivation and the crops were fine. Corn (Indian, broom and Kaffir), cotton, orchards and other products were grown, but I think the most luxuriant growth of all was the cocklebur. I am not sure that I ever saw finer. The sides of the road and some of the fields were full of them. Some very valuable ground seemed given over entirely to them. Out on the higher, dryer ground the sand burs had been so thick and aggressive that when we pulled out beside the road for lunch the tires were thoroughly coated with them, and their nauseous smell was very marked.

We camped early at Clovis and when we started to unload, discovered that I had failed to put on the tent poles this morning, so we are in the city camp hoping to cover ourselves with the tent without poles, and hoping the letter sent back for them will bring them to us tomorrow at Floydada, where we plan to visit for a day or two.

The speedometer reports 160 more miles today, making 10,527 since we left West Virginia.

CHAPTER TEN

Texas and Oklahoma

[LEAP LXXI,] IN WHICH WE SAW THE "GREAT STAKED PLAINS" OF Texas.

Come around some day and I will show you a geography such as was used in the schools of my day, and therein you will find what is now the "panhandle" of Texas labeled "Great Staked Plains." For many years after that it was considered as worthless as it is possible for land to be, and the state (which retained all its public lands when it was admitted to the Union, being a separate government) would have been glad to sell any or all of that land for a few cents an acre; but no one was foolish enough to pay real money for such lands. So they performed some service for the state, or failed to perform it and reported that they did, and the state generously endowed them with a lot of this unattractive domain.

For several years past at the state fair the sweepstake prize on agricultural products has gone to one or another of the counties which were formed of the "Great Staked Plains." Ground on which even a cow could not graze because she could find no water to drink was found to be under laid with a veritable lake only a few feet beneath the surface, and on some considerable areas the water is pumped to the surface and used for irrigation. Where it is too deep for that it is still in easy reach for the wind driven pump and there is an abundance of water for farm or town purposes.

Clovis is situated on the western edge of that region, and 10 miles east is the boundary fence of a farm which is also the dividing line between the Lone Star state and New Mexico, passing which we were into the home of Sam Houston and the Alamo. An empire in itself—possible the empire of which Aaron Burr dreamed—we were to spend days in crossing it and that merely across a corner.[1]

When we entered, it was the nearest level spot we had seen on the whole trip. While there is really a slight slope to the eastward, so that water falling from the clouds finally runs off in that direction, there is no grade noticeable, and in a run of over 100 miles that day it was hard to convince the eye that there was as much as 50 feet difference in elevation in any two places in the road. There was a considerable change in the character of the soil, although most of it appeared to be of high grade. Cotton, Kaffir corn, Sudan grass were the standard crops, with corn and wheat following well up, although we saw none of the latter. The year had been unfavorable so that the crop was light and it was harvested so long ago that all trace of it had disappeared. But the next year's crop was being planted, a number of drills being seen in operation, while other farmers were still plowing.

Tractors were common on the farm and also in pulling the road machinery which we encountered every few miles, repairing the damage caused by recent rains. But the standard motive power of the southwestern farm is still the mule. The automobile uses the road, yet in the two days approaching and leaving Santa Fe we saw more vehicles drawn by animals than in all the rest of the journey. The mule is still a very necessary part of the Texan life, even in the region where the Negro is almost unknown.

Cotton picking was just beginning. The plant does not grow high here, but sets a good lot of bolls, and produces a staple of good length, so it is about the best money crop. As yet no fertilizer is used, which materially decreases the cost of the crop.

Although the country was level, there were slight depressions and we still had the water gaps which had become familiar during the last few days. Even on a dirt road, there were low places where it was well concreted, and across these some wet weather stream would find its way across the road. Sometimes posts stood at the edge of the concrete, marked to show the depth of the water, so that the traveler could know whether it was safe to risk his car in. There were no culverts and no bridges.

In mid afternoon we arrived at Floydada, where mail awaited us as well as a refuge in the home of a cousin of Mrs. Clark, whom she had not seen since childhood. The speedometer reported 137 miles for the day, bringing the entire run up to 10,664.[2]

⁕

A day was spent visiting the Floydada cousins, which also gave us an opportunity to see more of the country and gather information regarding it. While Lena was having the surplus carbon removed, "all hands and the cook" boarded Cousin Smith's car and drove northward 30 miles through parts of three counties and visiting for a few minutes families of two other cousins who had settled in Texas way back when the world was young. The same general characteristics prevailed over all that distance, and would had we gone twice as far.

Every farm home has its windmill pumping water from a well, and many of them are allowed to run continually—or as much of the time as the wind blows—through the dry season. The immediate discharge of the pump is into a galvanized iron tank from which a pipe runs to the house. Another pipe will run to a yet larger tank so situated that stock from the barn lot, from the pasture, and perhaps from a field may all drink from it. Another pipe carries the surplus to a tank from which the garden is irrigated, or if there be no irrigation it may run to one of the lakes, almost every farm having one or more, which cover from one to two or three acres. It sometimes occurs that the wind does not blow for as long as three or four days, so these various tanks have to be of a capacity to carry water for that time. The water is quite cool and good to drink when first pumped, but of course, not constantly renewed, gets too warm to be pleasant.

The standard crops are milo maize, Kaffir corn, cotton and wheat. In years of sufficient moisture wheat produces enormous crops, and not infrequently after it is cut the stubble is hastily planted to one of the corns and a good crop of that produced. But the country is on the edge of an arid region and many years farmers are disappointed through lack of sufficient moisture.

The farms were of the regular western size of 160 acres each, with some of them doubling up, and we saw a few which contained several times that much.

The next morning we were on our road again, running nearly due east. Through a county or two there was little change in conditions although it seemed that the lakes were more plentiful. Then we came to the "rim," and slowly began the descent from the highland we had been traversing since leaving the Colorado river. This was accomplished very gradually, the country becoming more rolling and each hill a little lower than its predecessor.

The country at once became drier and all farming ceased. There was some stock but much of the land was unoccupied at this time, although evidently held for pasture in wetter seasons.

It was noticeably warmer on the lower ground, the evening at Vernon being the warmest of the whole trip, even Imperial valley not being an exception.

The flat tire came about two miles before we reached Vernon, due this time to a tack in the road, and it was readily fixed in camp, which is advertised as the best in the state, and which we found very nice except for the mosquitoes. The speedometer recorded 161 more miles, lengthening the trip to 10,825.

❦

All reports previous to arrival at Vernon were that the road from there to Fort Worth would be excellent, the only exception being a stretch of six or eight miles where construction work had been in progress and which might not be finished. But at Vernon the distance was increased and later a bit of evil omen asserted that there was no road in Clay county and we had to go clear through it. All of these unfavorable statements proved to be true. A few weeks ago roads might have been good, but rains have worked havoc with all dirt roads, injured gravel ones severely and did no good to the hard surfaced kind. As for Clay county, I feel safe in saying that but for crossing three or four streams, it would have been easier to have driven the 37 miles across it when Sam Houston first went to Texas than it is now.

There had been trouble fixing the flat tire in the morning, and it was late when we got away from camp. Since there was no community kitchen, we rented a cottage in which we could do our cooking. And it proved better on account of mosquitoes, which have become more or less prevalent through a wide region since the rains.

The scenic feature of the day was the cotton pickers. All day long we met them—white and colored—in rigs of all kinds, but usually in some automotive machine, the Ford truck being one of the favorites, although all were represented. We saw outfits consisting of such a truck loaded with kitchen furniture and bedding, the whole piled as high as the top over the driver; on top of that a half-dozen people, three more in the seat, and several others on the fenders and running board. I never knew a half-ton truck could carry so much. Practically all such outfits were going to some cotton field or else to a region where report had it that pickers were wanted.

We stopped for lunch at a wayside camp ground, which we divided with a doctor and his wife just starting on a vacation for two weeks. Like many such, they took along the family dog, but in addition also included the parrot—the only bird we have seen taking an outing, although at The Dalles we saw a car loaded with eight people and two cats, each with a litter of kittens.

We were getting into the heart of northern Texas as I had always understood it, and I was surprised to find so much waste land. Half the time that day, and down almost to Fort Worth, there was commonly untilled land on both sides of the road, and farm houses were few and far between. The land was all fenced and apparently pastured at seasons, but it was only native grass. Much of this north Texas is covered with Mesquite which is a pretty good pasture grass, but among the undesirable settlers is a good deal of Johnson grass, which has little if any value. Bermuda grass is also frequently found; an excellent lawn grass, but with no feed value, and hard to get rid of except by growing some crop which will shade the ground deeply all over. Scarce a tree is to be seen, and the few there are were too small to have any value, even for shade.

It was dark when we arrived at Fort Worth and we had a little difficulty locating Mrs. Clark's cousins there, but a warm welcome awaited us when we did find them.

The speedometer gave 188 miles for the day, making a total of 11,013.

⁂

It was a disappointment all around that we were not to see more of Fort Worth, but there was no time to delay. Texas is one of the few states following West Virginia's plan of not having one city far in the lead of all others, but instead has a number practically the same size. One of these is Fort Worth, the others being Dallas, Houston and San Antonio. More and more the oil industry of the state is centering at Fort Worth, and that city also handles a large part of the cattle trade of the state. By the way the "long horn" of a generation ago has entirely disappeared, not a single specimen remaining in all North America, even for museum purposes. In the main the white face has taken its place, offering more utility even though less picturesque.

There is much activity in oil now in various parts of the state, and if you want to buy stock which will increase in value at a wonderful rate, you will have no trouble in buying it in Fort Worth, without even the formality of an introduction, Dr. Cook having left several fellows to carry on the business during his temporary absence.[3]

We passed through one oil field the day before—one of the oldest in the state, where scores of wells were being pumped. They only went down to a shallow sand, and the wells are all pumpers, but recently somebody ventured down to a deeper sand and struck even better yields and a new drilling fever had struck the field, quite a number of new rigs being already at work. I learned there what I had not known before: that all the Texas drilling is done with diamond drills, a perfect core being taken out all the way down.

We were escorted to the city limits this morning—not by the police but by our cousins—and headed for Dallas, only 35 miles away, farther down the Trinity river. The country was thickly settled most of the way, and the land generally cultivated. This is some of the famous "black waxy" land of Texas, a heavy producer of cereal crops, easy to cultivate when containing the proper amount of moisture, but beyond navigation when too wet.

Dallas may be unfortunate in the way the *Blue Book* routes visitors through; it probably has some good wide streets, but we did not see any of them; all were narrow, crooked, crossing at all sorts of angles, and in general reminding us of the streets of Boston, which are the worst I ever saw.

We were in a purely cotton country when we turned north out of Dallas. Occasionally there would be a considerable field of corn, ripe long ago but sometimes still ungathered, and at rare intervals there were places where Milo maize or Kaffir corn had been planted, and so dry was the summer that it had died before it headed out. But the mass of the country was in cotton, and at every small town there was a number of gins, usually in active operation, although the number of pickers seemed to be small. On every farm there were fields of cotton, few had been picked, rarely were pickers seen at work, but everywhere the cotton was ripe. Possibly I was mistaken about those pickers in yesterday's leap, all headed north, where the cotton is just beginning to ripen— maybe they were getting away from the picking!

Once we saw a man sitting beside the road in a flivver looking disconsolate, and Florence drew up alongside, inquiring if there was anything we could do for him. He was out there watching for pickers and offered her a job. But she explained that the rules of her union would not permit her to take other work and we drove on. I think the women were really a little alarmed for once before I had refused an offer for them to pick prunes, and it might be that we would all have to go to work or suffer at the hands of indignant farmers. There seemed a little more haste in our flight after this episode.

Well along in the afternoon we paid 75 cents for the privilege of leaving Texas and entering Oklahoma. They called it toll on the bridge across the Red river which is the state boundary there.[4]

Durant was the first town in the new state. I call it new because it was new to us. Mrs. Clark had passed down through there in a wagon in the days when it was Indian Territory, and Oklahoma was not yet even a name, but to me it was an entirely unknown land. I believe the black waxy soil was all gone before that, but otherwise there was little difference for a time.

The land became if possible a little more flattened out—how much so I realized that evening when beside the camp fire I counted the box cars on a passing freight train and found one engine was pulling 112 of them. Presumably many of them were empty, being west bound, but they embraced all sorts of cars except coal and stock. In the days when we traveled along the Santa Fe road its freight trains were made up almost exclusively of refrigerator cars going to or coming from California orchards, but Oklahoma and Texas offered a more mixed traffic.

The women had never seen cotton ginned, so we stopped once during the day and watched a large gin for a time, the operation being a very fascinating one. Probably Eli Whitney would have trouble recognizing one of the modern machines as being his invention.

We were off the tourist trails now, and when we pulled into the only tourist camp in Caddo we were the only occupants, and on a world of high Bermuda grass we made our beds, rain threatening.

The speedometer had added 158 more miles, making it say 11,171.

༺ঌৢঁঌ༻

I had been sick ever since Saturday morning, and left Caddo Tuesday feeling no better.

At McAlester we turned east over a new road running directly into Fort Smith, Ark., the town where more men have been hung that any other in the United States. It was there that the custom of having all hangings on Friday was abandoned, it being impossible to hang them all on that day of the week and keep up with the work!

Really there were a great many. A United States judge there started in to clean up the condition of affairs in the Indian Territory, then the refuge of bad men from everywhere, and for several years it was admitted that he was much more feared there than the Almighty. It is a forceful example of what a man on the bench can do to better living conditions and secure observance of law if he wants to.[5]

Rain fell at intervals throughout the day, but always ahead or behind us, so our only trouble was when one of the rear tires picked up a ten penny nail and was not discriminating enough to pick it up lengthwise but took it point first with the usual disastrous results.

Our road was fine and it was still seasonable time when he pulled into the tourist camp at Fort Smith. With the ground wet and the certainty of rain we decided to engage a cabin for the night. But there was only camping space in the park, and it was the only park for tourists in a city of 30,000 people with good roads leading in at least two directions! We certainly were off the tourist routes—would have hardly been farther had we been in Philadelphia, where there was no camping place at last reports. At Vernon, Tex., the camp where we stayed had 40 or more cabins, and at least one other camp in town had some, and that town only 4,000 to 5,000 people. We were later to discover that Arkansas has a lot of beautiful scenery, but she hasn't told the world about it yet.

We camped beside a Methodist preacher and his wife from Mount Hope, W.Va., the first West Virginia car we have seen in a long time. Our speedometer had gone ahead to 11,360, the day having added 189 miles more.

CHAPTER ELEVEN

Arkansas to West Virginia

RENEWING OUR ACQUAINTANCE WITH THE FAMOUS ARKANSAW Traveler.

It will be remembered that the Arkansaw Traveler found that the native could not shingle his house when it was raining, and when it was not raining there was no need of shingles. So at Fort Smith with no cabins for the tourist the night we arrived, we knew none would be built the next day for it was raining. I woke in the night and it was raining, but I went to sleep again. Later I woke again and it was still raining, but another party of campers were getting up and having breakfast, their talk indicating they were getting ready for the day. So I suggested to Mrs. Clark that we get up and away as soon as possible. She agreed, and I dressed. Outside the tent it was still dark and I sat in the car where it was comparatively dry. Presently Mrs. Clark appeared at the door of the tent and asked the time. I switched on a light and saw it was 4:30. She went back to bed and I leaned back in the car and slept most of the time until 5:45. By that time the early risers were gone and another car load were at the fire getting breakfast.

We packed and got away shortly after, not stopping for breakfast until we reached a restaurant in Van Buren, on the opposite side of the Arkansas river. By that time it had settled down to one of the most peculiar bits of weather I have ever known.Until after 3 o'clock in the afternoon there was seldom a moment when fine mist could not be felt, the windshield needed wiping constantly, and yet it was not really raining. I doubt if a quarter of an inch of water fell in all day.

The road north was sloppy but it was a good road and we ran all day without chains. We were but a short distance from Van Buren until we began to climb, and the character of the country soon changed greatly. The plains gave way to hills, more or less wooded; cotton disappeared; orchards became more common. The land was much rougher, and we finally came onto a long ridge which we followed for miles finally coming to what was called the summit of the Ozark mountains. Considerable orchards, sometimes of peaches but more often of big red apples lined the road. Gardens were more numerous than they had been since leaving California. Tomatoes were grown in fields, probably for some cannery not far away.

We were fairly into the Ozarks, a region made famous by a few popular writers of fiction, and often exploited as a fruit country and resort section, the fruit investors usually living long enough the regret their expenditures.

The weather was too disagreeable for us to enjoy the scenery, although there was some which deserved attention. Several fair sized towns were passed, including Fayetteville, with a history running back a century, some of it quite tragic.

In mid afternoon we reached the home of an old friend who came to Bentonville from Tennessee a dozen years ago, there to spend the night. The speedometer had swelled its total to 11,468, the day's run 108 miles.

❦

Getting back once more into the "show me" state.

This morning of September 25, Jupiter Pluvius continued to play pranks on the weather man. Of all the departments of government, the one I pay taxes to keep up with the greatest unwillingness is the weather bureau. It may gather some statistics which are of value, but as a prognosticator of coming events it seems an absolute failure. On the Pacific Coast where it rains from November to March and then the sun shines from April to October, the weather bureau can forecast the weather just as well as the man who is not on the pay roll, but in regions where mixed weather comes at all seasons it does seem as though there were more misses than successes. In the case of this storm, at the beginning the observer at Oklahoma City reported rain falling and locally predicated a continuance—just as anyone would have done after a look at that sky—but his superior at Washington ignored the fact that it was raining over pretty much of a state and opined that fair weather would follow. For four days the rain continued to fall without ceasing, and in some places broke all records for quantity, and yet the direst thing that forecaster dared to predict was "probably showers." At one point in southwest Missouri there fell 9.92 inches of water in less than 12 hours, with an outlook favoring as much more in the next 12, and the weather man signed the pay roll for this week's compensation and told an anxious world: "Probably showers."

We started in the rain from Bentonville, Ark., and we ended in the rain at Rogersville, Mo., after running through the rain all day. It was a pretty country, part of the Ozarks, but of course conditions were not favorable for looking at it. Trees, so long absent, were here in profusion—almost too plentiful perhaps—and while the country had suffered from a drought during the summer, rains two or three weeks before had started vegetation to growing, and there was a pleasing freshness about everything.

Various parts of the Ozark region have been exploited for the growing of some particular kind of fruit. Thus years ago the Clarks spent two years at Koshkonong, Mo., then one of the peach centers, while only a mile or two away was the line of Howell county, heralded far and wide as "the home of the big red apple." Monett was the strawberry city, shipping hundreds of carloads each spring, and at Rogers was another peach section. There was little difference of soil, and none of climate between these sections, but the specializing was all due to the form of exploitation.[1]

Now we found the peach orchards at Rogers very rare, but the land was filled with the finest apple trees we had seen in a long time. Even the famous orchards of Washington and Oregon cannot compare in beauty with these of the Ozarks. The trees all look so clean and healthy; just as though they had come direct from a bath and a good scrubbing with a brush backed by plenty of soap and water.

It was apples, apples, apples everywhere, all of them red and all of them fine looking. A hard wind a few days before had shaken many of them from the trees—sometimes as many on the ground as on the trees—which had it happened early in the growing season might have been a blessing, but now it meant a heavy loss. Some of the windfalls were being shipped to nearby points, and everywhere cider mills were busy. Packing sheds at each station were the one busy place where rain had stopped every other industry.

So far as we learned—our opportunities to gather information being small—apple growing is not profitable, and we noticed few new orchards. Also the history of the country lends probability to the statements. Howell county, one of the big apple counties of the United States a few years ago, has almost abandoned their growth; Koshkonong has pulled up its peach trees; Monett no longer ships strawberries in any considerable quantity. Rogers has switched from peaches to apples, and is already beginning to wonder what it will try next. Any part of the country will grow any of the ordinary fruits, but the cost of getting it to market eats up the profits. Modern selling methods demand boxes within boxes; selection and re-selection; seller's salary and commission; freight charge; icing charge; drayage charge; from three to five profits before the consumer gets the fruit, considerable of which has rotted by that time. With so many paws to grab along the road there is little of the consumer's money gets back to the producer.

Before noon we crossed the line into Missouri, our road generally much better than we had expected to find, the only bad places being due to construction work. At Monett where we connected with the main east and west road of southern Missouri, we had a short detour, and between the rain and the detour we became thoroughly lost and could not find the business part of town, we wanting to get something to eat there. No one was in sight on the streets and [we] had to disturb a man in his home to learn the way to the town by which we were sur-rounded. It was the old case of "not being able to find the town because of so many houses."

Road continued good, rain continued bad and in due time we passed through Springfield, the metropolis of southwest Missouri, and stopped at a small hotel at Rogersville. It was harvest time with the hotel people, the rain driving so many tourists to shelter that before bed time it was filled to capacity.

The speedometer reading told of 149 miles over that rainy road, bringing the total up to 11,517.

⋅⋆⋅

Back again on old familiar ground.

The patter of the rain on the roof soon lulled everybody to sleep with a single exception. One there was who found Morpheus in no mood to be wooed. On her pillow one young lady tossed in fruitless efforts to forget the events of the day and sink in Nirvana. Strange itchings afflicted her and there were unaccountable twisting and twitching which prevented the absolute rest necessary to induce slumber. The clock struck the midnight hour, and then there was a discovery. A match was rubbed against the side of the box, the flame flared up, and there was a hurried scampering of frightened peoples whose domicile had been invaded by the young lady. Florence gave a yell—several yells—and everybody beneath the roof came to a degree of wakefulness which was astonishing compared with their condition a moment before.

The landlady was aroused, and when informed of the state of affairs, agreed sympathetically that "it sure wuz aggravatin!" She prepared a couch far removed from the populous couch, each article of bedding was scanned, and once more there was no sound other than the patter of the rain.

Our brakes had worn thin, so the next morning we had them relined and at 8:30 were out in the rain again with the weather man predicting "probably showers" for the next two days. Once in a while there was a bad spot in the road, but nothing at all dangerous to navigation until we reached Cabool. In the farther edge of that town was a creek of uncertain depth which Lena had to wade. It proved a little deeper than anticipated and we landed on the farther bank with the timer full of water and off duty until properly renovated.

However, that cost no time. Neither had the flat tire earlier in the day, although of course at the time we supposed it did. But a quarter of a mile after we got the timer to working again we came to a sure enough river with a number of cars lined up on either side waiting for the surplus water of that river to get safely on their way to the Gulf of Mexico!

The optimistic ones predicted that at the rate it was falling we could cross in from one to two hours, so we made use of part of the time of waiting by walking back to town and getting lunch.

Back once more at the flood we found that two or three venturesome drivers had already crossed, and the wings at the far end of the bridge were showing above the water. Two or three more crossed safely; a state highway truck ventured and made the passage. It appeared all safe except a drop of about a foot where the gravel had been washed away at the far end of the bridge. We decided that Lena should try it next. We ran down to the edge of the water, but a flivver had already started from the opposite shore, so we backed up out of the way and waited. Then one of the "gallery" announced that we had a flat tire!

By the time the tube was patched and the tire changed and pumped up all those 40 waiting cars had crossed and Lena was the last to reach the other shore.

Shortly before reaching Willow Springs we met a car just as we came to a detour sign. The driver advised us to stick to the road as he had done. There was bad road, but he had made it and he thought we could. The detour necessitated fording the creek twice and they were "pulling them out." We stuck to the highway, but got a puncture just as we ran into the bridge at the overhead railroad crossing near Willow Springs. A few rods farther back and changing tires would have been impossible.

I was on familiar ground now. Years ago I waited at Willow Springs one evening for a train to take me away, and as I was to deliver a speech in a few days, I improved those hours of waiting by wandering over the neighboring hills and whipping that talk into shape for use. But while I worked changing that tire and getting enough air pumped into the new one to carry us into town, there was no speech prepared. In fact the things which went through my mind at that time would not be proper to deliver from the lecture platform!

We had been promised a rather bad road—slick and sometimes rough—from West Plains to Koshkonong, and the promise was fulfilled to the letter. Just before sundown there had appeared a long streak of blue sky in the west, the sun appearing to end its day in peace and harmony, but where we were the drizzle continued and the windshield wiper was one of the most regularly employed parts of the car.

Dark came a little beyond West Plains, and we ran on over some of the slickest roads ever navigated. Only in a few places was there mud of consequence, but it was nearly impossible to control the car. We ran as slow as we conveniently could and in due time reached the home of our old friends, the Harrisons, who attend to the business of the Frisco railroad at Koshkonong, and soon unloaded Lena to give the tent and bedding its first chance to dry out since leaving Fort Smith. Except for a moment that evening we had not seen the sun for four days; it had rained almost constantly during that time and that unfaithful servant in Washington whose salary I am compelled to help pay had repeated with parrot-like regularity: "Probably showers!"

The speedometer had ground its way ahead until it showed 11,753 miles for the journey, 136 of them being for that day.

Another tire flat when we reached Harrisons!

AN INTERVAL

Two lazy days were ahead of us—a kind which seldom come on the road, where as a rule life was very strenuous. In this town of Koshkonong had been the Clark home for two years, during which they had tried to take their part in the activities of the town, so on Sunday morning the old Sunday School memories came vividly back. There were but two in the town then, both still continuing, but the one of which we had formed a part had seen the principal changes. We were not the only ones of the old attendants who had moved away in the last score of years, and now we learned that but one or two of those we had known as attendants were still to be found on its roll of members. The other school on the contrary, was still full of old friends, so it claimed us for that morning.

The children had grown up—quite a number of them had appeared on the scene since we left—but in the main it presented a very natural appearance, and the morning hour meant much to us besides the study of the regular lesson. The cashier of the local bank was still its superintendent, and after the study of the lesson he gave a new experience to me—he asked Mrs. Clark and Florence each to speak, the first time I had ever heard either of them address the public in words arranged by themselves.

The old trouble of all the visiting appeared when it was time to eat, for everywhere we had all been eating too much, and from the stores of the Ozarks we drew abundantly, with the hospitable insistence that we eat still more.

I said there were two lazy days to be spent there, but that was not literally true, for Sunday we visited as hard as we could with as many people as possible, while Monday morning the women did some necessary washing while I wrote the account of the last two days' run, and about noon we drove to a country home, Lena remaining to have some cleaning up done to his vital organ. In the evening we were driven back to another big feed, so the days (and we) were full to bursting with good cheer, friendship and pleasurable association.

⁂

Heading once more for the "Old Home Town."

It was 8:30 Tuesday morning, September 29, before we got away from Koshkonong after bidding the friends adieu, and we made five miles before we suffered a flat tire, hastily putting on our spare and running to West Plains to have the damage repaired. Our route was backtracking Saturday's run until we came to Cabool—where we had waited for the creek to run down—there turning east on one of the new roads of Missouri, mostly in good shape. The country was rather sparsely settled, and the towns were generally small as well as far apart. The hills were not very high nor steep, but the soil was stony and indifferent as to quality usually, although with the uniformly timbered hills and green grass everywhere, it presented a beautiful appearance. We found the cotton belt moved several miles to the north and a good many hundred feet higher up on the Ozarks since we had lived there, but still that region is best utilized when devoted to the growth of fruit or live stock, and of the really arable land which we saw on the whole trip, a little money will buy more here than anywhere else. At Koshkonong we were told of several farms with decent buildings, some orchards and much good pasture which were for sale at as little as $10 an acre—some of them even less. We probably passed farms that day which filled these descriptions and yet could be bought for half that price. Several dry years in succession are responsible for this condition; these same lands have sold up into the hundreds of dollars an acre, and probably in some cases will again before many years.

Rolla, reached late in the afternoon, is one of the old towns of southern Missouri, although probably at times it has numbered more than its present 2,000 people. The center of an iron mining region, its wealth attracted early attention, and in the days of the Civil War it was a place of importance, earnestly striven for by both sides. It is now the seat of Missouri's School of Mines, but its mining and smelting works are now of little importance.[2]

When we left there the clutch seemed to be working very irregularly and by the time we had run the 12 miles to Saint James we were a little uncertain about it holding to climb some of the larger hills. Locating a day and night garage, we arranged to have it put in shape and drove on to a camp ground, taking the car back after unloading it.

Through an oversight, part of the tent equipment was left on the car, so we arranged again to sleep under the open sky. After dark the mechanic from the garage came to us with the distressing intelligence that the clutch could not be repaired, but must have a new one. He could call the branch house in St. Louis and probably get the necessary part by the night train Wednesday night, only detaining us a day and a half, or he could call an auto supply house in Springfield who wanted business and were consequently accommodating, and the clutch would be there early the next morning—if they had it in stock, which was uncertain. We said try Springfield, for if that failed St. Louis could be called in the morning with hope that the part would be shipped in time to catch an evening train out of that city.

Then we went to bed with the tent spread over us, the speedometer saying 11,907 or 154 miles for the day, with considerable uncertainty as to when it would say anything more.

❧

Across the Mississippi again.

There was good news the next morning. Springfield did not have the clutch, but in some way the garage man had located one at Rolla and a boy had already been sent in a flivver to get it; the car would probably be ready to run by noon! But in the meantime there was another question to be settled. We were at the end of our road. The highway from St. James to St. Louis was closed (under construction) and the state highway department was directing travel to go north nearly to Jefferson City and here take a road intersecting with the regular highway at Union. It added some 50 or 75 miles to the distance. Travelers told us by no means to go that way. It was not only that much farther but the road was no better than the detours along the regular highway. Opinions were widely at variance, and I had time to make many inquiries. Opinions, advice and information generally were based on data several days old, since when there had been much rain. Every garage man in town advised going north as the state authorities said, but when I asked the man who was working on the car what he would do if he were going himself, he said he would go directly through. Then I met a car just arriving and the driver told me there was only one dangerous place, where I must avoid a mud hole with a rail sticking up in it as a warning.

At 11:30 I reached camp with Lena's "innards" in perfect order again and at 11:40 we were on the road again—the quickest "getaway" of the journey except possibly the time we fled from the Dakota mosquitoes. A few miles out the detouring began and it continued most of the way to Union. The road was rough, hilly and often muddy, but there was never a moment of doubt as to our ability to get through.

We got almost to St. Louis when a freight train kept possession of a crossing over half an hour, and by that time it was again raining hard. A little farther on came a flat tire, and by the time we reached the first street car track it was dark. Rain was coming down steadily and we were in doubt about our way across the city. The street signs did not agree with the *Blue Book,* but finally a colored truck driver told us the street had two names, so we were all right, and by 7 o'clock we were across the Mississippi and housed at a hotel, Lena occupying a stall in the hostelry's private garage in the rear. We had made 130 miles in spite of the hindrances, bringing our total up to 12,037.

❦

Rushing Homeward.

Our tent and bedding had been thoroughly soaked by the rain the evening before, so we decided to make Middletown before another stop. At 4:30 we arose and a half hour later were on the road, finding some difficulty in getting out of East St. Louis in the fog, which kept us from seeing street signs with only dim street lamps to read them by. After morning was fairly come we stopped for breakfast at a mining village restaurant, having had only one flat tire so far. The next one came a little later, and we lost an hour waiting for a garage man to repair it, finally doing it myself after he had worried with a loose rag around a sore thumb and failed to make the patch stick.

The road was just the same as that we had traveled going west in June, and there was no trouble until we got to Eaton, Ohio, and wanted to find the cut off to Middletown. One garage man even assured me that there was no way except around by West Alexandria, but having gone over the direct route, we could not agree with him. We finally found the way out for Gratis and got to Middletown at 9 o'clock, having driven 370 miles that day, the longest day's run on the trip, bringing our total up to 12,407.

❦

Friday and Saturday were spent with the children in Middletown, resting and telling them somewhat of the trip. Sunday, October 4, we left at 11:40, the children going in their Hudson to Columbus with us. The blow out came just before we reached Franklin, and while having the tire repaired at a garage there, another one went flat from a leaky valve. Still we reached the Hampton home in Columbus at 5:30, the speedometer showing 106 more miles, or a total of 12,513.

❦

HOME AGAIN!

The off front tire, which we had nursed so carefully for several days, blew out this side of Nelsonville, and when we came to put on our last spare, it was flat from a leaky valve. Our load was somewhat lighter, Florence having left us at Columbus the night before to go to Pittsburgh by train in time to see the Pirates win the pennant, so we pulled ahead and trusted to luck just as we used in the old days before we learned about flats.

Crossing the ferry into West Virginia about 5 o'clock with the speedometer showing 139 miles more, completing a journey of 12,652 miles, a trip it has taken longer to tell about than to make, even though it required 123 days.

I thank you.

THE END

Notes

Introduction

Carey S. Bliss's *Autos across America: A Bibliography of Transcontinental Automobile Travel, 1903–1940* (Austin: Jenkins and Reese, 1982) and Richard F. Weingroff's "From Names to Numbers: The Origins of the U.S. Numbered Highway System" (Washington, D.C.: Federal Highway Administration, 1997), found at www.fhwa.dot.gov/infrastructure/numbers.cfm, are both authoritative texts on early automobile history.

Before the trip W. C. Clark details in *Touring with Leaping Lena,* the newspaperman had written journals on two shorter auto journeys: *A Long Delayed Wedding Journey: Two Thousand Miles of Our Country Seen from a Flivver* (Ravenswood, W.Va.: privately printed, 1922; reprinted, Createspace, 2014), and *Flivvering along Ancestral Trails: Being an Account of a Vacation Trip Taken in the Summer of 1923* (Ravenswood, W.Va.: privately printed, 1923). A copy of *Flivvering along Ancestral Trails* can be found in the library at the Henry Ford Museum in Dearborn, Michigan.

Apology and Appreciation

W. C. Clark's "Apology" and "Appreciation" introductory notes transcribed from his original journal.

Chapter 1

1. Wamego, Pottawatomie County, Kansas, was platted in 1866 and named for an Indian chief. It is located in the broad Kansas River valley where alfalfa, sweet corn, maize, and wheat are grown. Cattle may be found in the rocky pastures of the hills around the city. The Clarks stopped in Wamego to visit with Hiram A. Long, who came from Ravenswood. He operated Wamego's Long Oil Company service station, opened in 1922. By the late 1920s, the Long Oil Company, owned by Hiram Long's brother, Archie, of nearby Manhattan, had nearly seventy stations located in cities and towns between Kansas City and central Kansas.

Chapter 2

1. There were many camping sites in and around Council Bluffs in 1925. The Clarks selected a site overlooking the city, which was named for an 1804 meeting

of the Lewis and Clark expedition with the Otoe tribe near modern Fort Calhoun, Nebraska, twenty miles to the north. Council Bluffs became the generic name for the area on both sides of the Missouri River, north of the mouth of the Platte River. The site was first settled by Sauganash and his Potawatomi band in 1838. Ten years later, the settlement that became known as Kanesville was established. It was named after Thomas L. Kane, who helped gain permission from the federal government for the Mormons to use Indian land along the Missouri River for their winter encampment of 1846–47. In 1852, the community was renamed Council Bluffs. It was a major outfitting point on the Missouri River for emigrants heading west and became an important rail hub after the railroad arrived in 1867.

2. The Custer Battlefield Highway was born in 1919 after an association of promoters of the same name proposed a highway starting at Omaha, Nebraska, running across the Missouri River to Council Bluffs, Iowa, north along the Iowa side of the river to Sioux City, and across the river into South Dakota. From there, the route would continue across South Dakota, Wyoming, and Montana, ultimately terminating in Glacier National Park close to the Montana-Canada border. In 1924, the highway was rerouted in Iowa to stretch from Des Moines to Glacier National Park. The highway was designed to promote tourism.

3. The Jim River is the James River, also known as the Dakota River. It joins the Missouri River east of Yankton, draining more than 20,000 miles of North Dakota and South Dakota and providing the main drainage of the flat lowland areas there. The James River was named after Jamestown, Virginia, by former Confederate general Thomas L. Rosser, who helped to build the Northern Pacific Railroad across North Dakota. Lawmakers in North Dakota renamed it the Dakota River in 1861, but the name never gained popular usage.

4. The Clarks probably viewed Bear Butte as a striking landmark. It is not known if they knew the million-year-old igneous rock formation was considered a sacred mountain by many American Indians. The Lakota Sioux called it "Mato Paha," meaning Bear Butte; the Cheyenne name was "Noahvose," meaning "giving hill." Many Indian tribes believe it is a place where the creator has chosen to communicate with them through visions and prayer. In places visitors may see prayers and offerings in the form of colorful pieces of cloth and small bundles or pouches hanging from the trees, but the Clarks may not have passed close enough to see such things. Additional information on Bear Butte may be found at www.pluralism.org/report/view/57.

Chapter 3

1. The Crow Agency, Montana, noted by Clark, has been located sixty miles southeast of Billings on the Little Bighorn River since 1884. Congress placed American Indian relations under the control of the newly formed War Department in 1787. By 1806 Congress had created a Superintendent of Indian Trade within the War Department. The superintendent was charged with maintaining the factory trading network of the fur trade. When the factory system was

abolished in 1822, the federal government licensed traders to have some control in Indian territories and to gain a share of the lucrative trade. Later, in 1849, Indian Affairs was transferred to the U.S. Department of the Interior, and other tribal agencies were soon established. For more on the Crow Agency, see wikipedia.org/wiki/Crow_Agency,_Montana.

2. The Lewis and Clark expedition passed through what is now the Billings area. Later, during Montana's territorial years, the area became known as Clarks Fork Bottom and was the hub for hauling freight to the Judith and Musselshell Basins. In 1877, pioneers formed the settlement of Coulson, the first town in the Yellowstone Valley. It was a rough town of dance halls and saloons, but no churches. When the railroad arrived and established nearby Billings, residents of Coulson soon moved to Billings, and Coulson began to die a slow death. Today, where Coulson once stood, a Billings city park called Coulson Park sits on the river bank. The Crow Indians have called the Billings area home since about 1700. The modern Crow Nation is just south of Billings.

Chapter 4

1. Wallace, Idaho, located in the Panhandle region, sits on the South Fork of the Coeur d'Alene River. It was founded about 1890 and named for Colonel R. W. Wallace, a land owner. Wallace, the principal town in the region's mining district, produced more silver than any other mining district in the nation but was the scene of much trouble between miners and mine owners. For more on Wallace, see wikipedia.org/wiki/Wallace,_Idaho.

2. Missoula is located in western Montana along the Clark Fork River near its confluence with the Bitterroot River and at the convergence of five mountain ranges. It was founded in 1860 as Hellgate Trading Post while the area was still part of Washington Territory. By 1866, the trading post had moved five miles upstream and was renamed Missoula Mills, later shortened to Missoula. The community provided supplies for settlers traveling through the area, and in 1877 Fort Missoula was established to protect the settlers. After the Northern Pacific Railway reached Missoula in 1883, the town grew into a city. A more complete history of Missoula can be found at wikipedia.org/wiki/Missoula,_Montana.

3. James F. Ailshie (1868–1947) was related to W. C. Clark through Ailshie's wife. Ailshie was born in Tennessee, taught school in Missouri, and then moved to Washington State, where he attended Willamette University in Salem, Oregon. There, he earned B.A. and LL.B degrees before moving to Idaho, where in 1902 he was elected as chief justice of the Idaho Supreme Court. At one time he was the youngest chief justice on any state supreme court. In 1913, he missed election to the U.S. Senate by just four votes in the legislature. He resigned from court in 1914, moved to Coeur d'Alene, and resumed his private law practice. For a time he owned a farm-ranch operation near Grangeville, served as president of the Grangeville Light and Power Company, and was director of a bank there. He again served on the Idaho Supreme

Court in 1939–41 and from 1945 until his death. For more on Ailshie, see www.accessgenealogy.com/idaho/biography-of-james-f-ailshie.htm.

4. Lapwai Mission on the Clearwater River was the first settlement in Washington State. The mission, located three miles above where Lapwai Creek joins the Clearwater River, was built in 1836 by missionary Henry Spalding. The word "Lapwai" means "place of the butterflies." More information on the Lapwai Mission can be found at www.nps.gov/nepe/learn/historyculture/henry-and-eliza-spalding-and-their-missions.htm.

5. The Battle of White Bird Canyon, the opening battle of the Nez Perce War, was fought on June 17, 1877. The original 1855 treaty between the U.S. government and the Nez Perces acknowledged the ancestral homelands of the Nez Perces, but after gold was discovered on Nez Perce land in 1860, miners and settlers swarmed into the area. Under pressure, the U.S. government in 1863 forced the Nez Perces to make another treaty, reducing by 90 percent the size of Nez Perce land. Some leaders of the Nez Perces living outside the newly assigned lands refused to sign the treaty, and the U.S. Army made several attacks to move non-treaty Nez Perces onto the newly assigned lands. Some Nez Perces wanted peace but others did not. After several Indians sought revenge for an earlier murder of an Indian and several settlers were killed, many Nez Perces moved to the southern end of White Bird Canyon. There they decided to stay. On June 17, 1877, a peace party of Nez Perces carried a white flag toward arriving soldiers in hopes of making peace. A civilian volunteer fired at the peace party and the battle began. Thirty-four U.S. soldiers were killed and four volunteers were wounded. Only three Nez Perces were wounded. A more complete history of the Battle of White Bird Canyon can be found at wikipedia.org/wiki/Battle_of_White_Bird_Canyon.

6. Lewiston Hill is located on the north side of Lewiston, Idaho, a community founded in 1861 and supposedly named for Meriwether Lewis of Lewis and Clark fame. The community is located at the confluence of the Snake and Clearwater Rivers, just east of Clarkston, Washington. Lewiston Hill's elevation is 2,756 feet. Residents called the early road through the area the "Old Spiral Highway." It was a serpentine road of 64 curves that opened in 1917 and remained the primary route north of Lewiston for more than half a century. A modern highway has replaced the old road, but more on the historic highway can be found at idahoptv.org/buildingbig/hiways/lewistonhill.html.

Chapter 5

1. Umatilla, Oregon, is a trade and distribution center named for the Umatilla Indian tribe. The Umatilla River, also named for the tribe, enters the Columbia River on the north side of the city. The city's first post office was established in 1851 and the town was incorporated as Umatilla Landing in 1864. Umatilla is thirty miles northwest of Pendleton, Oregon. See wikipedia.org/wiki/Umatilla,_Oregon for more on the history of Umatilla.

2. The Columbia River Highway, constructed between 1913 and 1922, is a scenic two-lane highway running the 75 miles between Troutdale and The Dalles in the Columbia River Gorge of Oregon. The highway was about three years old when the Clarks traveled it. Today it is called the Historic Columbia River Highway, with a walking and cycling trail alongside it called the Historic Columbia River Highway State Trail. For more information, see oregon.gov/ODOT/HWY/HCRH/pages/trail.aspx.

3. Long before the U.S. highway system was established, the original Pacific Highway was proposed as a national auto trail by businessman and good roads advocate Sam Hill to stretch from Blaine, Washington, through Oregon to the Siskiyou Mountains of northwestern California. At 1,687 miles, the highway was the longest continuous stretch of paved road in 1923, and it was later extended north to Vancouver, British Columbia, and south to San Diego in Southern California. Today the name Pacific Highway refers to several north–south highways in the Pacific Coast region of the United States.

4. Clark refers to the Hatfields, one of two West Virginia families that engaged in one of the nation's better-known feuds during the nineteenth century. The large Hatfield family lived along the Tug River in modern Logan County, West Virginia, while the equally large McCoy family lived on the other side of the river in Pike County. The families fought on opposing sides during the Civil War. For many years the families engaged in open warfare and feuding fueled by a Hatfield's clandestine affair with a McCoy girl, old grudges, and eventually, the Hatfields' killing of three McCoys. Late in the nineteenth century, some of the Hatfields moved to Oregon and settled at Centralia. For a history of the feud, see www.wvculture.org/history/hatfieldmccoy.html.

5. The Muir Shelter Cabin was constructed in memory of John Muir in 1921 as part of what became Camp Muir. The 12-foot-by-25-foot single-story one-room shelter for climbing guides still stands at an elevation of 10,188 feet. More information can be found at wikipedia.org/wiki/Camp_Muir.

Chapter 6

1. Astoria, Clatsop County, Oregon, is situated near the mouth of the Columbia River and named after John Jacob Astor, whose American Fur Company founded Fort Astoria on the site in 1811. The city was incorporated in 1876. The Port of Astoria is a deepwater port.

2. Monroe, Snohomish County, Washington, was named for the nation's fifth president, James Monroe. From its founding, its history has been intertwined with that of the Great Northern Railway, which pushed over the Cascade Range at Stevens Pass and wound its way down the Skykomish River Valley. By 1893 Monroe was an important stop on the railroad, and the city was incorporated in 1902. It is located about 30 miles from Seattle.

3. The Roosevelt Highway was an early name used to describe several north–south highways along the Pacific coast. Some of these highways were named

"Pacific Highway" either by legislation or by common usage. The original Pacific Highway (also called a "national auto trail") ran from Blaine, Washington, on the border with Canada, south into California. Later it was extended from Vancouver, British Columbia, south through San Francisco to San Diego near the Mexican border. What was formally known as the Roosevelt Highway ran through fourteen states, from Provincetown, Massachusetts, to Long Beach, California. Major highways were given official numbers in 1926, so by the time the Roosevelt Highway was completed in 1937, it was U.S. Route 6. A more complete history with contemporary photos of the Roosevelt Highway can be found at http://www.kcet.org/updaily/socal_focus/history/la-as-subject/from-the-roosevelt-highway-to-the-one-a-brief-history-of-pacific-coast-highway.html.

4. Reference to the Redwood Highway seems to refer to what is today the entire route of U.S. Route 199 from near Crescent City, California, south through the north coast region and Marin County to the present Golden Gate Bridge. That bridge, however, had not yet been built when the Clarks made their journey south along the Pacific coast of California.

5. Crater Lake became a national park in 1902. At 1,943 feet deep and 4.5 to 6 miles wide, Crater Lake is the deepest lake in the United States and one of the ten deepest in the world. A 33-mile rim drive encircles the lake with pullout points where the park's volcanic scenery can be viewed. For more information, seehttp://www.nps.gov/crla/index.htm.

6. Fort Klamath was the military outpost near the western end of the Oregon Trail, southeast of the modern unincorporated community of Fort Klamath. Clark mentions Captain Jack (Kintpuash), a Modoc chief who led a band of Modoc Indians in the killing of General Edward Canby and Reverend Eleazer Thomas during the Modoc War (1872–1873). Captain Jack and three other Modoc were arrested for the crimes and hanged at Fort Klamath. In 1890 Fort Klamath was closed as more settlers moved into the area. More information on Fort Klamath, the Modoc War, and Captain Jack may be found at wikipedia.org/wiki/Kintpuash.

Chapter 7

1. Santa Rosa, Sonoma County, California, was the home of Pomo Indians, also known as the Bitakomtara. After smallpox brought with European colonists decimated most of the Pomo tribe, Spaniards later settled the area and raised livestock. During the Mexican period, the family of Maria Lopez de Carrillo established their Rancho Cabeza de Santa Rosa just east of what later became downtown Santa Rosa. By the 1850s, a Wells Fargo post and general store were established in the area, and later, a grid street pattern including a public square was laid out, creating the town of Santa Rosa, which was incorporated by 1868. After California became a state, Santa Rosa grew in what was one of the most populous counties in the state. The 1906 San Francisco earthquake destroyed almost all of downtown Santa Rosa, as the town was located

just north of San Francisco. See wikipedia.org/wiki/Santa_Rosa,_California for a more complete history of the city.

2. Michael H. de Young (1849–1925) was the driving force behind the museum that carried his name. Born in St. Louis, he moved to San Francisco with his family as a young man, and in 1865 he and his brother founded the *Daily Dramatic Chronicle* newspaper, the predecessor of the *San Francisco Chronicle*. The M. H. de Young Museum, opened in 1895, grew out of the California Mid-Winter Exposition of 1894. Today, the museum showcases American art from the seventeenth through the twenty-first centuries, plus international contemporary art, textiles, and costumes along with art from the Americas, the Pacific, and Africa. A comprehensive history of the museum can be found at deyoung.famsf.org/about/history-de-young-museum.

3. Fish Camp, California, is a small community located just south of the entrance to Yosemite National Park. The name comes from a nearby fish hatchery. For more on Fish Camp, see wikipedia.org/wiki/Fish_Camp,_California.

Chapter 8

1. Walt Mason was born in Canada in 1862 and came to America in 1880. He worked for newspapers in Nebraska and Kansas, including William Allen White's *Emporia Gazette*. It was there he began producing prose that sounded like poetry. His rhymes were syndicated nationally, and he authored several books, soon becoming well known and respected. In 1921, he moved his family to La Jolla, California, where he lived until his death in 1939 at the age of 77. Exactly when Clark became acquainted with Walt Mason is not known, but both men were journalists and about the same age, and Clark admired Mason's writing skill. Two years before their trip west, Clark and his wife had made another auto trip through New England. He produced a narrative of that journey and included the following item by Mason titled "Flivvers," a term that might be used to describe the Clarks' vehicle on their 1925 western journey. Mason wrote:

FLIVVERS

By Walt Mason

The people who ride in the flivvers from trouble and worry seem free; they junket along by the rivers they teeter along by the sea; they stop when they're thoroughly shaken, they put up their tent in a grove and cook sundry rashers or bacon upon a collapsible stove. They always are joking and chaffing, though covered with road dust and grime, they always are joshing and laughing and having a bully good time. The people in sumptuous coaches are never so gay as they ride; whenever a grand car approaches I look for some soreheads inside. Oppressed by their opulent splendor and bored by the sameness of days, they haven't the spirit to render an anthem of pleasure and praise. They've ache in their hearts and their livers, they've pains in their blue-blooded toes; they look with disgust on the flivvers and journey in

choo-chooing rows. But happiness goes with the busses all rusty and bat-
tered with scars and most of the soul-weary cusses are riding in sumptuous
cars. The air of the countryside quivers with laughter, again and again; the
people who ride in the flivvers are making their camp in the glen.

A biography of Mason can be found at www.accessgenealogy.com/kansas/
biography-of-walt-mason.htm.

2. Barstow, San Bernardino County, California, is located 55 miles north of San
Bernardino and named for William Barstow Strong, president of the Atchison,
Topeka, and Santa Fe Railway from 1881 to 1889. The town was first settled in the
1840s on the Old Spanish Trail, which ran from Santa Fe to today's Los Angeles,
California. Barstow is close to the Mojave Desert where, in the 1860s and 1870s,
miners sought gold and silver in the Owens Valley and in the mountains to the
east. A Southern Pacific line, later acquired by the Santa Fe Railway, ran through
Barstow in 1883 from Mojave to Needles, developing Barstow into a transportation center. For more on Barstow, see wikipedia.org/wiki/Barstow,_California.

Chapter 9

1. Oatman, Mohave County, Arizona, located in the Black Mountains, was
an active mining town in 1925 when the Clarks visited. The town was named to
honor Olive Oatman, a young Illinois girl, taken captive by Yavapai Indians
during the nineteenth century and forced to work as a slave. Later she was
traded to Mohave Indians, who adopted her as a daughter and had her face
tattooed in the custom of the tribe. She was released in 1855 near the site of
modern Oatman, Arizona. Gold was discovered there in 1915, but nine years
later, about a year before the Clarks went through, the mines in the area shut
down. The town survived by catering to tourists traversing the National Old
Trails Road (later U.S. Highway 66). More on the National Old Trails Road can
be found at wikipedia.org/wiki/National_Old_Trails_Road.

2. For travelers on the National Old Trails Road in 1925, Pine Springs,
Apache County, Arizona, provided travelers with a chance to enjoy the cool,
alpine high country. The elevation is 6,968 feet.

3. Williams, Coconino County, Arizona, is west of Flagstaff. It was founded in
1881 and named after William "Old Bill" Williams, the early mountain man and
trader who trapped in the area. A large mountain south of town is named Bill
Williams Mountain. The town was incorporated in July 1901. A more complete
history of Williams can be found at wikipedia.org/wiki/Williams,_Arizona.

4. President Woodrow Wilson signed the legislation making the Grand Canyon the seventeenth national park in 1919, seven years before the Clarks paid
their visit in 1925. The National Park Service offers the natural and cultural
history of the Grand Canyon at http://www.nps.gov/grca/learn/index.htm.

5. The place "Maine," noted by Clark, was a railroad point on the Atchison,
Topeka, and Santa Fe Railway in the vicinity of Parks, Arizona, where the Old
National Trails Highway ran parallel with the railroad tracks.

6. Albuquerque, New Mexico, a Spanish colonial outpost founded in 1706 on the Camino Real (Royal Road), reportedly was named by the provincial governor to honor the viceroy of New Spain, the Duke of Albuquerque. Another legend says the name is derived from the Latin *Albus quercus* ("white oak"), referring to the prevalence of white oaks in the region. Still another legend traces the name Albuquerque to the Galician word *albaricoque,* meaning apricot, a fruit brought to New Mexico by Spanish settlers perhaps as early as 1743. This legend says the settlement was established near an apricot tree, and became known as La Ciudad de Albaricoque. In time the word became corrupted to "Albuquerque" because settlers were unable to correctly pronounce the Galician word. Regardless of the origins of the name, the community became part of Mexico in 1821, and after the Mexican War in 1846, it became part of the United States. It had grown to a population of about 8,000 people and added modern amenities to its infrastructure by 1900, thanks to the arrival of the railroad, and was becoming a modern American city by the time the Clarks visited in 1925. A more detailed history may be found at wikipedia.org/wiki/Albuquerque,_New_Mexico.

Chapter 10

1. Clovis, county seat of Curry County, New Mexico, is a largely agricultural community located in eastern New Mexico's portion of Llano Estacada, or the Staked Plains. It was founded in 1906 as Riley's Switch by the Atchison, Topeka, and Santa Fe Railway, but was later renamed Clovis by the station master's daughter. For more on Clovis, see wikipedia.org/wiki/Clovis,_New_Mexico.

2. Floydada, Floyd County, Texas, originally named Floyd City, was established in 1890 on 640 acres of land donated by James B. and Caroline Price from Missouri. After the town became the county seat and a post office opened, the town's name was changed to Floydada. The origin of the name is unclear. Some residents believe the name Floydada resulted from garbled communications with Washington, D.C, while others believe it is a combination of the county's name and the name of Ada Price, land donor James Price's mother. A history of Floydada and its origins can be found at wikipedia.org/wiki/Floydada,_Texas.

3. The Dr. Cook that Clark refers to is probably Frederick Cook (1865–1940), an explorer, physician and ethnographer who claimed he reached the North Pole in 1908, about one year before Robert Peary. Most authorities rejected his claim. In 1922, three years before the Clarks made their journey, Cook entered the Texas oil business. Relying upon his reputation as an explorer, Cook sold oil stock and was convicted in 1923 of using the mail to defraud investors by overstating the oil discovery prospects of his company. He went to federal prison and later was released on parole. Within a few years, Cook suffered a heart attack and fell into a coma. On his deathbed in 1940, President Franklin D. Roosevelt granted him a pardon of all offenses. Details of Cook's explorations and oil business may be found at www.pardonpower.com/2010/08/explorer-oil-man-liar-pardoned.html.

4. The Clarks drove from Dallas to Dennison, Texas, on a segment of the north–south Jefferson Highway. Near Dennison, they paid a toll to cross a bridge built in 1915 at the site of Colbert's Ferry, which was, during the nineteenth century, the primary crossing of the Red River from Indian Territory (by 1925, the state of Oklahoma) into Texas. After crossing the bridge, the Clarks headed north-northeast, following the route of the Old Texas Road, sometimes called the Osage Trace, a trail through the Cherokee, Creek, and Choctaw Indian Nations and the communities of Durant, Caddo, Atoka, McAlester, and Muskogee in modern Oklahoma. Then the Clarks turned northeast, entering Arkansas. A full history of the bridge can be found on the Texas State Historical Association's website at tshaonline.org/handbook/online/articles/rtc01.

5. Fort Smith, Arkansas, located at the junction of the Arkansas and Poteau rivers, was once called Belle Point. Fort Smith began as a frontier military post in 1817, and was named for General Thomas Adams Smith, commander of the U. S. Army Rifle Regiment headquartered near St. Louis. After the post was abandoned in 1824, John Rogers, army sutler and land speculator, purchased the property from the government and established the civilian town of Fort Smith. The United States judge Clark refers to was Isaac Charles Parker (1838–1896), a U.S. district judge who presided over the U.S. District Court for the Western District of Arkansas for 21 years (1875–1896). Parker, known as the "Hanging Judge," tried 13,490 cases, 344 of which were for capital offenses. Of 160 sentenced to death by hanging (156 men and 4 women), 79 were hanged. The rest appealed their conviction, died while incarcerated, or were pardoned. For more on Fort Smith's Judge Parker, see www.nps.gov/fosm/learn/historyculture/judge-parker.htm.

Chapter 11

1. Koshkonong, Oregon County, Missouri, is a small community named for its numerous sinkhole ponds and lakes that reminded a railroad supervisor of his favorite duck hunting spot at Lake Koshkonong, Wisconsin. A more complete history of Koshkonong, Missouri, can be found at wikipedia.org/wiki/Koshkonong,_Missouri.

2. Rolla, Phelps County, Missouri, was officially established as a town in 1858, and later became a transportation and trading center of the area. Legend suggests it was named when the settlement competed with nearby Dillon to become the county seat. When Dillon lost, its residents were allowed to choose the name of the new county seat. They named it Rolla, after a hunting dog. The more likely truth is that new settlers from North Carolina voted to name it Raleigh after their hometown, spelling the name phonetically. For more on Rolla, see wikipedia.org/wiki/Rolla,_Missouri.

Acknowledgements

A SPECIAL NOTE OF THANKS GOES TO ROB BENSON, SHERRI HEAVIER, and Maxine Landfried in West Virginia for their assistance in uncovering material about W. C. Clark and family. Thanks also to many others in local, county, and state historical groups who provided other bits and pieces concerning the interesting lives and times of W. C. Clark and family.

In addition, thanks to Jen Charney of Save the Redwoods League, Larry M. Kinsel of the General Motors Heritage Center, Jess Vogelsang of Northern Arizona University, Scott Daniels of the Oregon Historical Society, Colleen E. Curry of the Heritage and Research Center at Yellowstone National Park, Richard Weingroff of the Federal Highway Administration, Ginny L. Kilander and Bumma L. Hardy of the American Heritage Center at the University of Wyoming, Matthew T. Reitzel of the South Dakota State Historical Society, Tom Ferris of the Montana Historical Society, and Caitlin Lampman of the Arizona Historical Society for their assistance in locating and providing appropriate illustrations.

Also, many thanks to Byron Price, Charles Rankin, Steven Baker, Sarah Smith, and other staff at the University of Oklahoma Press for their work in producing this effort.

If Willie Chester Clark were still alive, I am sure he would join me in thanking all concerned for their assistance.

Index

References to illustrations appear in italic type.